To

Rebecca & Allen Hulbert

with gratitude and

good wishes from

Irving N. Fisher

My Father, Irving Fisher

My Father
Irving Fisher

---

by Irving Norton Fisher

It is better to live rich than to die rich.
                              Samuel Johnson

 A REFLECTION BOOK

COMET PRESS BOOKS   NEW YORK

For

My Wife

Virginia

Contents

Foreword

Several different books could be written about my father. One might deal with his professional achievements as an economist. Another might stress his devotion to a long list of good works. A third might show to what extent his life conformed to the American success story pattern. This volume aims to touch on these and other facets of his personality, without overemphasizing any of them.

Even the most cursory glance at his eighty-year career shows that he was a phenomenal dynamo of energy and an uncompromising seeker after truth. Never content with things as he found them, he constantly rushed in where angels feared to tread, but the ridicule which others sometimes heaped upon him for his pains never dampened his enthusiasm in the slightest. When his suggestions for remedying the defects in our creaking economy were given a cold reception, he continued expounding them to any who would listen and to many who wouldn't—especially if they happened to be members of Congress or residents of the White House.

The recognition accorded him by his fellow economists was cited by Dr. Royal Meeker in an *Appreciation* dated

January 22, 1947: "Economists at home and abroad agree that he has aroused the somnolent, unthinking 'thinkers' about money problems even though many disagree with his analysis and conclusions in respect to the role of money in human affairs. . . . His 'Compensated Dollar Plan' has been ridiculed as a woozy 'Rubber Dollar Plan.' The ridiculous ridiculers seem to be unaware that the venerated gold standard is a commodity standard—a *one* commodity standard and hence a very bad standard. . . . Professor Fisher has shown that the real 'Rubber Dollar' was and is the gold dollar."

A seven-column 1933 newspaper interview bore this headline: HE MADE THE DOLLAR WHAT IT IS TODAY; WE HOPE YOU'RE SATISFIED! If this was not literally true, he was certainly responsible more than anyone else for the public's realization that the dollar does fluctuate in purchasing power. Thus the influence of his thinking spread far beyond the realm of the usual college professor.

His participation in numerous controversies sometimes produced surprising invective from strangers. Once he was berated for claiming credit for an absent-minded-professor story, which his correspondent had seen in *Punch* twenty years before but which was entirely new to Irving Fisher. A West Virginia "doctor," referring to his article on "The Townsend Delusion" in a 1936 issue of the *Christian Advocate*, exploded: "If there were ever a liar, a cheat, a thief larger than you out of jail he ought to be in the penitentiary for life. You are not within a mile of the truth of the Townsend Old Age Revolving Pension plan. But you are just like all other hirelings of Wall Street and big business who are robbing and pilfering the general public."

He also received his full quota of adverse comment in the public press. At Battle Creek, Michigan, when a reporter asked him: "Professor Fisher, is 'Yes, We Have No Bananas' good English?" his matter-of-fact reply: "Yes, it would be correct, if the statement was preceded by the question 'Have you no bananas?' " produced coast-to-coast headlines, lampooning his pronouncement on the grammatical correctness of a current song hit and ignoring the vital core of the interview. Similarly his 1916 statement that infants were worth an average of ninety dollars at birth, lifted out of context, was greeted with a deluge of facetious newsprint. From as far afield as Fresno, California, he was castigated for setting a price on a newborn infant, when "all the wealth in the world could not buy it from you. Ninety dollars! Guess again, Professor Fisher!"

As for leaving the world better than he found it—a paramount consideration in his own eyes—one of his greatest strengths was in a sense one of his greatest weaknesses. He relied so much on logical argument in winning converts to his human betterment programs that he sometimes made insufficient allowance for the psychological. In a memorial article, Senator Paul H. Douglas wrote of him: "If we at times smiled over the lack of humor which sometimes accompanied his seriousness of purpose, we could only be reverent towards the total import of his life."

At his death he left four major projects under the heading of unfinished business: (1) the rough draft of five opening chapters for a book to be called *My Economic Endeavors*, portions of which have been incorporated in the chapters dealing with his professional work; (2) the basic material for an *Economic Primer for Laymen*, which was to be fashioned from a series of "Short Stories on Wealth," broadcast from 1928 to 1933 and syndicated in newspapers throughout the country; (3) an unfinished manuscript on *The Velocity of the Circulation of Money* which he had first discussed in a 1909 pamphlet; and (4) a projected autobiography, which was always being sidetracked in favor of more pressing matters.

Plainly this present undertaking bears little resemblance to the autobiography he hoped to write, except insofar as I have been able to tell the story in his own words. The book has also been written from the standpoint of a layman, rather than a professional economist, though I soon realized that more than a passing reference to his professional work would be necessary, or I would be guilty of leaving out Hamlet. In condensing his economic ideas, I run the obvious risk of oversimplification and misunderstanding, especially when the mathematical basis for them can scarcely be suggested in a book of this scope. The adventurous reader who craves the full treatment is referred to the originals. It is hoped, however, that even those who are already familiar with his work will find this summation helpful in evaluating his contributions to economics.

The book has three main sections: Part I records the details of the first thirty-four years and includes consideration of the first economic book; Part II covers a like span in more than twice the number of chapters, since most of his professional and extracurricular contributions were made during this period; Part III chronicles the final twelve years when two more economic works were added to make a total output of twenty-nine books. Within this framework, there is necessarily some overlapping between chapters, but on the whole there is a steady progression from one chapter to the next.

Father was a prolific letter writer, and by far the most important material in the book is contained in the passages quoted from his correspondence. This has been edited to some extent, mainly to reduce its bulk and occasionally to reorganize the paragraphs in a better sequence, and I believe that these changes would have met with his approval if he had been able to supervise the editing. The letters to my mother were obviously intended for her eyes alone, but —no doubt with posterity in mind—she carefully obliterated the most intimate passages by writing the word "apple" over and over again on top of his lines.

Another important source of material was his sixty-five-year correspondence with the Reverend William G. Eliot, Jr. of Portland, Oregon, which began when they were teen-age schoolmates in St. Louis. The passages from "Will" Eliot's letters were invaluable in reconstructing the early years. Manuscripts of his speeches on a wide variety of topics have also been a useful reservoir of material, beginning with an oration delivered at the time of his graduation from high school, and ending with one which he pronounced scarcely two months before he died.

In searching for a suitable device to use on his book-plate, Father selected the dolphin from the Fisher coat of arms, had it depicted with its tail curved to form a question mark so as to emphasize the interrogative aspect of his initials, and used these words for his motto: *Veritas, Sanitas, Serenitas, Utilitas.*

New Haven, Conn.
August 15, 1956

Acknowledgments

I am grateful for permission to use certain material, fully identified in the text, which was originally published in the indicated sources:

The American Economic Association, for Memorials of Irving Fisher, by Paul H. Douglas and Ray B. Westerfield in the *American Economic Review*, September, 1947.

The City Printing Company, for portions of *100% Money*, 1945, by Irving Fisher.

The Econometric Society, for passages from *Econometrica* by Irving Fisher, October, 1933, and by Joseph A. Schumpeter, July, 1948.

Harper & Brothers, for quotations from *Constructive Income Taxation*, 1942, by Irving Fisher and Herbert W. Fisher.

Liberty of Canada Limited, for an article by Irving Fisher in *Liberty*, February 22, 1936.

The Royal Economic Society, for an obituary of Irving Fisher by G. Findlay Shirras in the *Economic Journal*, September, 1947.

I am equally indebted to:

The Henry L. Stimson Collection of the Yale University Library and Mr. McGeorge Bundy, trustee of the Collection, for a letter from my father to Mr. Stimson, dated November 11, 1932.

My sister Caroline F. Baumann and my uncle Herbert W. Fisher for helpful suggestions when this project was in its early stages.

Royal Meeker and Leonard Bacon, neither of whom lived to see how materially their generous encouragement and constructive criticism helped in the final shaping of this book.

PART ONE

1867-1903

1. Looking Back

At a public gathering, following a dinner given in his honor by the members of Harvard's department of economics on the seventy-fifth anniversary of his birth, Yale's Irving Fisher found himself in the unaccustomed position of "looking backward instead of forward."

It made him feel like a mountain climber after an arduous ascent, who turns to look at the panorama spread out below and is astonished to see how far he has come. In trying to find "something to brag about," however, he could see little except for the fact that he was "still alive at seventy-five." Mentioning that he had entered economics through mathematics, he continued:

> The chairman has spoken of my output as having been prodigious. This reminds me that on the Fiftieth Reunion of my class, when visiting the Yale Library with some of my classmates, I found that it was the custom for the Fiftieth Reunions to exhibit in the Library the publications of all members of the class. I was astonished to see how much space my own exhibit took up and said to the attending librarian, intending to joke, that I must have broken the record. To which he replied that I had and for all time, even surpassing Billy Phelps (who had celebrated his Fiftieth the year before).
>
> The number of cards in the Library catalogue ex-

3

ceeded two hundred. Of these twenty-eight were books, eighteen on economics. But when one goes to shake down these large figures, to eliminate the popularizations, to take account of the many collaborations and anticipations, what is left shrinks to a small fraction of the original figure.

Washington Irving in one of his fantasies is supposed to doze off when in the British Museum and dream of the many tomes there from which he had borrowed material rushing upon him and running off with the passages of which he had made use so that when he awoke, still dreaming, he thought he had almost nothing left of his own. . . . So, despite my large output, the most that I can really claim is that of trying hard.

As a boy I was not interested in any sort of study and rather shirked it in school, much to the disgust of my father. But when a teacher got me started in the beauties of mathematics, I suddenly and thereafter rapidly took an enthusiastic interest in that subject, which lasted through college and graduate school.

In the prosperous nineteen-twenties, when he arranged for a full-scale genealogical investigation of his antecedents in an effort to disentangle the various hereditary strands which had gone into his being, the Fisher line could only be traced back as far as William Fisher, who was presumably descended from the Palatine Germans who migrated to Ireland in the sixteenth century, then crossed the Atlantic to New England in the eighteenth century. The earliest record referring to William Fisher described his 1766 trek in a covered wagon, with his fourteen-year-old wife, from Nine Partners (now White Plains) to Ashgrove (now Cambridge), where he established his new farm not far from the single log cabin which was the nucleus for Troy, New

York. Subsequently he fought for the independence of the colonies as a member of the Albany County militia.

William's son Zachariah married Delight Norton, whose line could be traced to Le Seignieur de Norville, Constable to William the Conqueror. Zachariah's grandson, who was destined to be Irving Fisher's father, was christened George Whitefield Fisher in honor of the eighteenth-century Calvinist. He was born in Cambridge, New York, on Christmas day, 1833. He graduated as valedictorian of his high-school class, but finances did not permit him to enter Yale until he was twenty-two. Enrolling then as a member of the Sophomore class, he became an editor of the *Yale Literary Magazine*, and was chosen class poet before his graduation in 1859. The photographs in this book give an impression of his intellectual brow, but do not reveal his hazel eyes and fair complexion. He was about five feet three inches tall, won a reputation as a wrestler and possessed a pleasant tenor voice.

After his graduation from Yale, George Fisher taught school for three years in two different New York state seminaries, in order to accumulate the wherewithal necessary for completing his ministerial education at the Yale Divinity School. While teaching Latin and English Literature in Charlotteville, New York, he was very much attracted to a pupil from Waterford, New Jersey, named Ella Wescott. One day, when she had given an obviously wrong answer to a classroom question, he noted that she joined good-naturedly in the laughter at her expense and he thought to himself, "That's the girl I'm going to marry," although she was his junior by twelve years.

The first Wescotts to reach America from England settled in Wethersfield, Connecticut, about 1636. Part Puritan and part French Huguenot, they took active part in town affairs, fought in the Indian wars, the Revolution and the

5

War of 1812. In contrast to the fair complexion of Ella's teacher, they were very swarthy, with black eyes, black hair and, in the case of the male members of the family, bushy black eyebrows rivaling those of John L. Lewis. Ella's brother John was destined to deliver the speeches which placed the name of Woodrow Wilson in nomination for the presidency at the Conventions of 1912 and 1916.

Ella was born on March 1, 1846, the daughter of John and Catherine Bozorth Wescott, a member of the eighth generation of Wescotts in America. She was seventeen when she married George Whitefield Fisher on July 1, 1863, at her parents' home in Waterford, New Jersey. Her husband had completed only one year of study in the Divinity School, so that the first two years of their marriage were spent in the shadow of Yale. To help meet expenses the potential preacher exercised his manual dexterity by making rustic furniture. Later he put his carpentry skill to further use in making improvements in his successive homes, and he devoted considerable time and effort to Scriptural research concerning the design and construction of the Mosaic tabernacle. With his own hands he built a meticulous scale replica which was eventually presented to the Yale Divinity School.

Ella's strict upbringing prepared her well for the role of a minister's wife. Although she and her husband were opposites with regard to complexions, they were nearly equal in height and their moral heritages were very similar. In assuming the duties of parson's wife she showed herself an apt pupil. She sang in the church choir and on one occasion even went so far as to deliver a sermon from her husband's pulpit, when he was incapacitated by illness. Instead of being shocked at her temerity, as one might expect of a Victorian congregation, her flock listened attentively and afterwards one parishioner pronounced her "better than the dominie himself."

It was one thing to defy the conventions in such an emergency, but in day-to-day living Ella was an uncompromising stickler for all the proprieties. In her later years, for instance, if anyone suggested an innocent game of cards on a rainy Sunday afternoon, she could not conceal her disapproval. I also remember the very real struggle she had with her conscience, whether or not to break the Sabbath by attending a special matinee of John Drinkwater's play *Abraham Lincoln*. In the end she yielded to our persuasions and salved her conscience by remarking afterwards that the play was "as good as a sermon."

George and Ella Fisher had four children. Cora, the eldest, was born a year before her father's graduation from Divinity School. The second child, named Lincoln in reverence for the emancipator, survived scarcely a month after his birth at Saugerties, New York, where the thirty-one-year-old preacher held his first pastorate. Early in the following year, still in the shadow of Washington Irving's Catskills, on February 27, 1867, the third child was born and christened Irving. A younger brother, Herbert, arrived seven years later.

From Saugerties the family returned briefly to New Haven, then proceeded to Peace Dale, Rhode Island, where the head of the house occupied the Congregational pulpit for a dozen years. Irving's earliest recollections, therefore, were of the parsonage in this small mill town, where the family thrust down their roots in the fall of 1868 when he was eighteen months old.

One of the embryo economist's first noteworthy Peace Dale exploits could be considered a rudimentary gesture in the direction of "book-larning." Having reached the stage when every piece of furniture was an invitation to adventure, he took it into his head to climb up the face of

7

his father's library bookcase as if it were a ladder. Frustrated at not being able to climb beyond the top, he wedged his head firmly between the final shelf and the ceiling. When his mother entered the room in response to his muffled distress signal, her heart leaped into her mouth. In her agitation she never could recall precisely what she did to rescue the young bookworm, but she always considered it a miracle that the whole structure had not toppled over and nipped his potential career in the bud.

As his horizons broadened still further, Irving decided one fine afternoon to go exploring in a nearby region known as Tower Hill, which afforded a commanding view across Narragansett Bay. Not being endowed with a good "bump of location" he soon got lost and his parents and their neighbors spent several anxious hours searching for him. When he was found and brought back to the parsonage, due to the intercession of his older sister Cora, his only punishment was to listen to the reading of the story of the Prodigal Son. At the conclusion of this lesson, the young truant solemnly inquired, "Did he go to Tower Hill too, Papa?"

Before long the youngster had other reasons to be impressed by the seriousness of life. He was only six years old when nine-year-old Cora contracted typhoid fever. As the crisis deepened, he could not help noticing his parents' mounting anxiety, and when Cora died he was both frustrated and angry that such a thing could happen without anyone's being able to prevent it. The loss of his older sister made an indelible impression on him, leaving him temporarily in the role of an only child. This memory was to be a contributory factor in his subsequent passion for preaching the gospel of good health.

Six months later he was surprised to be sent off to spend the day with neighbors. He was willing enough to go for there would be playmates there, but he was puzzled none the less and quite unprepared to discover upon his return that he had a new baby brother. Thus, although he was the third born in a family of four, he was the oldest of the only two offspring who were destined to reach maturity and thereafter he always took a protective attitude toward brother Herbert.

For more than a year after leaving Peace Dale the family lived in New Haven, where the elder son began preparing for college at the Hillhouse High School. Then they moved west to St. Louis to be near his father's sister, Mrs. George Jackson. For the calendar year of 1883 his father once more assumed the responsibilities of a parish, this time in Cameron, Missouri, until ill health forced his permanent retirement. He and Ella and Herbert then went to Berlin, New Jersey, to be under the care of his brother-in-law Dr. William A. Wescott, leaving Irving with his Aunt and Uncle in St. Louis to complete his preparation for college at Smith Academy. The friendship which he formed in St. Louis with William G. Eliot, Jr., who was also a clergyman's son and destined to become one himself, survived as long as they both lived, although their eventual homes were on opposite fringes of the continent.

Eliot and Fisher were active members of a debating society known as the Clay Lyceum, with Fisher serving as secretary. The subject for debate on May 30, 1883 was: Resolved, that it would be beneficial to the world if it were conducted on communistic principles. The chair decided in favor of the negative. Early in the following year Fisher wrote a newsy letter to New Jersey, describing his holiday social activities and subsequent participation in another debate on the subject of whether or not it would be practicable to build the Panama Canal:

9

Dear Parents:

Christmas night I went over to Norman Flagg's. When I arrived they had a house full of visitors. After running the gauntlet of two rooms' full of people whose names I forgot as soon as I was told them, I settled down to a game of checkers with Flagg. Mrs. Flagg wanted me to dance. I wished I could but I couldn't.

Saturday we all went to hear Mr. & Mrs. Scott who gave an elocutionary entertainment. We were all packed in a big peach wagon, nine of us. As we were riding over, I remarked that we would have a comedy all our own, if the wagon should break down. Miss Lathy thought that it would be a tragedy. We arrived spattered with mud and listened to a very fine program. When we rode back we had Mr. and Mrs. Scott in addition to the former load.

On the road to Flagg's, which is about three and a half miles from the church where we heard the Scotts, there is a very steep hill. In order to relieve the steepness, an embankment of earth has been made, which however was little wider than to admit one wagon. It was quite dark and the driver not seeing clearly did not steer quite straight enough and the wagon went a little down the side of the embankment. In trying to pull it up it seemed to go down more. The driver then stopped. The wagon was leaning at about an angle of forty-five degrees. We decided to disembark.

Mr. Cavender got out and called to Mrs. Scott to jump into his arms saying "come on, come on." And she came on. But, lo, as she gently lit in his embrace his feet were not under him and as he quietly reclined on that soft cushion, the mud, she gracefully spread herself over him. I picked her up, as best I could.

10

After we were all out and paddling with dignified mein through the semi-liquid earth, the wagon was restored to its normal attitude. Of course in being righted it was drawn a rod or two ahead, which distance its passengers had to flounder through. Mrs. Flagg got along worst of all for every two or three steps her rubbers came off and she had to stoop down to put them on. Luckily we had brought a step-ladder along, so in getting aboard again the passengers retained their dignity. We reached home about twelve o'clock. Next morning we had quite a time cleaning up but I guess Mr. Cavender's overcoat is muddy yet.

Flagg and I returned to school a day early to confer with our colleagues about the debate. I met Eliot (my colleague) at the depot. We went to his house together and I stayed all night. The debate came off next evening. It was below zero. We had an audience of twelve. The society sat on the platform. Ten on the platform and thirteen (including the usher) in the audience! But we carried it on as dignified as if there was a housefull. We had a nice debate, though we, Eliot and I, lost it. I think that the arguments were overwhelmingly in our favor, but the votes stood eight to four against us.

I asked Uncle Jackson what he thought about omitting a year before going to College and he denoted his approval. The more I think of it, I think that it is a good plan. Americans naturally want to do things in as short a time as possible. Their motto is "Hurry, Haste is speed." There are too many that graduate from College without knowing very much about the *common* branches of education. But I think if I get a good solid foundation in *these* branches and have a general knowledge of the literature of standard authors and be well *up with the times* in general which I am *not* now, that I would have an advantage

over some of my hurrying, cramming hasty classmates who think, as I did in the New Haven High
School, that if they keep well up in their lessons they
will have a finished education when they graduate.

The only *dis*advantage which I have as yet thought
of is that I would graduate a year later in life. But
Uncle Jackson thinks that the older I am the better.
I think that during that year I could earn considerable money and also learn some way by which I could
earn money after I get to college. There should be
an abundance of time to learn stenography or any
other thing. I have thought of another way—don't
laugh—if it wouldn't cost too much I *might* take
elocution lessons. During the summer vacations I
might give a sort of entertainment. If I could render
the "Raven" like Uncle John or Will (which is it?)
it *might* be a good plan.

If I could work on Flagg's farm I would have nice
people to live with and *all the books I want*. Perhaps
I could get a place at George Bliss' home, for his
father is a graduate of Harvard and so, I suppose,
has a nice library. There are numberless ways of earning money if I decide to omit a year. Please both
think it over and give your verdict with your reasons.

The debate on the Panama Canal was not the last occasion on which he found himself advocating the unpopular
side. The more he matured the more he seemed to thrive on
controversy, and this early forensic training undoubtedly
helped cultivate his natural aptitude for expressing himself
clearly in public. The authorities of Smith Academy evidently appreciated his effectiveness on the rostrum, because
they gave him the twelfth and final position on the program
of declamations and orations delivered at the commencement exercises in June, 1884.

The style and content of his composition, "Extremes Meet," bore as little resemblance to his subsequent out-pourings as the copper-plate hand in which it was written bore to the handwriting of his mature years. But, in the course of his remarks he contrasted the extremes of tyranny and democracy and made this precociously accurate forecast:

In those nations where tyranny holds sway, lurks danger which, if not forseen and provided for, is liable at any moment to change the too-restricted government into one of unlimited freedom—a freedom, indeed, so free that it loses all virtue of freedom. Men cannot enjoy the benefits of civilized liberty without restrictions. Law and Order must prevail, else confusion takes their place, and, with the coming of Confusion, Freedom vanishes. So, if the radical Nihilists should realize their designs to the fullest extent, there is reason to believe that Russia like France, would merely exchange a reign of Tyranny for a reign of Terror.

The question of whether or not to postpone college for a year was settled by events. Immediately after taking his last college entrance examination he joined his parents and brother in New Jersey. From there he wrote to Will Eliot, telling of his father's death from consumption, and mentioning his own invention of a device for improving the internal mechanism of pianos, the first of a long line of brain-waves with which he bombarded the patent office:

BERLIN, NEW JERSEY, July 6, 1884
DEAR WILL:
The next morning after examination I took train for the east and arrived here last Monday night.

13

Papa is much worse. Mamma was not very frank with me in her letters, until I was all through with examinations. She thought not to worry me before it was necessary and I suppose she did right. The truth is the doctors have given up all hope.

Papa is now reduced almost to a skeleton. He lives mostly on milk. The great trouble is he cannot digest. He eats enough and more to support him but his organs will not appropriate it. He suffers no pain. He has become very deaf which at present is a great blessing since it prevents him from being disturbed by any noise.

I received a certificate yesterday, admitting me to Yale. I have not yet decided to enter this class, though I think I shall. Everything is so uncertain.

My invention is getting along nicely. I have almost made a complete model but must make another better before I send it to the patent office. It is of the utmost importance to keep it secret and you will of course say nothing of it to anyone.

BERLIN, NEW JERSEY, July 14, 1884

DEAR WILL:

Two days ago my father left us. He was all that was noble and virtuous. As a father and husband he was kind, loving and thoughtful. He was particularly interested in my college plans. A short time before he died, when Uncle John asked him if he had any anxiety on his mind he replied: "No, except that I leave Irvy in the lurch."

Uncle John assured him that his children would be cared for. But papa partly provided for my college expenses and with this aid I think that in various ways I can pay my own expenses clear through.

The funeral will take place tomorrow after which the remains will be taken to Peace Dale. The trouble is hard to bear but it was inevitable. If there is a

14

place of rest for the righteous man I know that papa has attained a rich reward. The example he set will ever have a hallowing influence on my life.

The financial aid mentioned consisted of five hundred dollars which had been left in trust with a Providence classmate before the family moved away from Peace Dale. Six weeks later another letter was dispatched to Will Eliot from Uncle John's house near Berlin:

HADDONFIELD, NEW JERSEY, August 25, 1884
DEAR ELIOT:

My father's life and example were such that all could imitate with profit. We buried him in Peace Dale where he was pastor a long time. The funeral service was preached by a clergyman from a neighboring village—an old friend of papa's.

When I entered the church and saw the familiar pulpit where I had seen papa stand so often, an overwhelming feeling of sadness passed over me. I could fairly see papa rise from his accustomed seat and walk to the pulpit. The church was packed, for papa's influence was widespread.

We remained in Peace Dale about a week and then came back to New Jersey. In about another week I expect to be in New Haven. College begins September eighteenth. We return to the same quarters we left before going west—115 Park Street.

I have obtained a caveat at the Patent Office which prevents any one else from getting a patent on my invention without my knowledge. I need yet to complete some points and will apply for patent in two or three months.

Although his father's death thrust him into the role of chief provider for his widowed mother and ten-year-old brother, this did not swerve him from his determination to matriculate at Yale that fall with the class of 1888.

2. College Years

When Irving Fisher reached New Haven as Freshman and breadwinner, the third-floor rooms to which the trio reverted after their two-year absence were rented on credit. To help balance the budget one of his classmates was taken in as a boarder. The widowed mother also contracted to sew innumerable buttonholes for the dressmaker who occupied the lower floors of the house, and younger brother Herbert added his mite by delivering finished dresses to customers after school. But the older brother contributed the most to the family exchequer by tutoring in term time as well as during summer vacation.

From the first he was ambitious to do well in his studies, and financial pressure gave him an added stimulus toward scholastic achievement, since there were worth-while cash prizes to be won, particularly in his favorite subject, mathematics. It was rough sledding at first, for his constitution was not considered rugged. But his father's untimely death aroused an early awareness of the importance of keeping well through regular exercise. He won some distinction as an oarsman and was especially commended by the crew coach, "Bob" Cook, for devising an ingenious rowing indicator to help each oarsman cultivate a smoothly curved stroke. His classmates warmed to him slowly, however, partly because he was under the disadvantage of living off campus and also because the social graces did not come easily to him.

Having been brought up with a strong sense of right and wrong, he had little patience with those who conformed

16

merely for the sake of appearances. This did not prevent him from succumbing quite soon to the current fashion of sporting a mustache. It was a full decade, however, before he added his professorial goatee, after calculating precisely how much time he would conserve in an average lifetime by not shaving. As an undergraduate he earned the innocuous sobriquets of "Magnus" and "Piscates," and his class book gave these precise personal measurements: "Height 5 ft. 8¾ in.; weight 147 lbs.; chest 36½ in."

But the letters he wrote to Will Eliot in St. Louis provided more insight into his unfolding mind than any amount of statistics. He poured out his soul in them in a way which he could not do with his Yale contemporaries.

Several of these undergraduate letters covered a score or more of closely written pages and touched on such diverse topics as the Freshman Rush, Tap Day in Junior year, the progress of his mechanical invention, and the controversy between science and religion. The amount of space devoted to the latter showed how difficult it was for the Yale Freshman to reconcile the beliefs of his parsonage upbringing with the teachings of science:

NEW HAVEN, CONN., October 12, 1884
... College began on the eighteenth of September. We were all summoned into chapel at four o'clock to be given our seats. As we went in, a crowd of Sophs stood by the door to make fun of the green Fresh. "Take your hands out of your pockets."—"No newspapers allowed in chapel."—"Take off that hat." etc. were flung at us but received very good naturedly. . . .

Among my classmates are Henry Ward Beecher (related to the great one), Morison Waite (grandson of the Chief Justice), Henry L. Stimson, who passed his examinations without conditions a year ago but stayed out a year. He has been in Europe

17

three times and knows French and German. There is a Russian in the class, who comes to recitation with an old straw hat on and pants three times too big.

The night before college opened there was a "rush." I prepared before I went by putting on an old pair of pants. We formed a phalanx, each man linked his arm into his neighbor's and put his hand on the fellow's shoulder in front. The Sophs tried to break the phalanx, which they did quite successfully, all the time trying to pull off our upper clothing. The rags thus obtained are held as great trophies. I lost my coat and shirt and came home naked as far as the waist.

After losing my shirt, I was anxious to get ahold of one of my antagonists'. Many however wore canvas jackets which it is next to impossible to tear. Seeing a fellow with a shirt of material tearable, I asked him if he was '87 and receiving a somewhat reluctant "yes" I seized his shirt and dragged him toward the phalanx to which I was clinging. He called in vain for '87, and I guess he lost all his shirt. At any rate I got about a square foot or so.

As I was desirous to tutor in college my friends have spoken to Profs. Phillips and Beebe about it and a week ago Prof. Beebe recommended me to a fellow in the fourth division who needed tutoring in Geometry. So I have one pupil already. He pays me a dollar an hour. I hope to get more before long.

One of the features of college life is the class prayer meetings which are held twice a week. It is a good thing and I am quite struck with it. When I hear fellows of my own age speak with religious enthusiasm, I feel more well disposed toward christianity. However, I still adhere to this: that every belief should be controlled by the reason. I want to settle the question of religion but I want to settle it on grounds of truth.

18

The first question with a doubter ought to be: Are these religious teachings true? Does God exist? Is immortality a fact? Can he accept these beliefs on account of their advantages alone, even though his reason tells him that they are false?

NEW HAVEN, May 17, 1885

My sickness which I have just experienced was not brought on, the Doctor thought, by overwork, though it was aided by it. Of course, I could not study during those four weeks so that I have now a good deal of back work to make up.

I have been cramming up for a prize exam., which takes place during the next three days. It is on Latin prose composition, on Greek and on the solution of Algebraic problems. The person who stands first receives the income of $1000 annually during the four years of the course; the one standing second receives the same amount for one year; and the third receives the same as the latter.

I have a new room-mate. He is a classmate, who had accumulated so many bad marks that his father came on from St. Louis. He arranged with the faculty to put the boy in the room of some steady fellow, so it fell to me. Since then Graham (that's his name) has not improved much, but he is kind-hearted and very agreeable company.

His first summer vacation was spent partly in Saugerties and partly in Peace Dale, visiting his father's former parishoners. From each place he wrote long letters to Will Eliot, who was in Oregon with his grandparents. In these letters he continued the discussion of religious beliefs. His Peace Dale letter, in fact, consists largely of an Eliot-Fisher debate on immortality, nearly every paragraph containing a quotation from Eliot with appropriate rebuttal by Fisher.

19

Saugerties is my birthplace—papa's first parish. I am staying with some of his parishoners and I enjoy myself among them very much. The girls whom I have met here are pleasant and pretty and one or two have considerable character. When I fall in love she must be a girl of *pure morality, fine tastes* and *broad culture.* If you have a superfluity of that description in Oregon, send me word.

My life here is spent in boating, croquet, checkers and to some extent the three r's. Boating I consider the most important as it affords me easy pleasant, symmetrical exercise which I need so much. I go out every morning in the creek. The banks are very high and wooded. There is a mile and a half which is very straight and offers as good a rowing course as I have ever seen. I generally row three or four miles. Yesterday I made a quarter of a mile in 3.12.

The other night quite a party of us (seven, five of whom were ladies) took a very pleasant moonlight row. I find I have quite a passion for rowing. When I go back to college I think I shall join the Dunham Boat Club which will give me the privilege of using any of the Yale Boat House shells or barges. I have begun now for the first time to fully realize that it is neither politic nor right to study at the expense of one's health.

In "readin' " I am taking up *Innocents Abroad* and Dickens' *Martin Chuzzlewit.* There are many things of a more solid sort which treat on the controversy between science and religion. But as I have never read any of Milton, Byron, Tennyson, Thackeray, George Eliot, Carlyle, Johnson, Gibbon and many others, I feel as if I ought first to do some general light reading.

The "ritin' " refers to a very little scribbling I do in writing down some of my numerous thoughts for the purpose of making them clearer to myself. I am just beginning to realize the importance of clearness of expression. I congratulate you on your success in the Oratorical Contest. I took third prize in the Exam. of which I wrote you. In Mathematics I took first prize.

The patent business stands in this wise. I received an official letter containing a criticism of my claims and referring to some other patents. Prof. Phillips gave me a letter to a Patent Lawyer with whom he was acquainted. The lawyer looked up the references and found (who would have imagined?) that there are several contrivances already patented for the identical purpose as mine, some involving similar mechanism in some parts. I will say, however, that my contrivance is more perfect than any of the others.

I would give a good deal to be convinced of Immortality. When one contemplates the Infinite and Finite, the idea of a short *limited* life is *awful*. This fact is presented by many as an argument for believing in immortality. To let your beliefs be influenced by the pleasure or pain which they bring seems to me to be *immoral*.

I was trained to love the right and hate the wrong and now I have an earnest desire to be good and useful. A misspent life seems to me very repulsive, a well spent one like my father's has a pure and noble beauty. My motives for right doing are therefore both Duty and Pleasure, the only possible motives for doing anything. I write this about myself, that you might not think that because I am without Religion, I had weakened my principles of Morality.

PEACE DALE, R. I., September 3, 1885
Your long letter did me a great deal of good, though its arguments failed to convince me. I have

often wondered why you never expressed your opinions in some such way before. In your letter you gave me the reason: "I think there is nothing like discussion to confirm doubt." I quite agree with you excepting that I would add *belief* to doubt. That is one great reason, I think, why so many intelligent men seemingly capable of judging, differ so widely on many topics. It is harder to be a judge than a lawyer.

You "believe in immortality because of its *reasonableness*." It is a question in my mind whether it *is* reasonable and if so whether one should believe in it *implicitly*.

"To my mind absolute annihilation of my spirit is *as* unreasonable as to deny an axiom in mathematics." —I suppose you wrote that for emphasis, for I cannot believe that it is literally true. You must not think, however, that I demand to have a thing absolutely proven in order to believe it. If I were convinced of the reasonableness of immortality to the extent of probability I would believe it but not without doubts. There are different degrees of reasonableness. An axiom is reasonable to the extent of certainty.

When you say "How little we know" I agree, but it seems to me to have more force on the negative side of the question. When I consider how little we *know*, what a wee bit of an end of all truth we have hold of, and that it is even possible to question the authority of axioms, I find it hard to comprehend how people can put unlimited, unqualified, undoubting faith in things for which they can have very little foundation.

"I feel bound to put my trust and faith in immortality, as a necessity both in reason and in justice."— Justice implies the existence of a just God. I am inclined to think there *is* a God and perhaps a just one. But it seems to me to infinitely outreach the bounds of justice to reward a *finite* worthiness with *infinite* life. . . .

22

"My conviction of immortality *besides* being *tested* by its reasonableness is as much *in* me as the sense of duty is in either of us."—There may be something in that. I suppose you mean Man's innate longing for immortality, though the longing may not be innate but acquired. *Homines credunt quod volunt.* I have been speaking of the *longing* for immortality, not the *conviction.* I presumed that the former was the cause of the latter. Perhaps I was too presumptuous.

How I wish I could see you! We would accomplish more in a half-hour's conversation on this subject than we can by weeks' correspondence. But I would like to see you most just to see you. My natural inclinations prompt me to write love-letters to you, but as I have an impression that you do not like anything "gushing," I will forbear. The emotional lyric belongs rather to the opposite sex. I will content myself with the matter-of-fact:

Ed. Jackson, my cousin, has been visiting near Boston and a week ago I went up to Providence to meet him on his way back to St. Louis. We saw a good deal of Providence together, went through Brown University, saw Corliss's house and got a glimpse of Corliss himself riding by in a carriage. He is the inventor of the Corliss engine.

I came back via Newport and spent a day there looking at the empty display of fashion which I saw on a larger scale than I ever saw before. Showy equipages passed with marble-statue coachmen and footmen and a glittering harness whose jingling reminded me of a baby's rattle—some diverting little trinket to please the poor little minds of the devotees of fashion. (I am afraid I put that on too thick.)

I have finished reading Munger's article on "Immortality and Modern Thought" and found it intensely interesting. The attitude of my mind toward religion is becoming more favorable than it has been. Not long ago everything I hit upon seemed to argue against the religious belief in which I was trained. Now almost everything I come upon seems to point the other way.

P. S. on my way from Saugerties to Peace Dale, I stopped in New York a day to visit Piano Manufacturers. My visit confirmed my doubt of success. None of the men I saw expressed any encouragement.

During his remaining undergraduate years the letters to Will Eliot diminished somewhat in frequency as well as in loquacity. One summer vacation was spent soliciting book subscriptions and the others were occupied with tutoring, either in private homes or at a resort boarding house, where he lived at the expense of his employers.

Excerpts from some of his letters in this period continue the story of his undergraduate career:

NEW HAVEN, December 27, 1885

The semi-annual examinations were over the 22nd. I have worked as hard as possible consistent with health. The tutor in English told me that I passed the best exam. in the class. Now I shall tell you what else I know about myself. I am, I believe, undisputed monarch of the college in mathematics. Excuse me if I seem Egotistic. I think a man should rate himself just as he should rate another, viz. according to his *honest* judgement.

About my classmates: Graham, who rooms with me, has been doing better this year. His is a strange character. He has no good or noble ideal. He is doing well for *policy's* sake. Fellowes is an admirable character but seems hard for me to reach. Stimson is perhaps the brightest fellow in the class. He is popular and goes with all kinds. He is not *too* industrious,

24

though he must stand within the first three of the class. Thomas is a very good and agreeable fellow. He is a class deacon but is a hail-fellow well-met kind of man and enjoys jollity very much.

There is no one fellow who is especially adapted to my temperament or liking. You see I had before entering college formed my ideal of a man, an ideal which no one of my classmates comes up to.

NEW HAVEN, April 4, 1886

Perhaps you have already heard of the death of Graham, my room-mate. Four weeks ago today he was visiting some friends in the country. While riding home he contracted a severe cold. The next day he attended college exercises; that evening he felt very sick and never rose from his bed after retiring that night. He died the following Sunday. His father arrived Saturday night and was with his son six hours.

The funeral was held in the chapel. That evening Mr. Graham left for St. Louis. Two of the classmates, Stimson and myself, were appointed to accompany him as far as New York. He was utterly broken down. It was more terrible to see his suffering than to think of the death itself. Poor Graham had many very fine qualities. When he died he had a first division stand. I believe I forgot to say that the disease was Pneumonia.

BERLIN, N. J., May 29, 1886

You said the puzzle with you is to know what to do for a life-work. It is not exactly the same with me. I am almost decided as to my immediate and possibly permanent occupation after leaving college, viz. to teach mathematics. But the puzzle with me is about the vital principles of conduct of life. I want some meridian of reference to which to refer all the actions in my little sphere. I want to know the truth about philosophy and religion.

If I could only have a standard to which to refer all I do, I think I would not find much difficulty in deciding as to details. As it is I live a hand-to-mouth existence, sometimes acting from one impulse and sometimes acting from another, but with a main purpose to study and think about these things hoping for something more definite and satisfactory.

Pittsfield, Mass., July 25, 1886

I row an hour or two every day. I have a notion of entering for the races this fall. My main object is to get strong physically in order to study well next year. Now that I probably stand first in the class I better make an effort to retain my place. I shall not do it in a narrow way but shall make the intrinsic worth of my studies of the most importance.

How much there is I want to do! I always feel that I haven't time to accomplish what I wish. I want to read much, both in general reading and in history and in Science and Religion. I want to write a great deal. I want to make money.

Most of all I want to know what some great man (Goethe?) said was the one thing worth knowing. I feel that I have power and I want a worthy object toward which to direct it. How very very little we know about ourselves! Our minds! Our feelings! Our destinies! Why don't some one find out whether materialism, necessitarianism, atheism are lies or not?

I have been writing a little, but I haven't much confidence in myself. My chief fault is I lack ability to write conceits, turns of expression, and all the paraphernalia which makes up good skillful writing.

I always incline toward saying things directly and exactly instead of couching them in similes, etc.

NEW HAVEN, October 24, 1886

As soon as I got back to New Haven, I began practicing in the Dunham Boat Club and acquired the ability to row to advantage in a single scull. As the races approached it happened that no *good* oarsmen were training for the Cleveland Race and so I decided to enter and won it. In order to obtain the cup to keep, I must win it twice more in succession. It is a work of art. On one side is an engraving of Lake Saltonstall where the races are rowed and on the other are the names of the winners.

I have the same difficulty as you in finding companions that are thoughtful *in what they express*. There is a kind of atmosphere about college that prevents a man from talking very earnestly and soberly, especially in a company of more than two. But I find that many fellows who seem so careless are really much more sober and thoughtful in their innermost selves. It took me a long time to get on to this, but I am compelled to adopt a similar course and I find I get more at the real characters of my classmates than I did.

I am sorry there is so much made of popularity at Yale. It is the one essential of a "big man" and of a candidate for one of the two great Senior Societies: Skull and Bones and Scroll and Keys.

NEW HAVEN, November 14, 1886

Your announcement of your decision about your life work is indeed a surprise. I remember your telling me that your mother wanted you to be a minister but that you thought better of the law.

27

As for myself, I am not by any means decided, though I expect to be a teacher of mathematics for a time at least. The thing that is now engrossing my attention is the competition for the Editorship of the Yale Lit. I have handed in two pieces for the next issue. I have been refused twice. If I get rejected this time it will "settle my hash."

Those who associate the name of Irving Fisher solely with what has been called "the dismal science" may be surprised to learn that he first broke into print when one of these two items was accepted by Yale's undergraduate *Literary Magazine*. Here are the concluding verses of his twelve-stanza poem "Whispers of the Elms," which was published in the fall of his Junior year:

> Sacred records of the Past!
> How much History, how much Mystery,
> Your stalwart forms hold fast!
>
> And to me each nodding bough,
> Gently swinging, softly singing,
> Tells of one who is not now.
>
> One who thirty years ago,
> When he dwelt here, thought and felt here,
> Sung in measures sweet and low,
>
> Drawing from these things of Time
> Inspirations for creations
> Of melodious liquid rhyme. ⸢
>
> Over him and others, ever
> Gently swinging, softly singing,
> Chant these elms a hymn forever.

In the spring of 1887 he was one of eight who competed in a public-speaking contest known as the Junior Exhibition. Although his friend Stimson nosed him out for first place, his own discourse on "Liberal Education and Social Needs" was considered a close runner-up. To show the direction in which his thoughts were moving, here is the gist of his argument:

Division of labor implies cooperation, and cooperation implies unity in Social life. In the delicately balanced condition of modern supply and demand, the sudden failing of one class of men to contribute their expected portion transmits a shock throughout the Social organization. Society grows together as men's pursuits grow apart. To help this growth into an organism is the mission of liberal education.

To perfect the organization of Society, there must be, as well as leadership and sound philosophy, a framework of social restraints. It is strange that a liberal education should be necessary to make men accept common Social Conventions. But there is a class who have just reached the stage of theorizing. They are a strange excrescence of modern civilization, known under the various names of Socialists, Communists and Anarchists. We might almost hold our liberal education responsible for their existence.

They form incorrect notions of the province of government and boldly question the propriety of *all* restraints on personal liberty. These would-be reformers with their dangerous mixture of knowledge and ignorance and those of the labor leaders that without reason and without profit block the wheels of industry must have their eyes opened to the great *laws* they are violating. If we do not pull together, we may only succeed in tearing Society to pieces.

Two additional letters to Will Eliot describe the aftermath of his participation in the Junior Exhibition, and his personal impressions of Yale's traditional Tap Day:

NEW HAVEN, April 10, 1887

Your generous interest in my Junior Ex-ploit was very pleasant. The truth is I did not at first look at my defeat philosophically and I felt so ———— something, that I wrote you a note for the mere satisfaction of working off my feelings. I sealed it and forgot to mail it. The next day I tore it open to reconsider. It now lies before me destined for my waste basket. I am all straight again now but my ambitions had been so high that great was the fall thereof.

On the day of the speaking I was indiscreetly told that my piece was held the best by the chief of the judges. I was very much surprised and pleased for this man has never liked my previous writing. The thing that more especially inspired the unmailed letter was quite different. A day or two after the decision members of the faculty separately told me that my piece was considered the best, but that the prize was given to Stimson for the extraordinarily good delivery.

I was pleased at the faculty's attitude toward my efforts but my selfishness disliked the idea that the prize indicated one thing to the college and outsiders, but to the faculty was a symbol of *another*. If this had been straightened out I would care *nil* for the prize for I am not at all ambitious to be an orator.— I say I would care nothing for it except for the *money* and the admission to Skull and Bones which it generally brings.

NEW HAVEN, May 29, 1887

A week ago today I felt considerably battered. After the Junior Ex business, I had been through a series of defeats. I was going to write then but concluded to wait till after the Senior Society elections. In the Phi Beta Kappa elections I was defeated for the chairmanship by Stimson. This was a small matter.

Eight days ago the race came off for the cup which I then held. The day before the race in a practice pull the waves broke over my deck and through a hole in it swamped me and I had to swim ashore and walk one and a half miles with nothing on but shoes and kneepants through a tangled wood, to get to the boat house.

That night I slept only about three hours. When the time came for the race a wind came up which was unfavorable to me alone of all contestants, because my boat was adapted only to very smooth water being light and low, while the other boats rode high. The result was that I was virtually rowing with my oars under water, and the wind caught me and turned me around so that I had to pull almost entirely with my left oar. Then one of my row locks troubled me and all these things lost me the race.

These taken together with the fact that the crew captain had seemed to rather "sour" on my rowing indicator, for plotting a rower's stroke, gave me the feeling of "the man who failed." I thought I would wait till my next failure in Senior Society elections before writing, so that my stock would be complete. But the failure I looked forward to did not come.

These Senior Societies are one of Yale's traditional institutions. They tinge a man's actions with something like insincerity, for the incumbents have to become popular. Thence come forced friendships and cringing. In some cases it is said, friendships are broken up. An election is considered by the majority of undergraduates the "biggest college honor."

On Thursday last the college assembled in front of Durfee Hall. There was a sprinkling of ladies in the windows to see their gentlemen "taken in." A Bones man comes along with a sober face, hunts through the crowd until he sees the man for whom he was sent and then approaching him from behind if possible he claps his hand on his shoulder and mutters "go to your room." The man though often struck hard, never seems offended and obeys the arbitrary order while the crowd claps and the Freshmen inquire "who is it?" Then a Keys man comes round the corner and does the same act, and so on.

I thought my chances were about even at the beginning but after three men on the Bones list were taken they sank down to almost zero. After the ninth man was taken I had given up hope and was waiting for the show to stop, for the last half dozen men taken are generally "sure" men, which I was not. I was almost dreaming when Corwin, Captain of last year's Football team whose presence I had not observed, whacked me on the shoulder and sent an electric shock through me.

It is rather hard to describe my feelings. I am sorry for the disappointed men. I take a great satisfaction in my election to Bones for I felt it to be my first little conquest among men. As a Freshman I was afraid of my own voice and was as little prominent as a man could be. Sophomore year witnessed some improvement in the ability to converse and tell people my thoughts enough for them to know I had some, but I have during Junior year done the most growing in this direction. To have some tangible recognition of it is to me a great thing.

Then there was a long silence. Even commencement did not stimulate him to write to Oregon immediately. Perhaps he sent a newspaper account of the proceedings, but his personal impressions of the big day were not recorded until nearly the end of a Vermont tutoring assignment. The fact that Stimson had again won a coveted pregraduation oratorical contest was more than offset by Fisher's ranking highest in the class and delivering the valedictory:

GREENSBORO, VERMONT, September 2, 1888

Commencement was a gala day for me—my first experience of triumph. Two days previous on class day it was announced that I had taken a $200 prize for my mathematical solutions, which is twice as much as ever before given. I was also awarded a scholarship for post-graduate study yielding $500 a year. These made quite a prelude to Commencement.

My Commencement piece was on *Conservatism as Presented by the Comparative Study of Man*. It was attentively listened to and roundly applauded. Next came the address to the President and then to the class. I had put all my Yale enthusiasm into this and spoke simply and from the heart. I scarcely dared look at my classmates individually until I was nearly through and then I was half startled by suddenly realizing that they were crying.

When I stopped the people cheered and cheered and when I found myself loaded with five large flower tributes they rose on a tide of enthusiasm. As I walked down the aisle I found myself stopped all the way along by strangers who wanted to shake my hand. On my way home with my mother and our train of visitors we received ovations from the street corners even. From as many as half a dozen sources I heard that my Valedictory was "the best they had ever heard."

Perhaps you will think my head was turned. But I enjoyed my little college successes quietly, thankfully, and with a sort of association with my father's

33

memory, over whose grave I pronounced my address when I visited Peace Dale a few days later.

The people in this far away place have not yet learned what a boat is but have rectangular affairs warranted to row equally badly in all directions. I am more than satisfied with my summer; besides rest and the educating influence of my social and material environment I shall carry back nearly $200.

That fall he had a brief reunion with his west coast correspondent, before plunging into postgraduate work. They spent a large portion of one afternoon discussing religion on the summit of West Rock. Although no verbatim account of this conversation exists, subsequent references to it indicate that their basic beliefs were not far apart, although one of them was on his way to Harvard to study for the ministry, while the other was aiming for a career in mathematics. He served as part-time instructor in this subject during his postgraduate course, and for one term even filled a temporary vacancy in the astronomy department. His interest in mathematics remained a strong motivating force throughout his life, but it was fortunate for his own peace of mind that a combination of outside influences led him to select the comparatively uncharted sphere of mathematical economics for his own particular bailiwick. The next chapter will chronicle the details of this gradual metamorphosis.

3. Supply and Demand

After his first full year of postgraduate work he wrote an informative letter to the father of his former roommate who had died of pneumonia during Sophomore year. Before the letter was mailed his mother took pains to copy it in longhand, feeling that it should be preserved because it "showed so much well expressed thought and principles," for a young man of twenty-two. She neglected to note the precise date of the letter, but from the context it is clear that it was written early in the summer of 1889:

DEAR MR. GRAHAM:

In your talks and correspondence three years ago with my mother and myself, I was led to think you might, if ever I got in a tight place, help me out.

I am now undergoing the throes of choosing a life-work and my choice might be guided by an assured financial backing. I hope you will pardon me a frank letter about myself. After graduating last year I refused considering teacher's positions, finding that I could make finances go just as well by studying here another year on a scholarship of $500 ($400 above tuition) and what I could make by private tutoring. I have done this and finding I could keep my head out of water, I have decided to stay another year on an increased scholarship of $600 (net $500).

At the time of graduation I was almost fully determined to enter mathematics as a life-work. I was naturally led to this by the flattery of my instructors, who predicted great success in that line on account of my college record, which was the taking of every Math. 1st prize, ending with a $200 double first, twice in amount the largest prize ever before awarded.

My senior year, however, had roused an interest in other things. I have consequently used my graduate year as a period of reconsideration. I put my studies on a wide range to get a bird's eye view of the several departments—Mathematics, Social & Political Science, Law, Chemistry, Metaphysics.

After surveying these lines for a year and talking with friends I have reduced my possible future to three alternatives. Law practice, teaching and investigating Social Science and higher Mathematics. I intend to make definite decisions by September.

Mathematics I regard as a supremely grand study but a very unsatisfactory life employment. It gives delight as a dessert but little nutriment as the main course. By exercise it generates penetration but by neglect it tends to fossilization. It broadens a man as a thinker, but it narrows him as a factor in the world. Few realize what a terrible isolation a professional and devoted Mathematician must suffer.

Social Science has great attractions for me. It is the only study the teaching of which would be a pleasure aside from investigation. But it is peculiar in this; that the entrance to it is very difficult because it is a new study and an advanced one. I find teachers of Political Economy are either men who were wealthy enough to await a position and in no sense dependent on that position for support, or men who have gone into some other line first. Thus, unless some unexpected offer should be made me next year, I could scarcely hope to enter that branch except through some other preliminary means of support.

As regards Law, many things urge me toward such a life. It will require two years preparation after this coming year's study, and that study would be without

36

scholarship, as scholarships are given only for unprofessional study. After these two years preparation, I would have slowly to work up a practice and until my income reached $1000 I would scarcely make both ends meet. Of course I would earn a few dollars tutoring and some of my expenses could possibly be lessened or at an end when my brother is in college, and can support himself. It is obvious, however, that to go into Law means to allow expenses to exceed income for several years and I could do nothing but borrow money.

I write to ask you two distinct questions. First, could you aid me by a yearly loan of money, $500 at the least, beginning a year hence and lasting at least three years and on what terms? Second, could you (in case I get along as far as entering an office) probably help me in entering an office in St. Louis or elsewhere?

I write you now rather than after deciding my course, in order that your reply may be an item to be taken into account. I have taken the decision of my life work much more seriously than is usual. This I do because to me life is a sober thing to contemplate. I do not wish to fall into the vain regrets I find so common, nor do I wish to trifle with the especial duties to others I find allotted to me.

If you are to be in New York or Boston soon or after Sept. 18 and should care to talk with me I should like to come and see you; or, if you could be pleased to take the trouble, we would like to have you come and see us.

Very respectfully yours,

IRVING FISHER

Mr. Graham must have replied in the negative, for the record shows that the requisite financial backing was obtained elsewhere. One thousand dollars was borrowed from Rowland Hazard of Peace Dale, and duly repaid with six per cent interest before either party to the transaction had any inkling that the borrower was destined to become the lender's son-in-law.

During his second year of postgraduate work he wrote a paper on "Mathematical Contributions to Philosophy," in which he berated Kant for founding his theory of the universe solely on Euclidian principles, whereas "for aught we know we do live in spherical or pseudo-spherical space. The substratum of nature is for us always covered with the veil of thought. We can never hope to lift even a corner of this drapery and see the treasure it hides. But yet in some sense or other we have faith that there is something there. Beneath the cloak of phenomena there is some colorless, odorless, intangible something—an unknown X."

Such metaphysical speculations were a constant source of relaxation to him. More than once he mystified the family circle with involved discussions of the fourth dimension, whenever he could buttonhole a kindred spirit. Once I even accompanied him when he kept an appointment with Einstein in the mid-thirties at the latter's Rhode Island summer home, but their stratospheric discussion of the fine points of relativity was too erudite for me.

Two letters written on the same day, in the summer after his second year of graduate work, give further glimpses into his mental and physical activities. The first was written to Will Eliot and the second to brother Herbert at their grandmother's home in New Jersey:

NORTH OAKS, MINN., August 17, 1890
DEAR WILL:
I am tutoring for the summer twelve miles north of St. Paul. The youth I have had for five months

got several conditions on entering college. I am now at his father's summer home. He is J. J. Hill, President of the Great Northwestern R. R. and the richest man in the northwest. He has made all his money himself, honestly, and since he has reached his maturity.

This "Farm" of 4000 acres has a large house, a bowling alley (the boys and I live in the upper part), six or seven barns, numerous horses, fancy cattle, sheep, etc. There are in all nearly a hundred people here centering around Mr. Hill.

I tutor a good deal but have plenty of spare time. I am trying to make headway with a German mathematical book on Prices (by Auspitz and Lieben)— very interesting to me. I hope to write my thesis on something of that sort next year. Did I tell you I was re-elected Douglas Fellow and shall go back to Yale to study once more? This is of course made possible by tutoring. I shall have both the Hill boys to look after through the whole year, for which I shall receive $150 per month.

A week ago I went to St. Paul and spent Sunday with a classmate, Morison, and who should meet us at the depot but two well known friends. I haven't enjoyed myself in some time as much as we did that afternoon. We had some sport here last night, with the banjo and guitar and bowling. I hold all the records now in bowling.

My friend Morison is in Mr. Hill's office. I have been questioning and wondering what sort of a life railroading might mean for me? If I were sure I could succeed I should very possibly go into it. A man can't do all he sees done and would like to do but, if such was in my power, I would choose a sort of success similar to Sir John Lubeck's. To be a successful man among men and at the same time carry on my favorite studies with limited success—that would be my ideal.

DEAR BERT:

As to the concentration of wealth. Your grandma and uncles think that so much wealth as Mr. Hill has is "not a good thing" in one man's hands. Grandma and Uncle Will did not clearly conceive whether Mr. Hill's wealth was *an addition to or a subtraction from* the wealth of the world as it stood before Mr. Hill stepped on the stage.

If Mr. Hill's pile has been collected out of other people's certainly his fortune is a bad thing (for them). If his pile is a separate creation, he has not only not injured others but his wealth as capital has benefitted others.

Suppose two cases: First a group of ten men gamble. Each has a hundred gold dollars. Soon some one man gets way ahead; say wins $800. Before there were ten piles of $100 each; now there is one pile of $900, and $100 scattered over nine other piles. There is no more and no less total money than at the start. Here the concentration of wealth is by *subtraction* and injures nine people.

Now suppose ten men go to California and wash gold. Nine of them make $100 per week and the tenth, by greater skill and endurance, makes $150. The extra $50 is taken out of nobody else's pocket, but out of nature. Well, this man saves his extra $50 and buys a gold-washing machine which, for a consideration, he allows the others to use. Thus the extra $50 has become a means of enriching the other nine men. Say they can make $140 per week by the machine out of which they pay the owner $30. They still make $110, or $10 more than *before their companion got his capital.*

40

There are some men who get rich by the subtraction method. But most by the addition method, and so did Mr. Hill. When he got hold of his R. R., he more than *trebled its value, for he knew how to run it.* That is, through his *special sagacity*, its usefulness to farmers in conveying wheat was immensely increased. By constructing branches where the wheat could be grown best—by arranging the time schedules and the rates, he effected such a saving to farmers over what they had *before*, that they were willing to part with some of their extra produce to compensate their benefactor.

In the end, however, he was forced to revise his estimate of the railroader's personal integrity. Two years after writing the foregoing he wrote to Will Eliot in mock indignation: "Please don't refer to Mr. J. J. Hill as my 'friend.' He and I had a falling out. He is a shrewd man but unreliable to the last degree."

In the meantime, two outstanding members of the Yale faculty—Gibbs and Sumner—had been exerting a catalytic influence on his unfolding career. In his seventy-fifth anniversary talk at Harvard, he referred to J. Willard Gibbs as "the greatest mind which I ever met, except Einstein, and probably the greatest scientific mind which Yale has ever produced." Earlier he had helped establish the Josiah Willard Gibbs Professorship at Yale and personally financed the publication of his mentor's collected works. On the last day of 1929 he delivered the seventh Josiah Willard Gibbs lecture at Des Moines, Iowa, before a joint session of the American Mathematical Society and the American Association for the Advancement of Science, which included these personal impressions of the great physical chemist:

We think no less of Gibbs' greatness because he himself showed so little consciousness of it. He must have realized the fundamental character of his work, but his pupils often commented on his profound modesty. His chief delight was in truth seeking for its own sake. He had no time even to think of emphasizing the originality or value of his own additions to the great vista of truth over which his mind swept.

I remember hearing him say that when he wanted to verify another man's results he usually found it easier to work them out for himself than to follow the other man's own course of reasoning. This was said without any affectation, but simply in a jocular vein, as by one who would escape a difficult task by going his own way. But he founded a new era in physics and chemistry. . . .

Presumably Gibbs' greatest contribution to science was his application of the laws of thermodynamics to chemistry. He made this almost a deductive science, producing many deductions from a few general principles. His chief intellectual characteristic consisted in his tendency to make his reasoning as general as possible, to get the maximum of results from the minimum of hypotheses. I have often quoted an aphorism used by Gibbs, to the effect that "the whole is simpler than its parts."

Many other investigators instinctively seek to solve special cases before attempting to solve the general case. I remember Professor Bumstead, my fellow student at Yale, recounting with relish a conversation that Gibbs had with a youthful investigator who had made a laborious experimental study of certain relationships and who was, with pardonable pride, telling Gibbs of his conclusion. After listening attentively Professor Gibbs quite naturally and unaffectedly closed his eyes, thought a moment and said, "Yes, that would be true," seeing at once that the special result which this young investigator had reached was a necessary corollary of Gibbs' own more general results. . . .

Apparently I am the only one of his pupils who, after first doing teaching in mathematics and physics, became professedly an economist. After several years graduate study in mathematics under Gibbs, and in economics under Sumner, the time came for me to write my doctor's thesis and I selected as my subject *Mathematical Investigations in the Theory of Value and Prices*. Professor Gibbs showed a lively interest in this youthful work, and was especially interested in the fact that I had used geometric constructions and methods including his own vector analysis.

A decade after delivering this lecture he conducted a vigorous one-man campaign to bring about Gibbs' election to the Hall of Fame. To each of the hundred and twenty electors he sent a mimeographed brochure summarizing his mentor's achievements in the world of physical chemistry. This document included quotations from a long list of authorities, such as Lord Kelvin, Michael Pupin, Sir Joseph Larmor, as well as Professors Bumstead and Chittenden of Yale. Favorable replies were received from many of the electors, but Gibbs failed to poll the requisite number of votes until the 1950 election, so that his self-appointed sponsor did not live to see the fruit of this labor of love.

In contrast to Gibbs, William Graham Sumner was very well known to the generations of Yale students who attended his courses on the science of society. For many years he enjoyed the reputation of transforming numerous scions of wealthy families from protectionists to ardent free traders, with considerable annoyance on the part of reactionary captains of industry who sent their sons to Yale to acquire conservative educations. He coined the phrase "forgotten man" which Franklin Roosevelt later appropriated as a New Deal slogan. He also characterized socialism as a scheme for running everything by a committee, and in the event of its adoption he advised his pupils "to get on that committee."

Sumner and Fisher remained lifelong mutual admirers, but the extent to which their thinking ultimately diverged may be illustrated by this passage from the latter's speech on socialism, delivered before the Yale Socialist Club on November 14, 1911:

> I believe Sumner was one of the greatest professors we ever had at Yale, but I have drawn far away from his point of view, that of the old laissez faire doctrinaire.
>
> I remember he said in his classroom: "Gentlemen, the time is coming when there will be two great classes, Socialists, and Anarchists. The Anarchists want the government to be nothing, and the Socialists want the government to be everything. There can be no greater contrast. Well, the time will come when there will be only these two great parties, the Anarchists representing the *laissez faire* doctrine and the Socialists representing the extreme view on the other side, and when that time comes I am an Anarchist."
>
> That amused his class very much, for he was as far from a revolutionary as you could expect. But I would like to say that if that time comes when there are two great parties, Anarchists and Socialists, then I am a Socialist.

His Harvard talk, on the seventy-fifth anniversary of his birth, contained these further references to Sumner:

While I was still studying for a mathematical career, I took courses under Sumner, not because I ever expected to enter economics but because I wanted to meet such a personality before leaving Yale. The more I saw of him, the more I wanted to get his point of view, so that when the time came to select my thesis, I found I had devoted nearly half of my time to his courses.

I went to him and told him that I was perplexed as to what to choose for a doctor's thesis, since half of my time had been outside my field of mathematics.

He said, "Why don't you write on mathematical economics?"

I replied, "I have never heard of such a subject."

He said, "That is because I myself have never studied it enough to use it, but I can put you on to the literature."

The result was that I became fascinated with Cournot, with Walras, and with Jevons, not to mention Auspitz and Lieben, joint authors of a book which I studied perhaps more thoroughly than any other, though it has had few readers. This is how I happened to choose the subject of my thesis, which was founded partly on the work just mentioned, though chiefly on Walras and Edgeworth.

The influence of both Gibbs and Sumner can be discerned in the thesis which their pupil submitted for his Ph.D. degree in 1891. It was published the following year and it has since been translated into several foreign languages. English reprints appeared in 1925 and again in 1937.

After acknowledging his indebtedness to Jevons and to Auspitz and Lieben, he stated that certain equations developed in the course of Part I of *Mathematical Investigations* were found to be essentially similar to those of

45

Walras, which had been "obtained independently and by separate paths." Similarly: "Three days after Part II was finished I saw for the first time Prof. Edgeworth's *Mathematical Physics*," and he was "interested to find a resemblance between" some of the Britisher's geometrical figures and his own "total utility surfaces." But he considered Edgeworth's "foisting of Psychology on Economics" to be wholly "inappropriate and vicious." Others mentioned as having "contributed the most to the subject" were Cournot, Menger and Marshall.

From the standpoint of the general reader this initial publication of Irving Fisher is considerably more technical and abstruse than the majority of his later writings, so that it is difficult to summarize by means of excerpts and paraphrasing. The mathematically inclined reader who wishes the benefit of supporting formulae and graphs should refer to the book itself. These quotations are taken from the opening chapter:

> To fix the idea of utility the economist should go no farther than is serviceable in explaining economic facts. It is not his province to build a theory of psychology. It is not necessary for him to take sides with those who wrangle to prove or disprove that pleasure and pain alone determine conduct. These disputants have so mangled the ideas of pleasure and pain that he who follows them and their circular arguments finds himself using the words in forced senses.
>
> The last dollar's worth of sugar (we are told by Jevons) represents the same quantity of pleasurable feeling as the last dollar's worth of dentistry. This may be true as a mere empty definition, but we must beware of connecting it with the mathematics of sensations as did Edgeworth.
>
> It is difficult to see why so many theorists endeavor to obliterate the distinction between pleasure and de-

sire. Whether the necessary antecedent of desire is "pleasure" or whether independently of pleasure it may sometimes be "duty" or "fear" concerns a phenomenon in the second remove from the economic act of choice and is completely within the realm of psychology.

Stating that "each individual acts as he desires," he used this postulate as the cornerstone for his theory of marginal utility, that mysterious factor in commerce which induces a purchaser to buy just so many loaves of bread, pounds of sugar, or pairs of shoes—no more and no less. "Just as the tip of the scales is the test of equality or inequality of weights, so is the desire of the individual, the test of the equality or inequality of utilities."

If an individual consumes 100 loaves of bread in a year, the utility of the last loaf is greater than what it would be if he consumed 150 loaves. Their ratio is found by contrasting the utilities of the 100th and the 150th loaves with a third utility, say that of oil of which so many gallons have been consumed during the year. If the 100th loaf is twice as useful as the 150th when their ratio is defined in terms of increments of oil, it will also be twice as useful when the ratio is defined in any other commodity.

If the last loaf is sliced into 10 parts and these slices have different utilities, the marginal utility of bread is more nearly the utility of the last slice divided by 1/10, and so on ad infinitum. The utility of the 100th loaf per year may be regarded as the unit of utility, for a given individual at a given time. To get the total utility of a given amount of bread we sum up the utilities for the separate loaves. Or: The total utility of a given quantity of a commodity at a given time and for a given individual is the integral of the marginal utility times the differential of that commodity.

To illustrate his theories graphically he designed an elaborate hydrostatic mechanism to represent "in terms of mechanical interaction, that beautiful and intricate equilibrium which manifests itself in the 'exchanges' of a great city." With a series of interconnected cisterns, representing individual consumers and producers, he used the physical law that water seeks its own level to show that "a given amount of commodity to be consumed by a market during a given period will be so distributed among the individuals that the marginal utility measured in money will be equal. Furthermore the marginal utility thus determined will be the price. . . . The marginal utilities of all articles consumed by a given individual are proportional to the marginal utilities of the same series of articles for each other consumer, and this uniform continuous ratio is the scale of prices of those articles."

Not long before his death, in the rough draft of the first chapter of his proposed book *My Economic Endeavors*, Irving Fisher stated:

> The analysis in *Mathematical Investigations* differed from the analysis of Walras in several respects, in particular in the fact that the basic functions are marginal utilities as functions of the quantities of commodities, whereas Walras makes them functions of the mark-up prices. I feel that much of the classroom supply and demand analysis is extremely superficial and calculated to give the student the idea that mere supply and demand of individual prices are sufficient to fully determine said price, without having to take any account of money. . . . It is often ludicrous to note how confidently some of the writers

assert that there is 'nothing to the Quantity theory' of money when that or some equivalent is the very thing needed to make their own reasoning meaningful. . . . In the theory of money it is erroneous to say, as is often done, that the total volume of money (including checking deposits) is determined by the price level although each individual's cash balance is so determined.

Writing in the March 1893 issue of the *Economic Journal*, Professor Francis Y. Edgeworth of Oxford made these comments on *Mathematical Investigations*:

> The theory of Exchange which is based upon marginal utility has received from Dr. Fisher some very happy illustrations. Observing that most economists employ largely the vocabulary of mechanics—equilibrium, stability, elasticity, level, friction and so forth —and profoundly impressed with the analogy between mechanical and economic equilibrium, Dr. Fisher has employed the principle that water seeks its own level to illustrate some of the leading propositions of pure economics.
>
> We may at least predict to Dr. Fisher the degree of immortality which belongs to one who has deepened the foundations of the pure theory of Economics.

Quoting again from the uncompleted manuscript of *My Economic Endeavors*, the author of *Mathematical Investigations* made these references to Professor Edgeworth's enthusiasm for his thesis:

> To have my philosophy of utility accepted by Edgeworth and lead him to repudiate his own was a great satisfaction to me. He was certainly magnanimous in view of what was said of him in the Preface. He and I became lifelong friends. I was his guest at

49

Oxford and he was mine at New Haven, where he lost no opportunity to praise my work.

A similarly cordial relationship was maintained by correspondence with Pareto, who was nearly twenty years older than the author of *Mathematical Investigations*. One of the latter's most prized possessions was an eight-page letter in French from the Lausanne Professor, which was almost entirely devoted to a discussion of utility. After enumerating various points of disagreement as well as agreement with *Mathematical Investigations,* Pareto spoke scornfully of "the adversaries of mathematical methods," remarking dryly that to see the usefulness of these methods "it is necessary to understand them."

Pareto agreed that it was unnecessary to switch to another term to designate the utility concept, but advocated making a distinction between two types of utility: "(1) that which cannot be useful, and (2) that which is really useful." Toward the end of the letter he predicted: "It is precisely the young economists like yourself who will make the necessary progress in political economy, and who will make it become a true science. I hope to have made a first step, but you and others will make other steps even greater! In a period of fifty years, I believe that political economy will not resemble at all the science which now bears that name."

Half a century later the Harvard authority, Professor Joseph A. Schumpeter, wrote an appreciation of Irving Fisher, which first appeared in *Econometrica* for July, 1948, and was subsequently published in his posthumous volume *Ten Great Economists* in 1950. Here are some of his remarks on *Mathematical Investigations:*

> Full justice has never been done to it by the economic profession at large. Usually, even competent

theorists see Fisher's chief merit in having presented a succinct and elegant version of Walras's theory of value and price and in having illustrated it by means of ingenious mechanical models. But he did much more than reformulate, simplify, and illustrate Walras.

Fisher felt that "utility must be capable of a definition which shall connect it with its positive or objective commodity relations." But he ended up with results that go far towards the suggestion to do without any kind of utility at all; what is left is a concept that lacks any psychological connotation and contains the germs of all the pieces of apparatus that were to emerge in Pareto's wake.

Fisher, with unsurpassable simplicity and brilliance, supplied the theory of the measurement of this non-existent and superfluous thing by defining its unit under the restriction that the utility of any one or at least of one commodity depends on its own quantity only and is independent of the quantities of other commodities. The defects of the method indicated may be as numerous as were the defects of Columbus' flagship if judged by comparison with a modern liner. Nevertheless, it was one of the greatest performances of nascent economics.

In a letter to the author of this treatise, written soon after its publication, Will Eliot raised several questions which elicited this response:

PEACE DALE, R. I., September, 1892

I quite agree that given a certain commodity and price and even making a great many other limiting conditions, one cannot predict the conduct of a consumer precisely, even if there are a dozen apparently similar previous instances from which to judge. There is a kind of indeterminateness about our acts which

I have tried to state in the preceding sentence, without involving the question of the freedom of the will. The criticism you make is therefore a good one though I think you were wrong to connect it with the postulate: "Each individual acts as he desires."

The point at which, as it seems to me, you should have directed your attack was not the postulate but the assumption that the utility of a commodity was a function of the quantity of that commodity. The preference for the shoes was not only related to how many shoes I already had but to a million little circumstances which might readily be classified as "accidental." Yet, as I said in the book, this fitful quality tends to eliminate itself, though never entirely and we have to end in this as in every scientific investigation with giving it up.

And now I turn to a subject more interesting and more profound. I ask your congratulation on the greatest good fortune of my life, my engagement to Miss Margaret Hazard of Peace Dale. We were acquainted as children but she thought I was "the naughtiest little boy" she ever saw and though I never felt unkindly towards her, she never revealed herself to my boyish eyes.

But last fall I met her in New Haven and—will you believe it of your cold analytical mathematical friend —I loved at first sight. You will be interested to be told that I read the first of your letter before and the last after she spoke the magic yes. It seems a desecration to attempt a description of her transcendant character. I wonder if you remember in a letter I sent you about seven years ago an outline of my ideal girl? She is not only the complete realization of that ideal but is so much more that my uppermost and ever recurring thought is of my unworthiness to be her lover and destined husband.

In appearance she is very tall, just a third of an inch shorter than I, has dark brown eyes, dark hair, graceful figure and carriage and beautifully chiselled face, marred only by a little too Roman character in the nose, but when in motion displaying the most spiritual nature I ever came in contact with.

She is something of an artist and singer and has considerable creative faculty in music. She has firmness, decision, character but also gentleness, charity, and an infinite capacity for affection. She has originality in thought and a deeply serious nature, well endowed with thinking power, though not at all trained in exact or scientific knowledge. She is a lover of good poetry and can write very well either in prose or verse.

She has been the pet and youngest in an ideal home, is unselfish, unspoiled and genuinely modest. She has had every opportunity which a father's fortune could give and she gained by it all and never lost. She has met the best people and seen as much of the finest society as she wished but is as simple and innocent as a country maiden and has the greatest contempt for flirtations. She has been reared in the observance of every useful formality and yet has escaped all artificiality and remains a perfect child of nature.

She is deeply religious though she has never bothered herself about creeds. You may be surprised to learn that last Sunday I took communion from her hands in my father's old church. I have in no wise changed my views, which as you remember are essentially like yours, but your own loyalty to the church was one of the largest influences in showing to me the possibility of what I did.—If I should allow myself to talk of her to you as the impulse comes, you would surely classify me among those who have lost their minds as well as hearts.

4. *Happily Ever After*

He often related the story of that fateful afternoon in the fall of 1891, when he went to call at the Bushnell home, which faced the New Haven Green and is now the Graduate Club. He had been invited to meet a young house guest, whom he remembered dimly from his Sunday school days in Peace Dale. While removing his overcoat in the hall, he caught a glimpse of her smile through the partly open parlor door. It made no difference to him that her smile was directed at another caller, or that (as she later confessed) she was entirely oblivious to his presence in the hall; he knew when he stepped across the threshold that he was opening the door into another world. Not the least important element of her captivating smile was the angelic expression of her dark eyes. But every movement of her statuesque figure testified to the gentleness of her patrician heritage.

The first Hazard antecedent to reach New England landed at Boston in 1636 and three years later helped lay out the town of Newport, Rhode Island. His son, who had arrived at Boston with his father at the age of four, was the first of the family to settle across the bay in the Narragansett country, which is known colloquially as South County. There he acquired five hundred acres of the original Pettaquamscut Purchase in 1671.

Her great-grandfather, the first Rowland Hazard, named Peace Dale in honor of his bride, Mary Peace, when he brought her to Rhode Island from Charleston, South

Carolina, in 1794. The woolen mills which he established were to prosper under Hazard ownership for more than one hundred years. His oldest son, Rowland Gibson Hazard, was also known for his writings on *Language* and *Freedom of the Will.* By chance one of his volumes on the latter topic fell into the hands of Irving Fisher during one of his undergraduate summer vacations, and he read it with interest if not full agreement long before he had any ulterior motive for delving into the philosophic background of the Hazard family.

Margaret Hazard's father, the second Rowland Hazard, attended Haverford College, but completed his education at Brown University in 1849. His undergraduate friendship with James B. Angell, who became President of the University of Michigan, was responsible for the use of Rowland as the middle name of the future president of Yale. In 1854 Rowland Hazard married Margaret Rood, daughter of a Philadelphia parson. They called their new Peace Dale home Oakwoods. Built of native granite on a knoll at the edge of an oak forest, it overlooked the mill pond. All but the first of their five children were born in Oakwoods and it became the nucleus for a community of family homes somewhat reminiscent of feudal England. Early in June, when the native and imported rhododendrons bloomed along the edge of the woods, people came from miles around to stroll through "the place," as the family always referred to it.

The owner of Oakwoods began as superintendent of the mill and gradually assumed more and more community responsibilities. When the Quaker philosophy in which he had been reared became too narrow for him, he called a meeting in the Oakwoods parlor to organize the Peace Dale Congregational Church, of which Irving Fisher's father was the first pastor. Its founder also served for many years as moderator of the town meeting and was elected to the State Legislature both as Representative and as Senator. Republican by birth and conviction, he despised "boss" rule, and when his youngest daughter was eight years old he ran for governor on an independent slate in an attempt to overthrow the corrupt Republican machine. He won the popular vote, but by such a slim plurality that the decision—which rested with the legislature—went to the machine candidate.

Farther afield he acquired an interest in Missouri lead mines and defied no less a personage than Jay Gould in blocking the latter's efforts to defraud the Crédit Mobilier stockholders. When his youngest daughter was fourteen he established the Solvay Process Company for the manufacture of soda ash by the ammonia process in Syracuse, New York, following negotiations with the owners of the parent organization in Belgium. By this time his eldest son assumed some of the responsibility for the Peace Dale mill, while the second son went to Brussels to be groomed for the management of the Syracuse venture, which is now an important component of the Allied Chemical and Dye Corporation. In all these undertakings Rowland Hazard was a pioneer in instituting profit-sharing among the employees.

His eldest daughter Caroline, who was eleven years older than Margaret, was an accomplished water colorist, was destined to publish numerous volumes of verse and South County lore and served for a decade as president of Wellesley. The middle sister, Helen, married Nathaniel Terry Bacon and became the mother of the Pulitzer Prize poet, Leonard Bacon. The youngest daughter—known in the family as Margie—possessed an unusual soprano voice. She studied for a winter with Korbay in New York and sang in one of his student recitals in Chickering Hall in the spring of 1889. That fall she went to London, with sister Caroline as chaperone, to continue her vocal studies under Henschel.

They were scarcely settled in their London lodgings and had only been to Henschel for a preliminary audition, when the prospective pupil fell seriously ill with typhoid fever. In subsequent years she sometimes teased her husband by referring to the two dozen bottles of brandy which she consumed teaspoon by teaspoon during her long illness. His invariable rejoinder was that, if she hadn't been given the brandy she might have recovered that much more quickly. Because of the infectious nature of the disease, the sisters were obliged to move from their lodgings into a house on Half Moon Street, where such personages as the Dowager Lady de Ros and the Duchess of Buccleuch, hearing of the young American girl's plight, sent in their cards "to enquire" or brought offerings of hothouse grapes, which the patient could admire only from a distance. During the most critical period, straw was spread along the entire block in front of the house, to deaden the clatter of horse-drawn traffic on the inevitable cobblestones.

Sister Caroline kept her parents informed by cable, but they stayed in Peace Dale until after the birth of Helen's second child, reaching London for Christmas to find that the crisis was passed. In the spring they rented a house at Torquay for the final convalescence. To celebrate Margie's recovery, her father bought jewelry for all the family, as well as a tea service and Kings pattern flatware. During her illness she lost every scrap of hair from her head, and it grew back so slowly that she still wore it short in an almost present-day fashion, when her new suitor first glimpsed her smile through the partly open parlor door of the Bushnell home a year and a half later.

Soon after Irving Fisher's fate was sealed on the threshold of the Bushnell parlor, in the fall of 1891, he spotted a photographic replica of the magic smile on display in the window of a New Haven photographer. He felt he simply had to have a copy of that picture, and finally induced his mother to negotiate with the photographer. By this surreptitious means he became the owner of a photograph of his ideal girl many months before she herself offered him a duplicate of her own volition.

Late in the summer of 1892 he spent two days bicycling the hundred miles from New Haven to Peace Dale, with a determined gleam in his eye. When he appeared in church that Sunday his father's former parishioners gave him a warm welcome. More important for his immediate purpose, the eldest Hazard daughter unwittingly provided the open-sesame he needed by prompting her mother to invite him to Oakwoods for Sunday dinner. From then on it was a whirlwind courtship, though he carefully adhered to the custom of the day by securing the approval of the father of the house, before making his intentions known to the young lady. Then he invited her to go rowing with him on the nearby millpond and proceeded to a familiar spot, where the overhanging branches of a large maple provided suitable privacy, to make his earnest proposition. But he did not receive her answer until the next morning, September 24, 1892, when they returned to the same shaded bower to seal the pact.

Six weeks after announcing his engagement to Will Eliot in the letter with which the preceding chapter closed, he wrote again:

NEW HAVEN, December 11, 1892
I have been wanting to write you but the opportunity has not come till today. You see my sundays

have usually been spent in Peace Dale. Last Tuesday Miss Hazard with her family started for California.

And now dear friend I am going to surprise you again. I was admitted to the church last Sunday—my father's church in Peace Dale. You will take satisfaction in knowing too that it was partly through you. You remember our long religious talk on West Rock? It amazed me that you and I seemed to agree almost perfectly and there you were on your way to a Divinity School and I not even in a church. I thought it over a great deal and had there been a Unitarian church in New Haven I think I should have united with it two years ago.

I have long felt that I was in a more false light out of the church than in it, for I craved religious companionship. I found several other persons who were church members and yet had no more of the traditional creed than I and whose only difference from me lay in the fact that they had come into their present position, having been in the church before their change of belief came, while my change overtook me before I entered.

Next I found that Mr. Hazard was such a person. I consulted him and he advised me to unite. When the committee met it happened that Mr. Hazard had just been reading a letter (published in the Christian Union) which was accepted as a means of admitting a man to the *ministry* and which reminded Mr. Hazard strongly of my own expressions. I was admitted on the strength of this.

Margaret and I expect to be married next June. I would be so gratified if you could be there and I wish you would make a special effort to bring it about. I want you to be one of the three officiating clergymen! Please consider the matter carefully and do not say no at once.

The letters which the engaged couple exchanged during their five months separation were lovingly preserved for thirty years, then just as lovingly destroyed, being too intimate for any eyes but their own. In Santa Barbara, George Butler painted Margie's portrait and two of her mother, because he could not decide whether to depict her as a saint or as a great lady. Significantly the daughter selected the portrait which represented her mother as a saint for hanging in her future home. As the Hazards reached Chicago en route from California they were joined by their prospective son-in-law, so that the young couple might spend hours admiring the splendors of the Columbian Exposition, where a certain hydrostatic mechanism for illustrating price movements would have been exhibited if it had not been too bulky and too delicate to survive the journey.

June 24, 1893 was the wedding date. The Providence, Boston and New York papers all covered the "brilliant event," and sister Caroline contributed a full column account to the local *Narragansett Times*, the flavor of which may be suggested by these excerpts:

> The village of Peace Dale was in gala dress, for it was the wedding day of Miss Margaret Hazard and Professor Irving Fisher of Yale, whose brilliant career at Yale, as prizeman, valedictorian, instructor and now professor of mathematics has been eagerly watched with a feeling of pride, that Peace Dale shares in his successes.
>
> Through the crowded assembly the bridal procession moved. The Misses Betty and Peggy Hazard, nieces of the bride, wore pale green covered with white. The Misses Rood, cousins of the bride, followed in pale yellow with daisies.

Then came the Hon. Rowland Hazard with the bride in white satin. She wore heirloom lace which had been on her mother's wedding dress, and had been her grandmother's. Her only ornament was one of diamonds and pearls, the gift of the groom.

The service was begun by the Reverend J. W. Fobes. Then the Reverend Mr. Eliot, who came from the Pacific coast for the purpose, gave the direct questions. Dr. Vose continued with the vows and wedding ring and Mr. Fobes pronounced the final accomplishment of the ceremony.

The party drove at once to the Hazard Memorial, where the bride took her position under a great bower of laurel. The whole village came to congratulate her. The silent circle of King's Daughters, of which she was President, assisted her in cutting the great bride's cake weighing fifty pounds.

At Oakwoods she greeted the guests from out of town. Jaeger of New York served the collation there. Prof. and Mrs. Fisher are to sail for Europe in about a week, as Prof. Fisher has a year's leave of absence from Yale for study abroad.

The first week of their honeymoon was spent at the Hazard's shore cottage, only three miles from Oakwoods. While there the bridegroom wrote the following paragraphs to Will Eliot, in appreciation of the latter's participation in the wedding ceremony:

NARRAGANSETT PIER, R. I., June 27, 1893

You came a step nearer still to my heart at the moment when you shook hands with Margie in Church. The joy, kindliness, generosity and sweetness in your face is a living picture which I shall always associate with that moment of moments. I am glad I insisted on your helping in the service.

Margie and I were much pleased with the silver ladle. I hope some day you can see it on our table. I cannot but be sorry your life work appears to be fixed three thousand miles from mine, but we have a special guest chamber to welcome you always. Our house is already building in New Haven. It is the wedding present of Mr. Hazard. I have found it very hard to accept so much when I long to do everything myself for *her*.

I understand perfectly your sentiment about the "fee" and I was much touched at it. It was very hard for me to yield to it but I do and I hope you will give me credit for it. The draft which is enclosed is *not for you*. I want you to use it in your work as a minister of God in whatever way you think best.

Let me tell you how many sentiments there are in this money. I have worked very hard this winter in order to cancel an old score to the college for scholarships, to prepare for my wedding and to have a good surplus to give to *her*. Altogether I have given her enough to take us on our European trip.

Now, as you know, Margie needs nothing at all and *she* wants to use this money in fulfilling some sentiment. So this draft is in a way from her and she unites with me in the earnest wish that you can find some way to make it a real help in the prosecution of your life work.

Upon reaching England they enjoyed brief glimpses of Stonehenge, London, Oxford, where the young professor hired a single scull so that he might demonstrate his rowing prowess to his better half; then they went north to Scotland, from where he wrote Will Eliot:

EDINBURGH, July 30, 1893

We have shifted about from Southampton to Salisbury and thence to Oxford and up here. Tuesday we

62

sail to Norway, in the spirit of explorers and fired by the enthusiasm of several friends who have been there.

I made myself acquainted with the great physicist Prof. Tait here. He showed me his laboratory and explained his experiments on compressing water, determining the speed of a golf ball, etc., took me to the Royal Society here and gave me some of his publications.

The village where they spent most of August was called the Norwegian equivalent of *Fairyland*. It suited their idyllic mood to perfection and at first they welcomed the tasty Norwegian cooking, as a relief from Britain's plain fare; but after a steady diet of fish three times a day for three weeks, the visiting Professor made no secret of his longing for "a good tender beefsteak"!

When they returned to London he conferred with Professor Edgeworth of Oxford so as to plan his winter work to the best advantage. Since the terms of the British and Continental universities did not dovetail conveniently, he decided to divide his time between Berlin and Paris. In the former he heard the aging and feeble Helmholtz lecture and studied the theory of numbers with Frobenius. In Paris he studied the theory of probabilities under Poincaré. Before leaving London their suspicions were confirmed that there would be an addition to the family in the spring.

To avoid the severest part of the winter in Berlin, they went to Cannes for Christmas, where the American student found he could follow his courses just as well at long range, by having one of his friends in Berlin send him notes of the lectures. Before leaving Berlin they had invested in a small artificial Christmas tree with feathery branches which folded up like an umbrella for transportation. This little tree continued to serve as a dining table centerpiece for the next forty-five Christmas celebrations, following its initial use at Cannes.

The most important purchase, however, was a handsome volume, which had been bound according to the young wife's own careful specifications. It contained her husband's thesis, published the previous year, with blank pages inserted between the printed ones, in order that the author would have plenty of space for jotting down new ideas for a revised edition. On the fly-leaf she inscribed an affectionate jingle which ended:

> The white blank leaves are mine of course,
> The wise ones writ by you,—
> If space is *really* infinite
> Aren't mine with love, wise too?

The recipient was so overawed by the luxurious book-binding job that to this day the blank pages are as unsullied as when the volume was first presented.

His wife's parents joined them for a time in Cannes, so that he felt free to take a brief excursion into Italy to see some of his fellow mathematical economists. After reaching Paris he reported some high spots of his solitary side trip in this letter to Will Eliot:

> Paris, March 25, 1894
>
> From Cannes I made a circular tour through Monte Carlo, Genoa, Pisa, Rome, Naples, Florence, Venice, Vienna and Lausanne, partly to see sights and partly to meet mathematicians and economists. Monte Carlo is a place of most exquisite Riviera beauty, perhaps more picturesque even than Cannes, but the horrors and splendors of the place make an uncanny blending.

At Pisa I saw the old tower and thought of Galileo who had taken advantage of its leaning to deduce the law of gravitation. At Rome I found a world of interest mostly about two centers and two themes, the Vatican and St. Peter's with all the medieval glory and accumulation of the Infallible Church and the Forum and Coliseum with the fallen glory of ancient Rome. I could scarcely realize that I actually took the footsteps of the Caesars of whom I had read in Smith Academy. But descriptions are, without the thing itself, as dry as a guide book.

At Rome I met Prof. Pantaleoni with whom I had corresponded a little. He is much interested in mathematical economics, is editor of the leading Italian Economic Journal, as well as a business man. He was very kind to me and introduced me to the leading economists and statisticians, as well as to a Capt. Barone in Florence who is reviewing my little book for Prof. Pantaleoni's journal. It was a great encouragement to me to find that it had really made a small path before me.

At Vienna I saw the leaders of the Austrian school, Menger, Böhm-Bawerk and others, while at Lausanne I met Prof. Walras the father of Mathematical Economics and his successor Vilfredo Pareto. He does not speak English but his wife who is a Russian speaks fluently and interpreted. He is a man of forty with a high intellect and forehead and full of enthusiasm and good feeling. His wife is translating my book to be published in the *Giornale degli Economisti* at Rome. In the afternoon we all met again at tea. Mrs. Pareto smoked a cigarette!

Prof. Edgeworth at Oxford asked me nearly a year ago if I would not write something on Bimetallism using my method of fluid mechanics. I did this a month ago and he has accepted the article for his Economic

Journal. He now suggests waiting to publish it and that I read it first before the Economic Section of the British Association for the Advancement of Science, which meets at Oxford in August. Of course I feel much flattered. It will give me a chance to meet the English Economists also and they perhaps are the leaders of the world at present.

Like most prospective fathers he referred to the anticipated new arrival as "he," but after "she" arrived on the last day of April, he wrote to Will Eliot:

> PARIS, May 17, 1894
>
> I take pleasure and pride in presenting to you Miss Margaret Fisher, aged seventeen days. Her mother came through the ordeal safely and both she and the little one are "doing well." The latter resembles *all* her ancestors if I unite the divergent testimony of all who have observed her. She certainly is the most remarkable baby *I* ever saw and her mother makes me jealous by loving the little one. You see we are a happy family.

June and July were spent in Switzerland, from where the proud father wrote to Grandmother Fisher in New Haven about a week's scenic tour which he took alone, since his wife and child could not have stood the pace. This idyllic jaunt made a deep impression on him and he later referred to it in a surprising connection:

> LAUTERBRUNNEN, July 28, 1894
>
> DEAR MAMA:
>
> I started for Zermatt on Monday and returned last night. One day took me to the top of the Gemmi pass where I got a magnificent view of the snow

peaks and saw the sun rise on them in the morning. On my way there I visited "die Blaue See" a small pool of absolutely crystal water. It is the most romantic Wagnerian lake I ever saw. The water is really blue or rather the objects on the bottom look blue. I went around it in a rowboat and when the boat made ripples the objects on the bottom—sixty feet below— danced and became iridescent.

From the top of the Gemmi I went down the following morning by the path cut in the face of the cliff to Leukerbad a place where people go for skin diseases and bathe for hours at a time and to vary the monotony they keep each other company wrapped in bathing clothes and each one possessed of a floating table for his newspapers, coffee, etc.

From here I drove down to Leukwhenee, by train to Zermatt and by mule to the Riffel Alp Hotel. The next morning I went to the Gorner Grat a peak 10,000 feet above the sea and 4,000 feet above Zermatt, from which I got the most celebrated view in Switzerland. (Baby is getting her dinner and suddenly stops to see me write to Grandmama and her mother wants me to record the fact.) The view takes in snow peaks around the whole horizon and the great Gorner Glacier at the foot with its six tributary glaciers.

The next day I went by rail to Brig, thence by carriage to the Glacier du Rhone, a drive of eight hours. The glacier looks like a huge frozen waterfall. In it are grottos cut in the ice from which the light is seen in greens and blues. The next day I drove over the pass to Goeschenen, a beautiful drive first soft and fine then wild and bold with the road cut in the cliff or through tunnels even. At Goeschenen I took the train which emerges there from the St. Gotthard tunnel to Arth and got magnificent views all the way,

67

the last half along Lake Lucern. From Arth (which by the way lies over four villages buried in 1806 by a landslide bringing off the whole top of a neighboring mountain) I went up on a rack and pinion road to the top of the Rigi. It was not as clear as it might be but the view was wonderful and had the advantage of a beautiful lake in the foreground.

I came down the Rigi on the other side on the oldest mountain railroad in Switzerland if not in the world. This brought me to Vitznau whence a system of three connecting boats took me over the beautiful lake Lucern to Alpnech. There I took the railway to Meiringen. The views were fine and the cars made with an open vestibule on one side, so that you can stand and enjoy it all out of doors. At Merringen a horse brought me half over the Brunig pass whence I walked the descending half to Grindelwald and then drove here reaching Margie at ten.

From Switzerland the threesome proceeded to England for the delivery of the paper on bimetallism. The speaker's wife referred to it in this brief letter written to her mother-in-law:

OXFORD, August 12, 1894

DEAR LITTLE MOTHER:

It was the first time I had heard him do anything in public, and I confess I was a little anxious, but now I never will be again. The words came easily and Irving seemed perfectly composed. He did not read the paper, but "talked" it, and he had a large audience. After he finished, several men talked with him and I waited a little, but finally had to come back to baby.

On the way out I saw Professor Edgeworth and so introduced myself. He was very nice (but rather surprised I think at my speaking to him), but then he went on to say how "Dr. Irving Fisher is *soaring.*" They always call each other by their full name here.

When they reached New Haven at the end of August they settled at once into their new home at 460 Prospect Street. It seemed to them like another fairyland after a whole year of junketing from one hotel to another. The donors had promised to furnish it with "just the bare necessities," but the returning travelers found that this included "everything from a grand piano in the music room to soap in the soap dishes."

The house was so generously proportioned that any returning bride of today would contemplate it with terror. The main floor had a music room, a dining room, a library and a wide entrance hall, each with its own fireplace. The hall, which extended through the center of the house, was later transformed into a forty-foot living room with a large sunny bay window where the front door used to be. The second floor had five bedrooms and two baths and there were three children's rooms and three servant's rooms with two more baths on the third floor. Its spacious rooms now house a private school which has an enrollment of nearly two hundred.

Margie dated her first letter to Peace Dale "Fairyland" and spoke of "living in a beautiful dream. We go from one room to another and each time see some new beauty. When we walked into the Library for the first time, Irving fairly jumped at the kidney table and he still looks at it with almost loving glances. When he sat down in the platform rocking chair he exclaimed: 'Oh, this is such a luxurious chair!' I wish you could see our bewildered delight, our gratitude and our happiness." Irving wrote separately, "No other couple was ever so royally treated. Margie

69

thinks she does not deserve it, and I *know* I don't. The spirit of Oakwoods shows in every room and no home could have a more beautiful and refined atmosphere.—Margie is quite distressed that I forgot to mail her letter. It was sealed last night and written the moment she had time. I am very sorry and sorry too I could not finish mine sooner. Monday we will come to Oakwoods for baby's Baptism and to thank you all in person."

Most of the Peace Dale in-laws came to the Four-sixty housewarming on the second anniversary of Margie and Irving's engagement. Appropriate verses were read as hearth fires were lighted in the four main rooms. Here are the concluding lines of one composed for the library by sister Caroline:

> And here shall baby warm her toes
> And here the Mother take her ease;
> The master's volume may be prose
> Has he not poetry in these?

5. *Bitter Experience*

Before they had spent a full year on Prospect Street an unexpected opening developed for the head of the family in Yale's Department of Political Economy. At the faculty meeting when the decision was made to transfer him from the Mathematics Department, the heads of the two departments concerned nearly came to blows, each feeling that his own need was more urgent. How much the subject of the dispute welcomed the transfer was indicated in a letter to Will Eliot written from Peace Dale in the summer of 1895, where his mother-in-law lay in her final illness:

> Regarding my change from mathematics to political economy, I am delighted with the opportunity to be in touch with human life so directly and shall find no lack of opportunity to use my mathematical training. My one regret about a mathematical life has been its lack of direct contact with the living age.
>
> You speak of having been asked to advocate "bimetallism." I am now working on an essay *against* its expediency. That I sent you was *for* its possibility within limits. I wonder how you stand. I was never so *morally* aroused, I think, as against the "silver craze."
>
> Concerning social reform, I feel that the effort of philanthropists to apply therapeutics too soon is more likely to lead to evil than good. The very best the exhorter can do is to work *against* the "something must be done" spirit, and beg us to wait patiently until we know enough to base action upon and meantime confine philanthropic endeavor to the narrow limits in which it has been proved successful—chiefly education.... There is so much *specific* reform at hand to be done—in city government, suppression of vice, education—that the hard workers of humanity need not and ought not talk, until "little" things are done, on broad schemes for "society."

After his mother-in-law's death and the family's return to New Haven, he wrote in November, 1895:

> I have not yet gotten very far in opinions on *Political* questions. Being a "professor" now I am expected to have an opinion on them and some day I hope I will, and whatever I can contribute to their

71

solution will be more apt to be correct if I can keep my mind open until I plough my way through the preliminary questions of theory. That is the program I have laid out for myself.

About a year later he wrote in anticipation of Will Eliot's projected visit to Four-sixty: "We are both overjoyed. You must arrange to stay longer than a day or two. You know we could not possibly settle the great questions of the universe in a day or two, and it is of great importance that these questions be settled!" But these widely spaced "continued-in-our-next" discussions were never long enough to satisfy their mutual curiosity about what made the world tick.

1896 saw the publication of a textbook *Elements of Geometry*, written in collaboration with his former mathematics teacher and colleague, Professor A. W. Phillips. The next year he encouraged his brother-in-law, Nathaniel T. Bacon, to publish an English translation of Cournot's *Researches into the Mathematical Principles of the Theory of Wealth*. His contribution to this project was an exhaustive bibliography of mathematical economics, in which his European colleagues Edgeworth, Pareto, Walras and Pantaleoni gladly co-operated. At the same time he produced another mathematical text, *A Brief Introduction to the Infinitesimal Calculus*, which was designed to assist "those who lack familiarity with mathematics to follow the reasoning" of such writers as Cournot. This slim volume was also intended to widen the circle of his own potential audience, but it was chiefly in demand as a textbook—for a period of fifty years.

In June, 1897, his second daughter was born at Four-sixty and named Caroline in honor of her unmarried Peace Dale aunt. At the end of that academic year the predominantly optimistic Fisher outlook found expression in this letter to Will Eliot:

NEW HAVEN, June 25, 1898

I want to tell you myself before you are told by someone else that I have just been promoted to a full professorship. As you know, this is a life affair, whereas under the old terms I was only engaged for five years. The salary goes up a thousand too.

My old college friends are to be here in a few days. It is my decennial. We expect more than half of the men back and I shall have nearly a dozen staying at the house.

Yesterday was the fifth anniversary of the day you married us. They have been very happy years and we look forward to many more. We are getting to the time though when the phrase "the shortness of life" has real meaning and application. Life when ended will seem as a tale that is told. If only the tale may be worth telling!

Everything seemed to be breaking in his favour. He was fortunate in his family life, his material surroundings, his choice of career. He had achieved the coveted full professorship only ten years after his graduation from college, and yet his subconscious mind seems to have been vaguely aware of trouble ahead. That very summer, while the family was vacationing at Narragansett Pier, he had an experience which he believed might easily have ended his story. He was enjoying a solitary swim beyond the heavy breakers, but when he turned toward shore again he was amazed how far out the current had carried him. To regain the beach required every ounce of energy he possessed, and when he stumbled into the bathhouse he was in a state of nervous and physical collapse. In retrospect he considered this experience as probably a contributory factor—by lowering his resistance—in hastening his physical breakdown.

That fall, before he had reached thirty-two, he was troubled by a mysterious lassitude and a low but persistent afternoon fever, which completely baffled his family physician. At the patient's insistence, a specimen of sputum was finally sent to the laboratory for examination. The doctor was so chagrined when he received the report, which showed positive indication of tuberculosis, that he did not have the nerve to face the patient again. Instead, he broke the news to the wife in the privacy of the music room and departed without ever submitting any bill for his services. Her heart was heavy when she returned to the library, where the patient was reclining on a couch, to pronounce what then amounted virtually to a death sentence. He himself had little difficulty in visualizing the probable outcome, having witnessed his father's death from the same cause fourteen years earlier.

Although the outlook had suddenly turned grim, he rebelled strenuously against the fatalistic attitude of his physician, who suggested that he place himself under the care of Dr. Trudeau at Saranac, not so much because there was any expectation of a cure but more as a comfortable retreat in which to spend his declining years. With the vivid memories of the premature deaths of his sister, his college roommate and his father indelibly etched on his mind, he resolved to do his utmost to prevent such an outcome in his own case.

The two children and their nurse were dispatched to Peace Dale, where they helped Aunt Caroline adjust to the emptiness of Oakwoods caused by the recent death of her father. At Saranac the patient entered wholeheartedly into Dr. Trudeau's fresh-air regime. Since the thermometer often plunged below zero the program of outdoor living involved the purchase of a luxurious fifteen-dollar raccoon coat. Despite their isolated and Spartan existence, the couple later fondly recalled reading Whittier's *Snow-Bound* while living the actuality. Here are two letters written to Will Eliot during that first difficult winter:

SARANAC, December 11, 1898

Your letter was forwarded to me here, whither I have been banished by my doctor. The truth is I have a threatening of Tuberculosis. It has been caught in its early stages and, as you know, it is in such cases curable. I have been here three weeks and have regained my normal temperature and weight. The doctors fully expect me to get well but it takes time.

I have thought of going to Colorado Springs but am getting along so well here that I shall probably stay till March. Margie is with me and very well. The babies are at Oakwoods in Peace Dale and make the house less desolate for Miss Hazard

I am sitting out on the porch, thermometer is twenty and snow is two feet deep. I find ink freezes and so use pencil.

SARANAC, February 6, 1899

I hope you were not worried at my silence. After my trouble was reported in the papers, I soon got swamped with letters. Then Margie went to Peace Dale to attend memorial services to her Father and I wrote to her every day, then I had a lot of proof to look over, caught a cold and was laid up for a few days. I am now feeling quite well—as well as I have felt since November.

We have not absolutely decided yet, but fully expect to go to Colorado next month and stay a year or more. I am assured of keeping my place at Yale, as long as I have any chance of going back.

If I felt better, I would discuss Imperialism with you. I am an "Anti" of the blackest dye. Did you read Jordan's article on Alaska in a recent "Atlantic?" I would sell the Philippines to England if she would take them. She has the machinery, experience and genius to deal with the problem. We have none of these three essentials.

The worst of many bad features of the business is the initiation of the spirit of rivalry with Europe in heavy armaments. We enlarge our Army and Navy. England, Germany, France and Russia go us one better. Not to be outdone our jingos insist on "the greatest nation on earth" having the greatest warships. Then Europe meets us once more and so on until debt and taxation press and grind the poor into resistance and riot. Washington's farewell address applies today more than when he wrote it.

Tuberculosis kept him away from New Haven for three years and he always felt it took him three more years after that before he could work at full capacity. He looked back at this period of enforced idleness as a sort of purgatory. It conditioned his thinking and general outlook for the rest of his life. In the end it transformed him into a walking dynamo, as he tried to make up for lost time.

After five months at Saranac the family was reunited in Colorado Springs, where it was hoped the cheerful companionship of his small daughters would help him climb out of the slough of despond into which he had fallen. One by-product of the year spent in Colorado was his ingenious tent for tubercular convalescents, which was awarded a prize by the New York Medical Society.

From Colorado the family moved on to Santa Barbara for the final year of convalescence. It was there that I first tipped the scales at ten and a half pounds as a purely adventitious "native son" a few weeks before the turn of the century. By that time the patient's recovery seemed assured and he was looking forward to resuming his Yale duties in the fall of 1901.

In a speech delivered before the Yale Socialist Club a decade after his return to New Haven, he related this minor incident of his stay in Santa Barbara:

Discovering that the man who came to massage him was a Socialist and believed that "interest is the basis of capitalism and is robbery," my father determined to make the most of his pedagogical opportunity.

To the question, "How much do I owe you?" the masseur replied, "Thirty dollars."

"Very well. I will give you a note payable a hundred years hence. I suppose you have no objections to taking this note without any interest. At the end of that time you, or perhaps your grandchildren, can redeem it."

"But I cannot afford to wait that long."

"I thought you said that interest was robbery. If interest is robbery, you ought to be willing to wait indefinitely for the money. If you were willing to wait ten years, how much would you require?"

"Well, I would have to get more than thirty dollars."

With a gleam of triumph, Father thrust home. "That is interest."

In January 1901 he returned to Colorado Springs for a final check with his doctor, and to supervise the construction of another model of his tent for projected use in Connecticut. His doctor assured him that if he had come as a stranger for a life insurance examination, he would not have suspected any tubercular history. So a wire was dispatched to the Yale authorities, telling them that he would be available for classes that fall.

In May he and Mother spent a carefree fortnight in the Ojai valley near Santa Barbara. In a long letter written to his own mother in New Haven he gave an almost verbatim account of his talk on "Self Control" to the boys of the Thacher School in the local Congregational Church. He confessed that he "quaked a good deal at the thought of speaking on so short notice and in church which I had never done before, and after three years silence." However, he was able to repress his "excitement to a much greater degree than I would have been able to some years ago." At the end he added this postscript: "Please preserve. I might want to use again sometime." Here is the gist of his own summary of the talk:

Most people do not know how to relax. When a person first begins to ride a bicycle, he grips the handle bars and is tense all over. He uses ten times the nervous energy which is necessary to run the machine. If one learns the art of relaxation, and uses only the nervous energy that is needed, he will find that he can double his working capacity....

All greatness in this world consists largely of mental self control. Napoleon compared his mind to a chest of drawers. He pulled one out, examined its contents, shut it up, and pulled out another. Mr. Pierpont Morgan is said to have a similar control.

Besides controlling the direction of attention, there is also a very important control of the intensity of attention. The difference between the one who knows how to study and the one who does not, is that the real student learns to concentrate his thought, shuts out all the marginal images and confines himself almost exclusively to the one thing at hand, while the unsuccessful student permits his attention to wander over distracting objects.

But the most important use of self-control is in the formation of character. What we call the *life* of a man consists simply of the stream of consciousness, of the succession of images which he allows to come before his mind. We speak of a man's biography. We say he did this and that, moved from this place to that. This is not his true life; his true inward life is known only to himself and consists mainly of the images with which his mind is filled.

It is in our power to so direct and choose our stream of consciousness as to form our character into whatever we desire. This is especially true of the young. What you think repeatedly, that you become. There are certain images which young men find it difficult to keep out of their minds, but which they should train themselves to control. A pure mind will make a pure body.

In closing, I quote the lines of Henley:

> It matters not how straight the gate
> How charged with punishments the scroll,
> I am the master of my fate.
> I am the Captain of my soul.

The following month he went alone to the Yosemite, returning via Berkeley and Palo Alto. He wrote almost daily letters to his better half in Santa Barbara, which were reminiscent of his Lauterbrunnen-Zermatt expedition of eight years before in more ways than one. Here are some passages from one of these letters, and from another written to his mother after he returned to Santa Barbara:

PALO ALTO, June 19, 1901

What a joy it is to think and feel love and to be assured that this love that goes out is welcomed and is met by another love-flow. Do you feel it and do you love me, my Margie? It was dear to hear the music of your voice through the telephone. Its melodies were sweeter to me than the orchestra which was playing as I spoke.

The university here is much more imposing architecturally than Berkeley. Prof. Bannard (who is acting President as Jordan is in Hawaii) showed me about and let the cat out of the bag that Jordan called to see me in Santa Barbara to offer me a place!

Night before last I had a sort of inspiration about an important problem in economics. It is an idea I have hunted for, or rather waited for, for many years and when duly set forth will, I feel sure, solve the problem of "interest" and bring your old hubby some fame. Foolish boy, he is taking satisfaction already in it.

It is the third time such a thought has come to me in a flash and without effort, and the three times are connected in a natural series. The first was in Switzerland when driving from Lauterbrunnen starting for Zermatt. The second was at Narragansett Pier after several days' vain wrestling with a problem. Some day I'll go through the three with you. I'm not really so "stuck on myself" as all this sounds.

SANTA BARBARA, July 13, 1901

DEAR MAMMA:

At the Mariposa Grove it is impossible to realize the size of the big trees, they are so well proportioned. Yet there is a fine sense of the sublime. You remember that Darwin said his deepest sense of sublimity was reached in the forests of Brazil.

One's first view of the Yosemite is reached suddenly from Inspiration Point. The scenery reminds one a little of the Norwegian Fijords, except that the bottom is meadow instead of water. At Glacier Point there is an over-hanging rock from which one can look down in the valley. It gives a strange mixture of sensations—grandeur and fear.

I enjoyed seeing both the California universities, at Berkeley and Palo Alto. Then I went up Mt. Hamilton to visit the Lick Observatory. The director, Prof. Campbell, had received a letter from Prof. Cory telling him I was coming. Although they do not allow even distinguished visitors to look through the instruments, except on Saturday nights, I was allowed to on the ground that I was an astronomer!

Prof. Cory had mentioned the fact that I had taught astronomy in the Scientific School. I at once denied that I was an astronomer, but when I found that looking through the telescope depended on my being one, I loudly affirmed that I was. I told Prof. Campbell that having been given the title by the Lick Observatory, I should keep it, referring any skeptics to him.

The big telescope, which until lately was the largest in the world, has a lens a yard in diameter, and a focal distance of fifty-eight feet. James Lick, who gave the observatory $600,000, is buried under the large telescope, which is therefore for him a monument in every sense of the word.

En route from Santa Barbara to New Haven that fall the family paused briefly in Oregon to see the Will Eliots and spent a week at Banff inspecting Lake Louise. The long trek ended at Four-sixty on the day that McKinley died and Theodore Roosevelt succeeded to the presidency. Within a few weeks Father resumed his teaching duties on a part-time basis.

Whatever he undertook thereafter, his health history remained a lifelong conditioning factor. He bore the scars of his experience not only in his lungs but also in his mind. The memory of it spurred him to do all in his power to

81

compensate for the years wasted. He became a walking advertisement for the fresh-air cure, and was one of the prime movers in the founding—six months after his return —of the Gaylord Farm Sanitarium in nearby Wallingford, so that future Connecticut patients would have no need to go to Saranac or Colorado. To spread the gospel of good health became his guiding fetish.

He served as secretary of the New Haven County Anti-Tuberculosis Association, and in this capacity spoke on "The Modern Crusade Against Consumption" on April 26, 1903, in the United Church on the New Haven Green, stating:

> I know by bitter experience what it means to have Tuberculosis and also by a very happy experience what it means to get over it. Anyone whose head is held in this lion's mouth naturally becomes interested as to how to get it out, and after it is out he is still more interested in preventing other people from getting their heads into the same predicament.

Although his eyes were shining with an added luster, it was three full years after his return to New Haven before he felt that he was functioning anywhere near the 100% level. The gradual emergence of his new philosophy of life is revealed in a series of letters written during this transition period. One was written to his brother Herbert, another to his brother and mother jointly, and the rest to his better half while she was visiting her sister Caroline, who by then was president of Wellesley. The first letter in this series was written from Sugar Hill, New Hampshire, where we summered for a dozen years starting in 1902, because mountain air was considered more salubrious than seashore air for someone whose lungs had been affected. The recipient had gone to Rhode Island for the funeral of a contemporary cousin:

82

Tell sister I am reading the James book very carefully. It is just what I have been looking for. It is a joy to me to feel that I am in close sympathy with an actual religious movement, though many might deny it that name, and James calls it the religion of healthy-mindedness.

It seems to me that such a religion must always crop up in some form. Among the Romans it was Stoicism. Today there is a seething mass of literature, full of crudities, but representing a real experience. Many of the cases cited by James correspond to my own and I believe that the experiences are exactly the same as what men used to feel under older creeds.

Religion seems like a vine which will cling over any kind of creed. The creed is the bare wall and it little matters what kind of a wall it is so long as it is vine covered. To feel union with the infinite and submission and even joy in whatever fate is made for us is the key note. To be indifferent to pain, sickness, circumstances and death—to embrace what happens to us because it is ours just as we embrace our kinspeople, mother, brother, sister, because they are ours. This attitude tends to make evil disappear. Eliminate fear and regret and we have health of mind at once and probably, as a consequence, health of body too.

The more I read and study the more convinced I am that a wonderful source of power and peace is open to us. I don't practice all the time what I preach. But I have a vision of our growing "in tune with the Infinite" together, to increase in healthy-mindedness as the years go by in mutual support, harmony and love. . . .

The great test of the completeness of our attitude toward the Universal Being will come to one of us when the other is taken away. May we have the strength and sweetness to bear that as the one who goes would have it borne! While I am in this strain, I'll say how Prayer seems to me. It is the same thing as communion. For me it could never be a calculated request, for I feel that God's books for the future are already made up. But it is a mystic striving toward union with the Unseen and Unknown source of all things, speaking out of aspiration. The nearest it can get to asking is: "Oh, Father, *if it be possible*, let this cup pass from me."

That is simply a declaration to submit sweetly and not negatively or grudgingly but positively. I know that whenever I feel this unreservedly and joyously I am *well*, in body as well as mind and strength and endurance come.—The spirit moved me to write this. It's a kind of love letter, isn't it?

OAKWOODS, PEACE DALE, R. I., January 1, 1903
DEAR BERT:

I have developed a passion for out-of-door living. Last night at sunset I sat out here like an Indian, thinking of nothing, but *feeling* the serenity and power of the Universe. The joy of living and breathing is joy enough when living and breathing are normal.

Those sub-conscious impressions of three years or more of depression, fear and worry are still in my mental storehouse, but buried, I hope permanently. It has been only by hard work and the application of auto-suggestion that the blue devils have been crowded down at all.

I have to confess that the chief thing the matter with me after the first year was fear. . . .

In '96 the doctor frightened me about my heart. It had been strained by hill-climbing on the bicycle. I feared sudden death, and I feared to hear my heart beat on my pillow. The latter interfered with sleep and I ran down steadily for two years and then broke down.

84

Optimism is not a question of what evil exists nor of what we may expect of the future. A man may believe the world unhappy and that the earth will grow cold and dead, that he himself is to have pain, loss of friends, honor, wealth—and yet be an optimist. Epictetus lived in the degenerate times of Nero and was himself an ill-used slave. But he was happy as few men are, and he has contributed to the happiness of others as few men do.

Inward optimism often represents a reaction from or resistance to, outward misfortune, and Evil is a tremendous stimulus to good. Lucky is the man who learns some of these things without having to pay so high a price for them, who does not wait for the cruel goad of disease or failure to rouse him from lethargy.

Oakwoods, Peace Dale, R. I. Christmas, 1908

Dear Mamma and Bert:

Last night the children hung their stockings and this morning made me think of those far away days when Christmas toys and glitter were unalloyed bliss. Those days seem especially far away after my morning walk through the parsonage yard. I hadn't been inside in years and I found more change than I expected. It made me feel quite *mad* (not "Irate") to find the largest tree in the world no longer there, the grape arbor and fruit trees all gone. I didn't know before that I cared for the old place. But I see subconsciously I had all the time been counting on its keeping unchanged for me.

I kept thinking as I looked for one landmark after another: "What right had anybody to change all this without consulting me?" The Harrower's house seemed more like old times than the parsonage. From there I walked into the cemetery and visited the spots where papa and Cora and Margie's parents were laid away. The past is dead and yet lives in memory. Strange spectral past, to be true and untrue at once!

Of all the great mysteries the greatest to me is the mystery of history. Science explains the conditional, what would happen under different circumstances, but it does not explain the actual, what does and what did happen. When and how was the great machine we call the Universe set going and why was it pre-arranged in the particular way it was, so that out of it must have come all that did come out and will come out down to the minutest details. My running away to Tower Hill, for instance, and Cora's intercession in my behalf?

Whatever its meaning, of one thing I am convinced: That it is for us to approve and not disapprove. It is perfect because it is impossible of variation by a hair's breadth. The wheels of time never jump the track. What we call mistakes are deviations from our provisional programs. The Program of Fate is never altered. For man, to strive for his own plans is a part of that universal program but when they turn out unrealized, to drop them in favor of the Real is the part of the philosopher. To desire what we think may be, is permissible; but to desire above that the Real, whatever it has been or shall be is the highest and best that we can attain. So says Epictetus. And Now, having said it myself, I am no longer rebellious at the changes at the parsonage! Let them be!

And so let be all the illness and disappointments with which my cup of Fate has been filled, and so let come what will come! Robert Louis Stevenson said that it was the lot of man to fail but that he should fail contentedly. Nor does this attitude mean an easy-going lazy life—at least to me it doesn't. Napoleon was asked why, if he believed in fatalism, he didn't sit still and let empire come to him. He replied that he was fated to fight for it.

The spirit moves me to write you a New Year's letter. It means to express first of all my love for you, as a growing thing and to apply the experience of our past love-life together to a dream of the years to come.

Five years ago with the Saranac snow like that here today we dreamed, in sickness, of health and strength. Four years ago in Colorado we still dreamed of health for me but also of health for you. Three months ago I found I had blundered (about diet), and gave up my lectures to make you an Xmas present of a well husband. What I still dream of is even closer to my heart. It is that next Christmas you may give me a similar present.

I am not complaining, sweetheart, but you must let me suggest. That is the way we can help each other. I want you to help me that way and I'll promise to curl my moustache and learn all sorts of "young dog's tricks" for you, if you'll follow my suggestions, when you think they are good.

You, then are to take up the hygienic life more earnestly than ever before. I suppose you are right that you can never equal the alpine-climbing English woman. But let's see what a year of 366 days without a single day skipped will do. Then, if we are both here and this letter exists let us read it again and measure the progress. . . .

It is *in our power* to keep well continuously for many years. The effect on the children will be like that of sweet music. The effect on my work will be greater than you imagine. For this I dream of a book a year for three years and several articles, then a place among those who have helped along my science. It is hard to put it all in words, but whatever good there is in me you have helped to bring out. I believe there is more good in me still! And that you are the one who can bring it out. Is it wrong to tell you that I dream to outgrow my present self like the chambered nautilus? I want to be a *great* man. Is it wrong to say to you that I believe I can with your help?

If one little extemporaneous speech can do as much good as the United Church address seems to be doing, don't you think that with growing health, vigor and serenity I can find other and more powerful ways to make myself felt? I don't like to put it more definitely in words. It sounds conceited already. And your mission isn't simply to make a man better but also a son and two daughters. . . .

To do these things means to *be* what you wish the children to be. I don't know anyone who can fulfill their mission more easily than you. Most persons have to overcome boorishness, selfishness and pride. You don't. You scarcely know what these are as they exist in ordinary persons. All you need is the will to change slightly your health habits and to be less easily disturbed by servants' squabbles and children's naughtiness and a husband's loving interference.

But my own personal ambition for you is not the good you may do others but the good you may get yourself. Your joy is my joy and your discomfiture is mine. Hand in hand let us climb to the delectable mountains of serenity. Let us take ill fortune as it comes. But let us not invite any which need not be. Let us see how far we can go on our journey during 1904.

The singleness of purpose with which he devoted himself to his ambitious program, and the extent to which he succeeded in carrying it out, may be judged from the fact that the next seven years saw the publication of four of his most important books. The first two chapters of Part II, however, are devoted to rounding out the personal picture, as he reached the verge of real productivity.

PART TWO

1901-1935

6. *Under Our Roof*

At the outset of his Harvard talk on the seventy-fifth anniversary of his birth, Father expressed his appreciation of the invitation extended to him, then paid this tribute to Harvard's illustrious ex-president:

> When I think of Harvard, I always see in imagination the heroic figure of Charles W. Eliot. I have often spoken of him as America's leading citizen. No one outside of my immediate circle has had a greater influence on me, and there has been no one whose views on public questions I have so often followed. Perhaps it was from him that I first got the habit of not refusing a job because it was hard.
>
> Even when I was an undergraduate and read the debate between President Eliot and our own beloved President Porter, I thought that Eliot had the right of it in espousing more science as a part of the liberal education, in place of the classics. Afterward, when I came to know him personally, my respect deepened even further—especially after once I had him for a few precious hours all to myself under my own roof.

With the passage of time, an increasing number of visitors beat a path to our door. As Father's interests became more and more varied, Mother sometimes teased him about the uncouthness of certain additions to his "menagerie." If everyone who was ever entertained at Four-sixty could

91

be assembled at one time and place, there would be many furrowed brows, as each one wondered what common denominator had brought them together.

The roster included Michigan's President Angell as well as Yale's, Judge Ben Lindsey, Professor William Lyon Phelps, Governor Gifford Pinchot of Pennsylvania, Sir Horace Plunkett, the Irish advocate of agricultural cooperatives, and Surgeon General W. C. Gorgas, who was a Four-sixty house guest when Yale awarded him an honorary degree in recognition of his mosquito-control work during the building of the Panama Canal. Two fellow tuberculosis patients from Colorado, Roger Babson and Warren M. Persons, came to discuss business forecasting. Clarence Barron, another financial editor, enlivened the dinner table conversation by announcing his discovery of a sure cure for baldness, which involved rubbing the scalp every night with a generous libation of the best available claret. The department store magnate, Edward A. Filene, discussed economic problems in general and world peace in particular; and Horace Fletcher implemented his belief that most human ills are the result of inadequate mastication, by presenting his hostess with a five-pound box of Jordan almonds.

The boldest signature in the guest book belonged to the Oxford economist, Professor Francis Y. Edgeworth. After his first sojourn at Four-sixty in December, 1902, he absent-mindedly missed his steamer in New York, and so was able to return to New Haven a fortnight later to address a meeting of the Yale Political Science Club. Prior to the meeting his host and hostess gave a small dinner in his honor.

When the guests entered the dining room, the severity of the high-backed carved oak chairs, with their black leather upholstery surmounted by fearsome dragons, was softened by a cheerful hearth fire. The table was set for eight with the gleaming white damask, branched silver candelabra and finely cut crystal goblets, which characterized the era. There were wine glasses at each place, since the host's convictions on the subject of total abstinence had not yet eliminated alcohol from the Four-sixty menu. While servants glided noiselessly around the heavily-carpeted room, offering unpretentious but delectable viands, the only jarring note was an occasional rumble from the dumbwaiter as it hoisted the next course from the basement kitchen. Detecting a look of inquiry on the face of one of her guests, Mother laughingly set his mind at ease by assuring him that the disturbance was not due to an unseasonable thunderstorm.

This was the order of seating, beginning with the guest of honor at the right of the hostess and continuing in a counterclockwise direction: Professor Edgeworth, Professor Sumner, Professor Schwab (the current head of the department), the host, President Hadley, Professor Emory (a promising young economist whose career was to be cut short by death) and Professor Farnam. It was the invariable custom of the house for the host to pronounce grace, although constant repetition had reduced this ritual to little more than a perfunctory gesture. But the hostess prevented the ensuing conversation from lapsing at once into rarefied shop talk, by a simple and entirely characteristic stratagem. At each guest's place was a verse which she had composed for the occasion, gently poking fun at his particular specialty or failing. As a sample, here is the one which applied to the guest of honor:

> The Theory of Chances is all very well
> We firmly believe it is true.
> The chance we like best

Is when our good guest
Returns after bidding adieu.

The reading aloud of these jingles, under Mother's skillful stage management, formed a surprising but appropriate prelude to the main business of the evening, when Professor Edgeworth addressed the members of the Political Science Club on "The Relation of Statistics to Political Economy."

Another category of house guests included Yale classmates and fellow Bones men like Henry L. Stimson and Amos Alonzo Stagg. When '88 celebrated its fifteenth reunion, the generous facilities of Four-sixty were taxed to the bursting point. Here is the host's account of this reunion, contained in a letter to his mother:

NEW HAVEN, June 30, 1903

DEAR MAMMA:

Margie has written you of our festivities and has told you of how much we enjoyed them and how little fatigued we were. I was up until midnight or later four or five nights, yet I feel as though Commencement had done me good. All the men seemed to have a very good time, especially the Bones men who stayed with me. On Wednesday night there were twenty at supper, and sixteen guests slept here that night, making twenty-four souls under our roof.

After supper I announced that the day was not only the Fifteenth anniversary of my graduation, but also the tenth of my wedding. Fred Solley then played "Lohengrin" on the pianola. He was our best man, you know. Then at the suggestion of Waite we played the other wedding march, Mendelssohn's, and marched, husbands and wives together, the order being Mr. & Mrs. I. F. first, followed by the rest in the order of marriage.

94

Later in the evening Cooley, Roby, Stagg and I formed a sort of quartet and sang college songs in the music room. This seemed to impress Margie about as much as anything connected with our reunion, especially when we put our hands on each other's shoulders and sang "When Freshmen First We Came to Yale," ending with "The Saddest Tale We Have to Tell." The tears came into Margie's eyes. She commented on the beautiful quality of Lonnie Stagg's voice. He, by the way, although forty-one years old, looked the youngest of the crowd.

Our class uniforms consisted of white linen dusters with tall white hats, with blue '88 numerals on the front. In this garb we went to the ball game Tuesday afternoon. From the house there were two carriages, and one man had to sit on the box of each. As we passed the college, some of the colored sweeps seemed scandalized to see a Yale Professor in that rig. But if dignity was to be lost, it was certainly entirely gone at the game, where it rained all the time and we had not even umbrellas. I sat through five or six innings and then brought some of the men home, who seemed in need of a stimulant. I took none myself, and no ill results came from the wetting. Harvard won the game, so that our enthusiasm was dampened in more ways than one.

Still, the class meeting in the evening was the most enthusiastic we have ever had. We did not sit down until after eight o'clock. About sixty were present, and we were nearly equalled in number by the Providence band of forty-four pieces, which played with enough power to fill Woolsey Hall. The speeches were for the most part very good, and the men listened with the greatest attention. The contrast between the seriousness of Quindecennial and the childishness of Triennial shows what age will do. . . . It is a good

thing, in keeping the men together, to have a big
house where we can all be, and Margie and I enjoyed
it as much as any of them.

Ten years later a similar number of classmates descended
on New Haven for their twenty-fifth reunion, this time accompanied not only by their wives but by their entire
families. As usual, after the baseball game the returning
classes marched to the president's house, where President
Hadley who had taught many of '88 as undergraduates
greeted them in his inimitable manner. Here are his remarks, as they were reported in the contemporary *Alumni
Magazine:*

> This brings us back to the old ground-floor room
> where we tried to find out whether Henry George's
> land ownership scheme was the best policy or other-
> wise. We had some very active discussions there, and
> I particularly remember the originality of some of
> the economic theories of three of your men. Well, you
> have something to show for it in applied political
> economy.
> There is Harry Stimson there who has been apply-
> ing political economy; and there is Irving Fisher in
> theoretical economy. The only thing that makes me
> hesitate to allude to these things in this way is that
> Irving Fisher thinks Harry Stimson's political eco-
> nomy is theoretical and Stimson thinks Irving Fisher's
> is applied. If there is anything that either of them
> cannot tell us about the subject, we should have to go
> outside of Webster's Dictionary to find it.
> I congratulate you heartily upon the way in which
> you have carried out the principles of Yale in public
> service, and I hope when you come back as graduates
> of fifty years, instead of twenty-five, that we shall

respect you even more than twice as much as we do now.

Throughout the college year a steady procession of students and faculty newcomers shared our bountiful midday Sunday dinner, and in the afternoon Mother presided over the tea table, seldom at a loss to deal with the unexpected. Once she was nearly caught off guard, when an Oriental student called and presented her with a gaudy tea set. His lack of subtlety is what saved her. After a brief presentation speech, he sucked in his breath and bowed toward Father with the sly query: "And I hope I will pass my examination?" The tea set was politely but firmly declined and he failed to pass his examination.

There were many other community responsibilities which Mother assumed, in addition to those of a faculty wife, such as serving on the local boards of the Y.W.C.A. and the Visiting Nurse Association. She was an active member of the Colonial Dames and the Daughters of the American Revolution, until the latter organization blacklisted Father and a blue-ribbon roster of alleged subversives such as William Allen White and Presidents Jordan of Stanford and Neilson of Smith. The resulting furor precipitated the resignation of Mother, Mrs. William Lyon Phelps and ten other New Haven D.A.R. members, in protest against "tyrannical suppression" of free thought. The *Outlook* summed up public reaction with this blunt comment: "It is a little sad that these twelve ladies have been forced to withdraw from an organization in which membership has meant so much. It is far more sad, that only twelve have felt it necessary to do so. Once, or so the public believed, the ladies of the D.A.R. were gallant ladies. Apparently there are but a dozen."

Strangers often turned up at Four-sixty without warning, sometimes from remote corners of the earth. Some came like pilgrims, anxious to meet and talk with the originator of economic theories which they had admired at long range. Others came on the flimsiest of excuses, and Mother's intuitive reaction to some of their nebulous schemes often proved to be more reliable than Father's purely rational estimate. In many cases, he had to admit afterwards that it would have been better if he had listened to her gentle word of warning, instead of yielding to the persuasive logic of the visiting fireman.

Whenever people arrived on our doorstep who were in any sort of real trouble, both my parents were generous to a fault. In one instance, they devoted many hours over a period of years trying to legalize the position of a previously unknown young matron who had escaped from an out-of-state mental institution to which she claimed to have been irregularly committed. Similarly, Father spent a whole week end conferring with law enforcement authorities about the son of a former acquaintance who had blundered his way into the county jail. And when an impecunious relative from the backwoods of Pennsylvania underwent the ordeal of a wholesale extraction of teeth and the fitting of a new "store set," he and his wife spent four months at Four-sixty. A more distressing crisis arose when a young graduate student with a wife and two children suffered a complete nervous breakdown. Since no other solution presented itself, Father accompanied the deranged patient to a Vermont retreat, while Mother took the children temporarily under her wing.

A different sort of crisis confronted Father on the bitter morning of March 5, 1904, when a servant pounded on his bedroom door, shouting "Fire! Fire!"

He dressed hastily and calmed the servant's panic simply by the matter-of-fact way in which he organized our evacuation, almost as if he had rehearsed the whole thing in advance. After assuring himself of the safety of every member of the household, Father groped his way through the smoke-filled central hall, sprang onto the davenport and carried the heavily-framed painting of his mother-in-law to safety, although it required the combined efforts of three men to rehang it. Mother's portrait and one or two other items of sentimental value were then salvaged before he turned his attention to his irreplaceable books and papers. Meanwhile neighbors arrived to help remove other furnishings, including the Steinway baby grand, which was carried out through the oversize front door and deposited on the lawn. The calm and efficient manner with which Father directed these activities evoked universal admiration, despite the thinly-veiled sarcasm which crept into this newspaper account of the fire:

> The Yale Professors on Prospect Hill got out of bed this morning to fight a fire which broke out at 6:30 o'clock in the home of Prof. Irving Fisher of the economics department.
>
> With the thermometer near the zero point they formed a fire brigade under the direction of Prof. John C. Schwab, head of the political economy department, and T. G. Bennett, president of the Winchester Repeating Arms Company.
>
> One of the first on the scene was Prof. Schwab, who picked up a wheelbarrow on his way to the fire.
>
> "Where is your silver?" shouted Prof. Schwab.
>
> "Never mind the silver," said Prof. Fisher, "save my books."
>
> His library, one of the largest and finest in the city, occupied two rooms, but Prof. Schwab and Lewis S.

Welch, editor of the *Yale Alumni Weekly*, carried all the books away in the wheelbarrow.

Mr. Bennett, with a valuable Turkish rug over his shoulders and two statues under his arms, carried several rare paintings to his home across the street. Everything was taken out of the house except a bed and a cookstove.

The house is on the top of a long hill, and the fire department had great difficulty in reaching the blaze, as the horses could drag only part of the apparatus up the slippery hill. When the firemen finally arrived they could get little water pressure.

Four maids carried the three young children, who were ill with the grip, across the street to the Bennett's. Mrs. Fisher left town in the early part of the week for Florida for her health.

Aside from the fact that there were no statues, that no one had the "grip," and that the three children were transported to the Bennetts in a carriage, with the curtains drawn so that they might not see their home in flames, this report may have been fairly accurate. Mother had gone to St. Augustine to accompany her sister Caroline, who was taking a breather from her duties as president of Wellesley. Father later joined them for a few days' respite, after seeing his children safely installed at Oakwoods in Peace Dale.

The Four-sixty fire became a reference point. Things happened either before or after it, and when we searched fruitlessly for some well-remembered item we would sadly conclude that it had burned in the fire. By coincidence it also marked a turning point in Father's work. He came through the physical ordeal with flying colors, which so encouraged him after operating on one cylinder for six long years that he quickly moved into high gear. This was bad news for his offspring, who found it increasingly difficult to pry him away from his desk for juvenile frivolity.

In the after-supper interval, we and our neighborhood playmates especially relished a diversion known as "Giant." It was played virtually in the dark, with all the main-floor lights extinguished and only a dim circle of illumination filtering down at one end of the living room from the multicolored lantern on the stair landing. When we had found suitable hiding places, underneath the piano or even under Father's desk in the sanctum itself, he would stalk us with exaggeratedly heavy tread, simulating the gait of a giant and intoning in a deep base voice:

> Fee! Fi! Fo! Fum!
> I smell the blood of an Englishman;
> Be he alive, or be he dead,
> I'll grind his bones to make my bread.

As he approached the spot where one of us was hidden his mumbo jumbo reached a terrifying crescendo which sent delicious tremors tingling up and down our spines. Each captive was then transported in turn to the davenport and bound with imaginary fetters, while the giant went foraging for other victims. As soon as his back was turned we scuttled off to a new hiding place, so that the game could be indefinitely prolonged. When he had had enough— we were never satisfied—he would return to his desk and resume working where he had left off. Five minutes later he would have completely forgotten our blood-curdling pastime.

He was proud of his single-track mind, which enabled him to switch his attention from one channel to another with a minimum of waste motion, but he also recognized its disadvantages. There were many times when his thoughts remained stubbornly in fixed channels, and Mother had to resort to a gentle "ahem" and a pleading look, which the rest of us were supposed to ignore, before his attention could be brought back to our inconsequential dinner-table chatter. When the bars were down, however, there was plenty of *en-famille* hilarity, and numerous instances when the laughter was at his own expense, perhaps because of his professorial absent-mindedness. On such occasions he always joined good-naturedly in the general merriment.

Once while Mother was out of town she wrote asking him to send flowers to one of her friends who was entertaining at tea on a certain day, as an expression of regret at not being able to be present. Father decided not only to send the flowers but to do the thing up brown by attending the party himself. He was sure that it would please Mother to have him represent her. At the tea party he enjoyed himself for a full half hour before it penetrated that he was the only male present. He apologized to his hostess for crashing her party, but she graciously replied that she couldn't remember ever having seen such a lively and successful affair, largely because of his attendance.

A more serious consequence of his single-track mind was the loss of his brief case, containing a nearly completed book manuscript, which was stolen from between his feet while he was using a telephone booth in Grand Central Station in New York. Even in his distress over this incident, he could laugh at the thief's imagined disgust when the bulging brief case yielded nothing more lucrative than a treatise on economics. It took him nearly a year to rewrite it, and thereafter he always deposited a duplicate copy of his current opus in a safe place at home, before taking the working copy with him on his travels.

To minimize the disadvantage of not being able to take his desk with him, he evolved a special technique for not wasting any precious brain waves, whenever and wherever they might strike. In his left coat pocket he always carried a small scratch pad, to jot down ideas as they occurred to him. Whether he was at the dining table, in the dentist's chair, or listening to a sermon in the college chapel, he would whip out his pad, scrawl something on it and transfer the memo to his right coat pocket. When he returned to his desk each memo would be carried into execution. Sometimes, when he followed this routine in the bosom of the family, we might inquire what he had written, but we could never discover any link between his memo and the preceding conversation. Mother deplored the bristling pencils in his breast pocket which this technique required, and he himself complained that his memory was deteriorating to a pencil-and-paper level.

For evening relaxation he often read aloud to Mother from such classics as *Lorna Doone, Moby Dick* and *Vanity Fair,* and he felt a special affinity for the nonsense world of Lewis Carroll. But it took a major effort to persuade him to spend an evening at the theatre. Tragic performances such as Sarah Bernhardt's *Camille* and Walter Hampden's *Cyrano* were less to his liking than such a comedy as *Lightnin'* or an evening with Ed Wynn. He might well have been the "grey-bearded professor" mentioned by William Lyon Phelps in an essay on modern dramatists, who remarked to his wife during Maude Adams' performance of *What Every Woman Knows,* while tears coursed down his whiskers: "I thought you said this was a comedy!" As for music, he once remarked that nothing composed since Beethoven made any sense to him. He dreamed of collaborating some day with a qualified musician in studying the mathematical basis for music, so as to ferret out a rational explanation for the difference between what is great and what is mediocre.

Such festive interruptions as family birthdays and Christmas scarcely interfered with his work schedule, since he left all the details to Mother and remained at his desk until the last possible moment. Each year the collapsible Christmas tree from Berlin reappeared as the centerpiece for the dining table. Another important element of the Four-sixty Christmas was the party given for the household and office staffs. Besides the family there were usually present either an Irish or a Swedish cook, two Scotch maids, and Charles the furnace man, a West Indian Negro who remained a fixture in the household for more than thirty years. He always referred to Father as "Governor" and one or another of his small sons provided the high point of the occasion by reciting "A Visit from St. Nicholas" (" 'Twas the night before Christmas . . ."). There were also several helpers from Father's office, the number depending on whether or not there was a new book in the works. To break the ice there was a strenuous session of "drop the handkerchief" in the living room, then the sliding door of the music room was rolled aside to reveal a large Christmas tree. Everyone joined hands and danced around the tree singing "ring-around-a-rosy." Finally presents were distributed and we all sang Christmas carols. Altogether it was a curious mixture of feudalism and democracy, which Father would not have undertaken without Mother's guiding spirit.

This brief record of social activities under our roof would be incomplete without mention of one memorable dinner party given prior to a Yale prom. The dozen or more guests were formally attired in ball gowns or white-tie-and-tails. As they found their places at the table, one of the young ladies gasped involuntarily and raised her hand to her breast, too late to prevent her brooch from unclasping and rolling under the table. Her observant escort dove gallantly to retrieve it and was still under the table, when Father—bringing up the rear of the procession from the living room—arrived at his chair, sat down and said grace. It is hard to tell which was more startled, the young man under the table, or Father when he caught sight of the red-faced victim emerging from the lower depths. There is no doubt, however, that the dinner party was a great success.

Father appreciated in his heart how much Mother contributed to the aura of hospitality which pervaded Four-sixty, although he was inclined to take the unseen mechanics of housekeeping too much for granted. Everything flowed so effortlessly that it was many years before he realized how much she dreaded the ordeal of entertaining visiting dignitaries in the wilting heat of commencement week, and longed to escape to the White Mountains where the family spent a dozen summers before reverting to the Rhode Island seashore.

7. *Biologic Living*

Whenever people expressed astonishment at the volume of work which he turned out, Father offered this simple formula: First, always delegate to assistants whatever can possibly be delegated; and second, apply the rules of hygiene to one's daily life so as to keep one's working capacity as close as possible to the one-hundred-per-cent mark.

105

The importance he attached to the second part of this program constantly increased as he felt his own vigor being steadily renewed. In the spring following the Four-sixty fire, he wrote to Mother reaffirming the general philosophy previously outlined and indicating his increasing preoccupation with personal hygiene:

May 11, 1904

With the realization of my bald spot comes a consciousness that time is passing and that much time has been wasted. I feel as though my real life had scarcely begun yet and that all which has gone before was only introductory.

I have very definite ideals now of what I want to do and be. To reach distinction is not one of them, though I have little doubt that some measure of that will come if I really attain the other. Will you walk with me and help lead me? All that I have attained of true progress has been brought out with and through you.

My greatest ambition is to live and have you live and get others to live a sane and complete and unified life and die a natural death, not one of disease. I think the next ten years will see an immense increase in our knowledge and in the successful application of it. I want to be in this movement and to help it on.

At the same time that Four-sixty was being rebuilt, "Edgewood Camp," our new summer home at Sugar Hill, New Hampshire, was also under construction. We had spent the two previous summers in a nearby rented cottage, to test the theory that mountain air is better than seashore air for someone who has been through the tuberculosis mill.

Designed for simple living, the house had eight rooms and two baths. In fine weather the wide barn doors, with large panes of glass, could be rolled back to throw the porch and living areas together. It commanded a sweeping view of the Presidential range, with the sun rising directly over Franconia Notch and Mount Lafayette in the foreground and Mount Washington faintly visible to the North. Most of the structural joists and studs of the house were exposed and unpainted, while the natural pine logs, which were used for the posts and railings of the extensive porch, oozed pitch on our hands and clothing summer after summer.

One built-in feature of the three main bedrooms, which all overhung the porch, always flabbergasted our guests. In line with his enthusiasm for fresh air, Father had six-inch slits cut in the bedroom floors, extending in a band around three sides of each bed, to encourage an upward current of air for each sleeper on the same principle which had been utilized in the prize-winning Colorado tent. In cold weather these slits could be closed with hinged lids and when they were open a heavy wire mesh prevented our stepping through and breaking our legs. It was not long, however, before sleeping porches were added to all three bedrooms, somewhat marring the exterior simplicity of the original plan but providing much more elbow room inside.

An additional cabin was also built at the rear of the two-acre lot for Father's summer office, so that he could keep his New Haven staff busy by remote control. At the foot of the slope below the main house, an orchard of fifty-two crab apple trees made an ideal playground. The natives told us it was a sight to behold at blossom time, but we only saw the fruit and enjoyed the jelly which we cooked up to carry back to New Haven for the winter.

In the winter of 1904, after attending the annual meeting of the American Economic Association at Chicago, he visited the Battle Creek Sanitarium to meet Dr. John Harvey Kellogg and learn all about his system of "biologic living." En route from Chicago he wrote to Mother:

NEARING BATTLE CREEK, MICH., December 31, 1904

I am on a quest, not like Ponce de Leon for the fountain of youth, but for ideas which may help us to lengthen and to enjoy youth.

Tomorrow begins a New Year. For us I hope it does not contain as many or as great mishaps as this one, but even with all its disappointments, the closing of the year seems like the closing of one happy page of life. The lamp of Love makes darkness disappear and while I have felt all sorts of shortcomings as measured by ideals, the year has been a step forward not back.

May the next one be a longer step in the same direction. With you by my side and the love light in our eyes, we can't help going forward *inside* even if houses do burn and books don't get written. Much as I long to take a bigger part in the world's work, it is enough if I have your approval and that of my own soul.

He approached Battle Creek with some misgivings, mistrusting a vegetarianism which stemmed originally from the religious scruples of a Seventh Day Adventist, but his misgivings melted away before Dr. Kellogg's rationalization of his position and they became lifelong mutual admirers. Here are his first impressions of the sanitarium founder, written to Mother a few days after his arrival:

Dr. Kellogg is short like Chittenden, very quick and energetic. I don't think I ever saw a man with his capacity for work. After operating yesterday afternoon for hours, he arrived an hour late for his usual

lecture to his sanitarium "family" and made one of
the best exhibitions of popular science teaching I ever
saw, entirely in answer to questions propounded on
the spot.

His talk was easy, clear and to the point as well as
interspersed with anecdotes and other devices to keep
up the eager attention. After the talk was over I
overtook him walking down the corridor and he took
me to his office where he insisted on talking with me
for a half hour or more, though he must have been
tired and certainly was busy. I must say, the man as
a man has captivated me completely.

I have come to the conclusion that the "crankiness"
which I had expected is mostly a myth. He has found
the extreme vegetarianism impracticable and now differs little from Chittenden. He is certainly a wonderful advertisement for his own theories. I never saw
such a tireless steam engine before.

Father was especially impressed by Dr. Kellogg's rational approach to the health problem. Far from being
offended when his host criticised his posture by calling attention to the wrinkles in his vest, Father was quick to
see the point and thereafter always shunned the enervating
slouch. He appreciated the thoroughness of the routine
examinations which all newcomers underwent during the
first few days, no matter what the previous diagnosis might
have been. In this respect the sanitarium was pioneering
in procedures which are largely taken for granted today,
and the staff often succeeded in putting its collective finger
on an unsuspected tooth infection, for instance, as the
source of some apparently unrelated symptom which had
baffled all previous diagnosticians.

While waiting in line to be examined in the successive
departments—blood count; eye, ear, nose and throat; den-

tal; X-ray, etc.—Father occupied himself by correcting proof or catching up on his correspondence. For the rest of his stay he entered wholeheartedly into the prescribed daily program: setting-up exercises before breakfast; conferences with members of the medical staff; midmorning treatments, such as hot and cold fomentations applied to the abdomen, sweating sessions in an electric cabinet, or some form of hydrotherapy followed by a swim in the pool; and winding up the day with a brisk march and drill in the gymnasium after the evening meal. He did not hesitate to suggest to his host that the sanitarium put too much stress on water therapy and too little emphasis on fresh-air therapy, but on the whole he subscribed enthusiastically to nearly every aspect of Dr. Kellogg's biologic-living program, and before the family quite realized what was happening we found ourselves making periodic visits to Battle Creek, just as routinely as other people visited their family doctors.

Our first family pilgrimage to the sanitarium took place about a year after Father's indoctrination. On our second day there I developed whooping cough and had to be placed in isolation. Before I fully recovered, Dr. Kellogg strapped me on his operating table to remove my tonsils and a swollen gland in my neck, but I don't recall feeling rebellious about our subsequent visits to Battle Creek. Father's rational attitude persuaded us to accept the routines as a matter of course. During that first visit Dr. Kellogg also performed a minor operation on Mother, so that she and Carol and I remained several weeks longer than we had planned, while Father and Margaret returned to New Haven in time for the resumption of his Yale classes.

This was the year he conducted some experiments in endurance with a group of nine student volunteers to test the validity of the meatless diet. He also taught them to use Horace Fletcher's system of mastication, and they nicknamed themselves the "Munch Club." The endurance tests consisted of deep knee-bending, raising one's legs while lying prone, holding one's arms out horizontally to the limit of one's ability, etc. The newspapers treated the experiments rather flippantly, but Father considered his findings important enough to publish in a small book, *The Effect of Diet on Endurance* (1907), which was reprinted a decade later as a guide for soldiers in World War I. Here are some pertinent paragraphs from his contemporary letters to Mother at Battle Creek:

NEW HAVEN, February 7, 1906

This afternoon I took the first test with a Yale athlete. I tried him in holding his arms out. He had the reputation of great endurance and I tried to make him do his best by saying I wanted Yale to make a good showing in these tests.

I also took the test with him beginning at the same time. His time was 8 min. 54 sec. I had expected of course to drop out first, being no athlete and only an old professor. When 22 minutes had passed, I wanted to quit but had not the slightest necessity to and so kept on to 36 min. 34 sec. The runner was surprised and crestfallen but he was not as surprised as I.

March 23, 1906

It is good to hear you are keeping calm and getting extra "control." You always have been a controlled person, but we can't get too much. I sometimes think that we get diverted too much to the thought of physical hygiene, and away from the supremest thing of all, the mental serenity for which all the physical is sought. To adjust ourselves at once to the situation in which we find ourselves is the important thing.

Margaret is a great comfort and is going to be a real "charmer" one of these days. She said today, "I want to grow up and say 'I was never sick in my life,' " to which I jokingly replied that if she could say that when she was a hundred years old I would give her a penny, only added "I won't be alive then."

She protested, "Papa, yes you will!"

"But," I said, "I'd be one hundred and twenty-seven."

"Well," said she, "didn't anyone ever live that long?"

"Yes," I said "but I won't."

"Papa, don't say that. Those people lived that long just by accident, but you know how to live and so can live that long on purpose." Then she added, "Papa, I like to hear you laugh."

Today I had an endurance test for my diet squad which has been the first opportunity to see what Fletcherizing has done for their working power. One man showed no improvement. The other eight showed distinct improvement, in some cases over 100%, though usually less than 50%. Naturally, I feel quite elated.

GRADUATES CLUB, April 24, 1906

I am sitting in the room where I first fell in love with you nearly fifteen years ago. I brought down some paper as I thought I would not be home in time to get a letter into tonight's mail.

I had my lecture this morning, then went to the Gymnasium. I saw Secretary [William Howard] Taft, who is here lecturing on civic duties. He was crossing the campus and I buttonholed him and asked him why he didn't try the Chittenden scheme in the army. He himself is evidently very high proteid. In the course of the talk he asked, "What is proteid?"

While I'm writing, I hear a Doctor telephoning his patient or nurse: "Give him only sterilized food, such as beef tea, etc." He came out of the telephone room with a cigar in his mouth. Well, we'll reform him if he lives long enough!

May 1, 1906

, I think with you that the Battle Creek Sanitarium doesn't know it all and I don't want to tie to that or to any school but just keep on learning with an open mind from them and from others.

It was twelve years ago yesterday morning that I wondered whether you would live through the bearing of Margaret. I remember praying that your life might be spared. Margaret, little stranger, had then small place in my heart. Both she and you have a larger place today and yet I believe that when God asks me to part from one or both of you, whether by my going or your or her going, I can acquiesce better than I could have then.

There is a mist in my eyes, but I mean what I say. Yet we will plan for many happy and busy years before that day of good-byes comes.

The quest for hygienic truth was an endless one, and Father was never satisfied merely to practice what he preached. Others had to be persuaded to follow his example. In one instance, a visiting British physician who disagreed with some of his precepts had to be almost rude before Father realized that he had been overbearing. He couldn't understand why his irresistible logic failed to convince all comers. He did prevail upon his mother and Aunt Caroline to go to Battle Creek, but the institutional regimentation was more depressing than helpful to them. Occasionally someone like his Yale colleague, James Harvey Rogers, became equally enthusiastic about the sanitarium, but most people were like Professor Sumner, who took

113

Father's proselytizing good-naturedly without altering his self-indulgent eating habits in the slightest. In Father's estimation, a brilliant career was thus ended prematurely at the threescore-and-ten mark.

Although diet was the keystone of biologic living, the Battle Creek regime was not vegetarian in the strictest sense, since eggs and milk were permitted. The most important point was to adhere to an aseptic or poison-free diet, and the sanitarium chefs dreamed up surprisingly realistic meat substitutes, with peanuts featured prominently as the basic ingredient of their synthetic steaks and cutlets. Great emphasis was also placed on raw foods —fruit, salads, nuts, etc. Tea, coffee and cane sugar were on the forbidden list, and so of course were alcohol and tobacco.

Contrary to the usual impression, Father never adopted vegetarianism *in toto*. While at the sanitarium, he followed the regime to the letter and he was never guilty as some were of sneaking out to Mr. Post's Tavern or the still-nearer Little Red Onion, to kick over the traces with a thick juicy steak. But at home we nearly always had roast chicken on Sunday and red meat was not entirely absent from our table. However, the Battle Creek meat substitutes became a definite part of our scheme of living, and as time went on Father added numerous other innovations from a variety of sources. For example, because a New York dentist believed that people should eat fruit at the end of the meal instead of at the beginning, Father instituted this breakfast procedure which remains a Fisher idiosyncrasy today.

To supply more roughage or bulk for the first meal of the day, Father was at a loss to find a satisfactory substitute for eggs, until he happened to hear that Emily Post considered it perfectly *comme il faut* to serve anything at all for breakfast *except* salad. Thereafter he gleefully defied convention by starting the day off with lettuce, liberally sprinkled with lemon juice and milk sugar. This did not appeal to the rest of the family, so bulk was absent from our breakfast menu, until Mother hit upon a solution which pleased everyone. Inasmuch as coffee was not served at our table except to guests, she was determined to provide at least one hot item for the morning meal. For lack of a better description, it came to be known as "the baked dish." Never the same twice, its foundation was either cabbage or some other leafy vegetable, and it included whatever leftovers there happened to be in the refrigerator. These ingredients were blended together with Savita sauce, a Battle Creek product with a surprisingly meatlike flavor, although—to Father's considerable amusement—it was actually a brewery by-product. The Fisher "baked dish" was a perennial conversation piece for house guests, and a surprising percentage of them, who regarded the idea skeptically at first, took second helpings.

Exercise was the next most important aspect of biologic living and Father was always seeking more efficient ways of getting a good workout. Golf took too much time, but riding a bicycle to and from classes appealed to him because it accomplished two things at once. Our neighbors also grew accustomed to seeing him jog around the block in shorts. When time permitted, however, he preferred hiking to the top of East or West Rock. At the suggestion of a university associate, he once experimented with squash, but an unfortunate occurrence during his first game prevented his ever playing again. As he stood in the forward receiving position, he was puzzled because his opponent's serve took so long to materialize and he turned involun-

115

tarily to see the reason for the delay. No one had specifically warned him against doing this, and as luck would have it the ball struck him in the eye, coming directly from his opponent's racquet. For the rest of his life there was a blind spot in the center of that eye's vision, which made it hard for him to judge distances. With practice, however, he learned to minimize this handicap of seeing things with only one eye, by looking at them obliquely instead of directly. This partly accounted for his preoccupied expression, though few of his associates were aware that there was any underlying physical explanation for his absent-minded look.

He deplored the ultraconservative attitude of the run-of-the-mill medical man, and often remarked that the majority of them were "fifty years behind the times" because of the time lag between the making of new discoveries and their general application. To try to reduce the gap he joined forces in 1913 with Harold A. Ley to found the Life Extension Institute, and persuaded ex-President Taft to accept chairmanship of the board. This non-profit organization aimed to make periodic health examinations available at moderate cost to many people who could not afford annual visits to such a place as the Battle Creek Sanitarium. It was hoped that life insurance companies would make this diagnostic service available to policy-holders, and thus prolong life by uncovering minor ills before they became chronic.

Two years later he collaborated with the director of the institute, Dr. Eugene Lyman Fisk, in writing *How to Live*, which was "primarily concerned not with disease but with health." The book was written in consultation with a Hygiene Reference Board of close to one hundred authorities in a dozen different fields. In his Harvard talk on the

116

seventy-fifth anniversary of his birth, he made these references to it: "I never hesitate to praise this book, because it represents a composite of the best authorities. A friend who did not understand what such team-work really signified upbraided me for not taking any royalties, pointing out, since the book had had a sale of nearly half a million copies, that I might have received $75,000 if I had not given it all to the Life Extension Institute. I pointed out, however, that in that case I would not have received the support of the co-author, of the contributors to the appendix, nor of the Hygiene Reference Board, and that a book by me alone could not have had such a vogue."

Some of the ideas which were assimilated into his personal health philosophy were gathered from highly unorthodox sources. It made no difference to him who originated a new technique, provided it worked. Unlike Mrs. Malaprop, who thought that everything new was scandalous, he was convinced that each discovery was a potential elixir of youth until it was proved to be otherwise. As his open-mindedness in this respect became generally known, a constant stream of sure cures was brought to his attention, with especial emphasis on health foods, cold remedies, vitamin preparations and mechanical exercise contrivances.

He was especially vulnerable to the latter, because of his own inventive bent, and a top-floor room at Four-sixty was eventually transformed into a gymnasium. At one time or another it was equipped with: Indian clubs, dumbbells, weight-lifting devices, a rowing machine, an electric cabinet, a sun lamp, a vibrating chair which bore a striking resemblance to its execution-chamber counterpart, and an outlandish mechanism for administering an all over rhythmic massage, known as a pneumocardian. When fully zipped into this device, the user resembled nothing so much as a recumbent deep-sea diver. Whenever we expressed amusement over his latest acquisition, he took our jibes in good part but remarked that skeptics had also made fun of the first automobiles and airplanes.

Sometimes, after remaining faithful to a new health idea for a considerable period, he would be disappointed to discover that the originator had violated his own strict ethical code, and the offender would be summarily crossed off his list. This happened in the case of a certain Canadian physical culturist, much of whose program had appealed to Father, until he learned that the Canadian had exaggerated his age by at least five years in order to capitalize on his youthful appearance. After that Father considered him little better than a charlatan, although he continued to use his particular brand of health shoes to the end of his days.

His participation in Professor Leo F. Rettger's experiments with acidophilus buttermilk was on a much higher scientific plane. As I understood the theory at the time, Professor Rettger believed that Metchnikoff had discovered only part of the story when he extolled the virtues of bulgaricus sour milk. Under the microscope the two bacilli, bulgaricus and acidophilus, look as alike as Tweedledee and Tweedledum. Consequently the supposed beneficial effects of bulgaricus milk could well have been due to the accidental presence of a fair proportion of the still more benign acidophilus. Professor Rettger therefore propagated his own elixir in a Yale laboratory and supplied it gratis to anyone who was willing to participate in the experiment.

This entailed calling daily at the laboratory to pick up a fresh flask of very pink milk, similar in consistency to the stuff which is used for applying wall paper. The acidophilus milk which later became available commercially was a pale imitation of its laboratory progenitor. The aroma of that laboratory in old Sheffield Hall is still vivid in my memory, since each member of the household had to fetch and carry at one time or another; or Charles, the furnace man, would be pressed into service for this errand when no one else was available. At stated intervals telltale cartons containing fecal specimens also had to be delivered to the laboratory, so that Dr. Rettger could determine the exact potency of his concoction. Father didn't consider it incongruous to call at the laboratory even on Sunday, dressed in his cutaway, en route to or from college chapel. As far as he was concerned, furthering the noble cause of science lent the chore sufficient dignity.

While these experiments were in progress, he usually had to forego the ice cream and cake of Sunday dinner in favor of his proper quota of acidophilus, so that his total caloric intake would not be excessive. He appeared to enjoy it, and he was convinced that it benefitted him greatly. He was aware that some authorities regarded the acidophilus bacillus as a primary cause of tooth decay, and his own losing battle against this scourge might seem to corroborate such a theory, but to him the benefits far outweighed the disadvantages. In *How to Live* he devoted considerable space to the subject and took personal credit for assisting the recovery of the Dionne quintuplets from a serious intestinal illness at the age of four months, by suggesting to Dr. Dafoe that they be given acidophilus soy milk, a Battle Creek refinement of Professor Rettger's original preparation.

Probably the strangest and most unorthodox contribution to Father's health philosophy was made by Gerald Stanley Lee, an amateur relaxation expert whose per-

119

sonality was so divergent from his own that it was amazing they remained *en rapport* as long as they did. In spite of Mr. Lee's dilettante approach and his esoteric thought processes, Father was convinced that he had stumbled on something really worth while and engaged him to spend a month with us at the seashore, imparting his relaxation technique to the whole family. He was a cadaverous-looking individual who needed only a stock and a stove-pipe hat to approximate a comic-strip prohibitionist. He had once written a best seller called *Crowds*, which was always cropping up in the conversation. He expressed himself haltingly, with long pauses at unexpected places as he sought the exact word to convey his precise meaning, and when he had finished you were usually at sea as to just what he did mean.

His "discovery" was an indirect by-product of a serious illness, during which he had grown so weak that he could scarcely raise his head from the pillow, but by concentrating mentally on doing things in the most relaxed way possible, he soon astonished his attendants by his physical accomplishments. After his recovery, he continued perfecting his technique and applying it to the ordinary business of walking, rising from a chair, etc. Eventually he described his system of relaxation exercises in a book, *Rest Working*, and for a few years he enjoyed a vogue along Park Avenue, where he helped many tense people toward a saner way of life. During his month with us, we all became surprisingly adept at walking up and down stairs, with books or oranges balanced on our heads. Then we graduated to stepping gracefully over rows of evenly spaced chairs, without losing the book or orange. But the ultimate accomplishment was to be able to rise from a squatting position, without touching one's hands to the floor or losing the orange, while bearing the whole weight of the body on one foot. None of us achieved our teacher's proficiency in this stunt, but for beginners we didn't do too badly.

One morning, while Father was having his relaxation lesson in the library, the local expressman arrived with a typewriter, which had been shipped from New Haven. Without giving Father or Mr. Lee a thought, I ushered the expressman with his heavy burden directly into the Library, where I knew the typewriter was to be placed. At the moment Father happened to be lying on his back in the middle of the floor, with his head resting on a book. By repeatedly allowing one's head to roll off the edge of the book, one was supposed to cultivate that relaxed feeling in the neck toward which Mr. Lee wanted us to strive. The expressman took no notice of teacher or pupil and departed promptly after depositing the typewriter in the designated corner. I could see from the color of the pupil's face, however, that he was anything but relaxed. When the expressman had gone, Father said rather sharply: "Irving, don't ever bring anyone in here again when I'm having my lesson!"

I apologized lamely and closed the door, but his reaction took me completely by surprise. He had always pooh-poohed the importance of "appearances," so it never occurred to me that he would mind being seen in an unconventional situation. The expressman had known us for a long time and was better informed about our little foibles than Father realized, so that I was reasonably sure he would not have been surprised to find us all standing on our heads. It was a revelation to me to discover that Father did after all sometimes consider appearances, in spite of his protestations to the contrary.

In the end he lost patience with Mr. Lee, because of his vague intuitional approach and his reluctance to reduce his system to a rational scientific minimum. In the mean time Father had run across a book called *Progressive Relaxation*, by Dr. Edmund Jacobson of Chicago, which tackled the same problem from a more orthodox standpoint. True to form, Father tried repeatedly to bring Lee and Jacobson together, on the logical but impractical assumption that they could be induced to pool their ideas and come up with a well-balanced program. He might as well have tried to bring about a meeting of the South Pole with the North Pole. He never succeeded in scheduling even a preliminary conference, and the next revision of *How to Live* devoted several pages to Jacobson without making any mention of Lee.

But twenty years before he ever encountered Mr. Lee, he was readying for publication the two economic books which are to be considered in the next chapter.

8. *New Definitions*

In the fifteen-year interval between the publication of *Mathematical Investigations* and the next major work, he contributed numerous essays to economic journals on both sides of the Atlantic, which foreshadowed the forthcoming works. But it is debatable whether or not his breakdown appreciably postponed their publication. Perhaps such basic concepts required a prolonged period of gestation before they could be crystallized in book form. Once physical recovery was achieved, however, it is certain that his "bitter experience" served to accelerate the gestation of the two books which appeared in 1906 and 1907: *The Nature of Capital and Income* and *The Rate of Interest*.

In his unfinished manuscript *My Economic Endeavors,* he confessed that at the time of writing *Mathematical Investigations* he had not appreciated the need for drawing a fundamental distinction between capital and income, with respect to the element of time. Just as "accountants distinguish sharply between capital accounts or balance sheets relating to a point of time and income accounts relating to a period of time" he came to realize that the theory of capital and income should be built along similar lines. But when he had first joined Yale's department of political economy in 1895, "economics and accountancy were almost total strangers to each other."

The importance of this distinction with respect to the element of time first dawned on him in the summer of 1894, as he drove from Lauterbrunnen toward Zermatt: "It suddenly occurred to me while looking at a watering trough with its in-flow and out-flow, that the basic distinction needed to differentiate capital and income was substantially the same as the distinction between the water in that trough and the flow into or out of it."

In his December, 1896 paper in the British *Economic Journal,* "What is Capital?" he sought to dispel the current confusion over the meaning of the term. He argued that: "We should as reasonably expect to establish the theory of conservation of energy without clear ideas of energy, as to set up an authoritative doctrine of capital before conceiving what the term capital precisely signifies." He considered most rival definitions unsatisfactory:

> Previous to Adam Smith the tendency had been to set [a stock of] wealth lent at interest over against the [flow of] wealth or interest which it thus earns. According to him a stock may earn [a flow of] wealth or "revenue" in many other ways than by being lent.

The only essential feature is that it be so employed as actually to earn a revenue. Any such stock is capital. Here is certainly a latent consciousness of the antithesis between stock and flow.

But we are told expressly that not all stock is capital. Adam Smith appeared to reason that, since capital is opposed to income or revenue it cannot include all stock, for there would then be no room left for revenue. In fact he expressly states that the portion of stock which is not capital consists, among other things, in his revenue "as it gradually comes in."

But how can one's "stock," or any part of it, consist of something *gradually* coming in? Stock refers to an instant, while "gradually" indicates duration. The use of this time-word "gradually" shows that Adam Smith felt instinctively the necessity of describing the peculiar relation which revenue bears to time; while the fact that he includes revenue in stock shows that he had not worked out this relation.

His own first definition of capital as "a stock of wealth existing at a point of time," was revised a year later in the same journal to read: "a flow of services (including uses of capital) through a period of time." Fifty years later he wrote in *My Economic Endeavors* that he "never found any need to recede from the concepts of capital and income then adopted," although he had to "elaborate their application."

When he gave this subject its full-scale treatment in 1906 in *The Nature of Capital and Income*, there was still widespread confusion over the time element. Commenting on this point in *My Economic Endeavors*, he wrote: "Economists have introduced, in place of the fundamental distinction between fund and flow, and between wealth and services, the merely relative distinction between one kind of wealth and another. Among the many confusions which have come from overlooking the time distinction between a stock and a flow was the famous wage fund theory, that the rate of wages varies inversely with the amount of capital in the supposed 'wage fund.' "

McCulloch had calculated that if "the capital of a country appropriated to the payment of wages" amounted to ten million quarters, and if the number of laborers in that country were two million, then the wages of each laborer "would be five quarters."

"But five quarters in what time?" asked the writer of *My Economic Endeavors.* "Five quarters per hour, per day, or per year? Divorced as it is from any time concept, this definition is meaningless."

In speaking of the gradual acceptance of his theories he cited William Smart's prediction that the book "would mark the beginning of the end of the old controversies over how to define capital and income," and the old confusion as to "what part of wealth is capital and what part is income" has nearly disappeared. In the preface he expressed the hope that *The Nature of Capital and Income* would form "a sort of philosophy of economic accounting, and supply a link long missing between the ideas and usages underlying practical business transactions and the theories of abstract economics." Here is a condensation of his summary of the subject, taken from Chapter XVIII:

> The parts of the material world which [man] appropriates constitute wealth, whether they remain in their natural state or are "worked up" by him into products to render them more adapted to his needs. . . . By means of land he is enabled to increase and improve the growth of the vegetable and animal kingdoms in such a way as to supply him with food and

the materials for constructing other instruments. By means of dwellings he is enabled to divert the elements from contact with his body and with the objects of wealth which he stores in them. By means of machinery, tools, and other instruments, he is enabled to fashion new instruments to add to his stock. By means of final finished products which minister to his enjoyments, he is enabled to consummate the objects for which the entire mass of wealth is produced, namely the satisfaction of his desires. . . . We thus see in the mind of man a microcosm of the objective economic world, consisting of desires, efforts, and satisfactions, corresponding respectively in the objective world to capital, outgo, and income.

To describe in a few words the nature of capital and income, we may say that those parts of the material universe which at any time are under the dominion of man constitute his capital wealth; its ownership, his capital property; its value, his capital-value; its desirability, his subjective capital. But capital in any of these senses stands for anticipated income, which consists of a stream of services or its value. The causal relation is not from capital to income, but from income to capital; in other words, the value of capital is the discounted value of the expected income.

This book was dedicated "To William Graham Sumner, who first inspired me with a love for Economic Science." When the completed manuscript had been sent to the publisher in March, 1906, he wrote to his wife:

The dryness of my book is in the *subject*. It's all finished and planed and polished and not hastily put together. You know it was written once a year ago and has been under revision at intervals ever since.

I meant (when I said I did not care about its reception but was glad I had done *something*) not that I had written it as some students do a thesis just to do "something" but that at last I was glad I had done my part toward putting out a beginning of my life-work and that, having done the best I could, I wasn't bothering about whether the world will make much or little of it. That's beyond my power and therefore not to be worried about. I haven't heard yet from Macmillan. They may reject it you know!

Forty years after its issuance under Macmillan's imprint, Professor Schumpeter made these comments on it in *Econometrica* for July, 1948:

> Most people saw nothing in it but a continuation of the time-honored discussion of these two concepts of which they had every right to be tired. A few, Pareto among them, admired it greatly, however. [Fisher] deduced rationally a set of definitions of Wealth, Property, Services, Capital, Income that was new by virtue of the very fact that it fitted a rational schema.
>
> It produced the definition: earned income equals realized income less depreciation, or plus appreciation of capital, which is associated with the much-discussed proposition that savings are no proper object of income taxation or that the taxation of savings spells double taxation.

In a footnote to this passage, Professor Schumpeter remarked:

> Fisher has invariably won out, by virtue of his impeccable logic, in the controversies that arose on

the subject. But it is for me a source of wonder how he can have believed—as he evidently did—that this logic would convert anyone who wishes to see savings taxed or be needed by anyone who does not. I mention this because belief in reason was so characteristic of this modern Parsifal. This bent of his made him, perhaps, a bad adviser in the nation's or the world's affairs. But it also made him still more lovable than a more worldly Fisher would have been.

During the year which intervened between *The Nature of Capital and Income* and the publication of his next book, fate came close to diverting his energies into somewhat different channels, since his name was one of several which were considered for the secretaryship of the Smithsonian Institution. The election of a new incumbent was scheduled for January, 1907. A thirty-page mimeographed brochure was prepared for the board of electors, summarizing his career to date and containing excerpts from reviews of his writings as well as twenty-three "Expressions of Opinions by Representative Scientists" as to his fitness for the post. These included statements from President Hadley, Professors Phillips and Beebe, his former mathematical teachers and colleagues, Professor Sumner and Henry L. Stimson, who was then U.S. District Attorney in New York. But the most underscored item in the brochure was this recommendation from Dr. Kellogg, founder of the Battle Creek Sanitarium:

Professor Fisher would fill the position more efficiently than any other man who could be found. He is possessed of excellent, one might say extraordinarily good health, and so gives promise of many years of active usefulness.

Just before the election the candidate confided to Will Eliot in Oregon: "I am not at all sure that I want the position if it should be offered to me." And when the choice fell elsewhere, perhaps because it was feared that Irving Fisher would be too idealistic and forthright for his own good or for the comfort of his potential associates in Washington, he wrote again to Will Eliot:

> January 23, 1907
>
> I have received the news that Walcott has been elected Secretary of the Smithsonian. It would have been an interesting position and I should have much liked to have it, but of course shall content myself as it is.

While the decision still hung in the balance he was putting the finishing touches on *The Rate of Interest,* which went to press in July of the same year. This book was the inevitable outcome of the definitions formulated in *The Nature of Capital and Income.* Together these works elaborated the threefold series of inspirations which began in Switzerland in 1894, were continued in Rhode Island and reached their culmination in California in 1901.

His earliest expression of opinion on interest was an address delivered at the annual meeting of the American Economic Association in Indianapolis in the final week of 1895. Using the bimetallic controversy as his springboard he spoke on "The Relation of Changes in the Volume of the Currency to Prosperity." Years later he noted in pencil across the first page of the stenographic report of this talk that the material was "all substantially contained in *Appreciation and Interest* (1896), and later in *The Rate of Interest* (1907)."

At a British parliamentary hearing on the depreciation of Indian currency, Alfred Marshall of Cambridge made this reference to the 1896 monograph: "One of the ablest of the younger school of American Economists, Mr. Fisher of Yale, has written a book on *Appreciation and Interest,* which bears very closely on this matter.... I am not sure that it might not be worth while for the committee to reproduce some of Mr. Fisher's tables which bear upon this subject, [although] he takes the question of rupee paper only incidentally." In a personal letter to the author, Byron W. Holt wrote: "I consider your discussion of *Appreciation and Interest,* if not the greatest, at least one of the greatest, contributions ever made to monetary science."

When this theme was treated at greater length in *The Rate of Interest* (1907) it was dedicated to John Rae, who in 1834 "laid the foundations upon which I have endeavored to build." Indebtedness was also acknowledged to Landry and to Böhm-Bawerk, and the author stated that his own theory of interest "differs from former versions of that theory by the introduction explicitly of an *income concept*." He was not concerned, as some of his predecessors had been, whether the rate of interest is "an agio, or premium, for of this there can be no question," but rather "upon what does that agio depend and in what manner? Does it depend on the volume of money, the amount of capital, the productivity of capital ... or upon some other condition? The solution here offered is that the rate of interest depends on the character of the income-stream, its size, composition, probability, and above all, its distribution in time."

He submitted the manuscript of this book to a considerable list of friends and colleagues for criticism and suggestions—a procedure he followed with all his subsequent major works. He especially welcomed any adverse comments, and he was anxious to secure the reaction of as

130

many laymen as possible, so that the published book might be correspondingly more comprehensible to the general public. The preface of *The Rate of Interest* mentioned nine such critics, including one to whom a presentation copy was duly inscribed: "To my brother Herbert, who more than any other person has helped me in my attempts to set forth a difficult subject."

These paragraphs have been condensed from the summary chapter:

It is clear that the rate of interest is dependent upon very unstable influences, many of which have their origin deep down in the social fabric and involve considerations not strictly economic. Any causes tending to affect intelligence, foresight, self-control, habits, the longevity of man, and family affection, will have their influence upon the rate of interest.

So far as the effect of the monetary standard on the rate of interest is concerned, the prospect of depreciation of gold tends nominally to raise the rate of interest, but practically to make the rate of interest really not only low, but lower than it otherwise would be. . . . It is commonly assumed that the rate of interest is a phenomenon confined to money markets and trade centers, and the public approval or disapproval of the rate usually takes its cue from the sentiments of the borrower. If "money is easy," he is content.

The truth is that the rate of interest is not a narrow phenomenon applying only to a few business contracts, but permeates all economic relations. It is the link which binds man to the future and by which he makes all his far-reaching decisions. It enters into the price of securities, land, and capital goods generally, as well as into rent, wages, and the value of all "interactions." It affects profoundly the distribution of wealth. In short, upon its accurate adjustment depend the equitable terms of all exchange and distribution.

Twenty-three years later, while preparing a new edition of *The Rate of Interest*, his colleague and editorial assistant, Dr. Royal Meeker, urged him to turn this revision into a major reworking of the subject. The resultant book, *The Theory of Interest*, was published by Macmillan in 1930 and was reissued in 1954 by Kelley and Millman in their series, *Economic Classics*.

In the preface the author explained that he had postponed revising the earlier book for more than two decades, because he "wished to revise the presentation, and to rewrite those portions which, if I may judge from criticisms, have not been understood. . . . Though, in substance, my theory of interest has been altered scarcely at all, its exposition has been so amplified and recast that it will seem, to those who misunderstood my first book, more changed than it seems to me. . . .

"Years after *The Rate of Interest* was published, I suggested the term 'impatience' in place of 'agio.' This catchword has been widely adopted, and, to my surprise, has led to a widespread but false impression that I had overlooked or neglected the productivity or investment opportunity side entirely. Thus I found myself credited with being the author of 'the impatience theory' which I am not, and not credited with being the author of those parts lacking any catchword. It was this misunderstanding which led me to adopt the catchword 'investment opportunity' as a substitute for the inadequate term 'productivity' which had come into such general use. . . . If this combined 'impatience and opportunity' theory can be said to be at all distinct from all others, it is because it explicitly analyses opportunity, and fits together impatience and opportunity and income. I venture to hope that the theory, as here presented, will be found not so much to overthrow as to co-ordinate previous theories, and to help in making the chain of explanation complete and strong."

Part I of *The Theory of Interest* reviewed the ground previously covered in *The Nature of Capital and Income,* which by that time was out of print. Part II set forth "the theory in words" while Part III explained the theory in mathematical terms, and Part IV contained the summary. from which these paragraphs have been condensed:

> The value of capital is derived from the income it yields by capitalizing it at the prevailing rate of interest. To reverse this process by multiplying the capital value by the rate of interest gives the original income, as long as the capital value remains stationary. It is this income which affords the basis for the determination of the rate of interest, and of capital value. The final enjoyable income of society is the ultimate and basic fact from which all values are derived and toward which all economic action is bent.

> The main problem of distribution is concerned with the determination and explanation of the amounts and values of capital and incomes possessed by different individuals in society. . . .

> The rates of preference among different individuals are equalized by borrowing and lending or, what amounts to the same thing, by buying and selling. An individual whose rate of preference for present enjoyment is unduly high will contrive to modify his income stream by increasing it in the present at the expense of the future. The effect will be upon society as a whole that those individuals who have an abnormally low estimate of the future and its needs will gradually

part with the more durable instruments, and these will tend to gravitate into the hands of those who have the opposite trait.

This progressive sifting, by which the spenders grow poorer and the savers richer, would go on even if there were no risk element. But it goes on far faster when as in actual life there is risk. While savings unaided by luck will ultimately enrich the saver, the process is slow as compared with the rapid enrichment which comes from the good fortune of those few who assume risks and then happen to guess right. Likewise the more rapid impoverishment comes from guessing wrong. Henry Ford and others grew rich not so much because of thrift as because they took advantage of unusual investment opportunities, in which the rates of return over cost proved to be many times the market rate of interest.

There is another factor closely associated with the process of accumulation or dissipation. This is habit. If a man has been accustomed to simple and inexpensive ways, he finds it fairly easy to save and ultimately to accumulate a little property. If a man has been brought up in the lap of luxury, he will have a keener desire for present enjoyment than if he had been accustomed to the simple living of the poor. The old adage, "from shirt sleeves to shirt sleeves in four generations," has some basis in fact.

It is true, as the socialist maintains, that inequality is due to social arrangements, but these arrangements are not, as he assumes, primarily such as to take away the chance to rise in the economic scale; they are, on the contrary, arrangements which facilitate both rising and falling.

Professor Schumpeter, in his July, 1948, *Econometrica* paper, referred to *The Theory of Interest* in these words:

134

The book is a wonderful performance, the peak achievement of the literature of interest—a pedagogical masterpiece. It teaches us, as does no other work I know, how to satisfy the requirements of both the specialist and the general reader without banishing mathematics to footnotes and appendices, and how to lead on the layman from firmly laid foundations to the most important results by judicious summaries and telling illustrations.

The work is an almost complete theory of the capitalist process as a whole, with all the interdependencies displayed that exist between the rate of interest and all the other elements of the economic system. And yet this interplay of innumerable factors is powerfully marshalled around two pillars of explanation: Impatience and Investment Opportunity.

Splendid wheat, all this, with very little chaff in between . . . and we should be further along if we had chosen Fisher's work for the basis of our own. This, however, has not been done to any great extent.

Having thus established the foundation of his economic philosophy in these 1906 and 1907 books, he next directed his attention toward the broader field of pure pedagogy.

9. Purchasing Power

The next item on the agenda was *Elementary Principles of Economics*, which made the name of Irving Fisher familiar to many generations of students at Yale and elsewhere.

In his exposition of "the science of wealth," the author sought to take "due account of those ideas with which the student's mind is already furnished," and then gradually progress from the familiar to the unfamiliar. He shunned the "tendency to run after remedies before formulating principles." Instead he urged "the student first to master the fundamental economic principles on which all or most competent economists can agree, and then to take up *some one* moot question—some burning issue of the day—and, so far as possible, master that also."

Some of the old guard looked down their noses at the book's "expediency." Whereas many previous writers had used technical terms like assets, liabilities, cost, income, etc. virtually "without discussion or even definition," the author of *Elementary Principles* was determined to progress from fundamentals to clear and concise definitions. He believed that "when the usage of academic economics conflicts with the ordinary usage of business, the latter is generally the better guide," in contrast to the ivory-tower approach of his predecessors.

Although it was intended for use in elementary classes, the book amounted to an abbreviated recapitulation of the author's economic philosophy as set forth in his previous writings. At the outset he stated that economics is the science of wealth, then proceeded to discuss it under three main headings:

(1) The Foundation Stones, in which he introduced the student to the concepts of wealth and property, benefits and costs, price and value, capital and income. In particular he showed that capital is the net discounted value of future benefits and consists of "concrete physical objects" while income consists of "final satisfactions."

(2) The Determination of Prices, which was subdivided into the determining of "price levels" and of "individual

prices." With respect to the former he stated that normally the price level is "proportional to the quantity of money, and inversely proportional to the volume of trade. The velocities of the circulation of money and of deposits subject to check are also important factors. The disturbance of the normal condition of the magnitudes in the equation of exchange has much to do with periodical crises and depressions of trade." In determining individual prices the problem was further subdivided into: "the prices of individual goods, and the rate of interest." The key to the first is "marginal desirability," to the second "marginal impatience."

(3) The study of the results of these forces on "the distribution of income, relatively to its sources and owners." Distribution by sources was divided into "*profits* (whether the profits are from capital or work or both), *capitalists' stipulated income* (whether interest or rent) and *labor's stipulated income* (wages)." The distribution by owners "depends on inheritance constantly modified by thrift, ability, industry, luck, and fraud," which led finally to a consideration of "the effects of the ownership of wealth on social welfare."

This whole study was admittedly "cold and impartial" and did not include any "practical application of the principles." The student was warned against taking any partisan position on economic questions until he had some grounding in economic principles. But after laying these foundations the chief object of the author was to place the student "in a position to study and help solve the great problems of money, tariffs, trusts, labor unions, housing and hygiene, wealth and poverty." The book ended as it began by urging the student to "take up *some one* of them for thorough study."

137

Toward the end of the opening chapter of *My Economic Endeavors*, the author linked this elementary textbook somewhat unexpectedly to *Mathematical Investigations:*

> When my colleagues at Yale requested me to write a textbook on elementary economics, I took occasion to insert in it some of my most cherished ideas on prices. Thus, although it was intended primarily for elementary students, there are in it (see Ch. XVI) a few features on price theory which are not to be found elsewhere and which may be considered original contributions.
>
> These points were discussed with various correspondents including Pareto, Marshall, Edgeworth, and Taussig. Pareto wrote that the big and imperfectly solved economic problems were largely concerned with the variations in the marginal utility of money. Marshall sent me his exhaustive but unpublished supply and demand analysis for international trade. Edgeworth said he felt that the non-existence of supply and demand curves applicable to all the possible equilibria under all possible values of the variables involved should not deter us from utilizing them. Taussig used my *Elementary Principles* only for his advanced pupils, believing some of the analysis too difficult for elementary classes.
>
> I believe there is much still to be done on individual price theory. This will utilize but extend the excellent work already done by Cournot, Walras, Marshall, Edgeworth and others on competition, monopoly, price policies and strategy, the effects of taxes and tariffs, the interrelations of individual *prices* and price *levels*, the effects of mass production and of spreading information (and misinformation) especially through advertising and salesmanship.

An illustration will serve to show one point I have in mind. A midwestern concern dealing in a machine used in business offices, finding itself "in the red" asked an expert salesman to become sales manager. He replied, "Yes, on one condition—that you double your price." The company demurred, saying "That's our trouble! Our price is already so high, we have too few customers." He replied, "I need that 100% extra margin to pay my selling costs." Finally the Company accepted his terms, with the result that they have become one of the largest and most prosperous concerns in the United States.

Moreover, the public benefitted. Although the price was doubled, probably a hundred times as many people obtained help from the machine as could have done so without the price rise. Most of these would never have heard of it without the costly advertising and salesmanship. This principle is overlooked by those who regard advertising as waste and propose that government grading should replace private brands. This might hamper progress. It seems to have done so in Russia.

While *Elementary Principles* was undergoing its first revision, the author was also working on another major project, *The Purchasing Power of Money*, which was first issued in March, 1911. In this book he was practicing what he preached in the preface and on the concluding page of the elementary textbook, by devoting himself to what was for him the most "burning issue of the day."

He set his sights on the controversial topic of currency stabilization, which was an especially timely one in 1911, since there had recently been a spectacular increase in the cost of living. Even the most economically uninformed housewife was alerted by the high prices she had to pay for food. True to form, the author set about his task blandly assuming that if he called attention to the great harm done by "periodic changes in the level of prices, producing alternate crises and depressions," it would only be a question of time before the general public would be sufficiently aroused to insist on some sort of remedial action. In the preface he stated:

The main contentions of this book are at bottom simply a restatement and amplification of the old "quantity theory" of money. What has long been needed is a candid reexamination and revision of that venerable theory rather than its repudiation.

In making this attempt at reconstruction, I have the satisfaction of finding myself for once a conservative rather than a radical in economic theory. It has seemed to me a scandal that academic economists have, through outside clamor, been led into disagreements over the fundamental propositions concerning money. This is due to the confusion in which the subject has been thrown by reason of the political controversies with which it has become entangled.

Since the quantity theory has become the subject of political dispute, it has lost prestige and has even come to be regarded by many as an exploded fallacy. The attempts by promoters of unsound money to make an improper use of the quantity theory—as in the Bryan campaign—led many sound money men to the utter repudiation of the quantity theory.

The study of the principles and facts concerning the purchasing power of money is of far more than academic interest. Such questions affect the welfare of every inhabitant of the civilized world. At each turn of the tide of prices, millions of persons are benefitted and other millions are injured. For a hundred years the world has been suffering from periodic changes in the level of prices, producing alternate crises and depressions. Only by knowledge, both of the principles and of the facts involved, can such fluctuations in future be prevented or mitigated.

It is not too much to say that the evils of a variable monetary standard are among the most serious economic evils with which civilization has to deal. I have proposed, very tentatively, a remedy for the evils of monetary instability. But the time is not yet ripe for the acceptance of any working plan. What is at present most needed is a clear and general public understanding of principles and facts.

A year later the second edition brought the tables and diagrams up to date and included alterations from such widely scattered readers as Professor Wesley Clair Mitchell and Carl Snyder in New York, Professor Warren M. Persons of Colorado Springs, John Maynard Keynes of Cambridge, England, and Major W. E. McKechnie of India. The author regretted being unable—without radical alteration of the plates of the first edition—"to meet a criticism of Mr. Keynes' to the effect that while my book shows *that* the changes in the quantity of money do affect the price level, it does not show *how* they do so." For the explanation readers were referred to Chapter XIV of *Elementary Principles*.

Here is the gist of *The Purchasing Power of Money*, with direct quotations from and paraphrasing of Chapter II, where the argument was summarized for the benefit of "the cursory reader":

He defined money as any commodity which "is generally acceptable in exchange for goods." Its acceptability may be "reenforced by law," to make it "legal tender," but "whatever the substance of such a commodity"—whether it is gold dust on the frontier, tobacco in the colony of Virginia, or wampum among the Indians—what makes it money is its "general exchangeability." Of the various "degrees of exchangeability, perhaps the *least* exchangeable is real estate. A mortgage is one degree more exchangeable." This is less exchangeable than a good "corporation security." A government bond is more exchangeable, a sight draft still more so; "while a check is almost as exchangeable as money itself. Yet no one of these is really money for none of them is *generally acceptable.*"

Bank deposits, by means of checks "do actually serve as a medium of exchange." But a check is not money, while "a bank *note* is both circulating medium and money. Between these two lies the final line of distinction between what is money and what is not.... The total amount of circulating media in the United States is about 8½ billions, of which about 7 billions are bank deposits subject to check, and 1½ billions money." (1911 figures.)

The "quantity theory" of money "is correct in the sense that the level of prices varies directly with the quantity of money in circulation, provided the velocity of circulation of that money and the volume of trade which it is obliged to perform are not changed."

Suppose that a person buys 10 pounds of sugar at 7 cents a pound. In the mind of this buyer, 10 pounds of sugar have been regarded as equal to 70 cents. This may be expressed algebraically: 70 cents equals 10 pounds of sugar multiplied by 7 cents a pound. All other "sale and purchase" transactions may be expressed similarly, and "by adding them all together we get the equation of exchange for a certain period of time in a given community."

To state the equation of exchange in algebraic form, M is used to express the quantity of actual money, and V to express the velocity of circulation of this money; while M' represents the total of deposits subject to check and V' the velocity of circulation of those deposits. P stands for a weighted average of the prices of all goods, and T for the sum of all the quantities of goods. P then represents in one magnitude the level of prices and T represents the volume of trade. Using these symbols, the equation of exchange reads:

$$MV + M'V' = PT$$

Stated in words: "the total circulation of money in the sense of money expended is equal to the total money in circulation multiplied by its velocity of circulation or turnover. . . . Under the conditions assumed, the price level varies (1) directly as to quantity of money in circulation (M), (2) directly as the velocity of its circulation (V), (3) inversely as the volume of trade done by it (T). The first of these constitutes the *quantity theory of money*."

"In short, the quantity theory asserts that (provided velocity of circulation and volume of trade are unchanged) if we increase the *number* of dollars, whether by debasing coins, or by increasing coinage, or by some other means, prices will be increased in the same proportion. It is the number and not the weight, that is essential. This fact differentiates money from all other goods and explains the peculiar manner in which its purchasing power is related to other goods. . . . The quantity theory of money rests, ultimately, upon the fundamental peculiarity which money alone of all goods possesses—the fact that it has no power to satisfy human wants except a power *to purchase* things which do have such power."

Next he considered "several methods by which a government might regulate the quantity of money relative to business so as to keep the level of prices constant," such as: making inconvertible paper the standard money, and to regulate its quantity; or issuing paper money redeemable in varying amounts of the basic precious metal, so as to keep the level of prices stable. His own proposal "to adopt the gold-exchange standard combined with a tabular standard" was considered briefly, but full-scale treatment was reserved for later works, since he fully appreciated that the adoption of such a remedy lay far in the future and that "for the present there seems nothing to do but to state the problem and the principles of its solution in the hope that what is now an academic question may, in due course, become a burning issue."

Referring to this 1911 book in the July, 1948, issue of *Econometrica*, Professor Schumpeter wrote:

> Like most great system builders, Fisher felt the impulse of treating the problems of money in all the pomp and circumstance of a central theme. This he did in his *Purchasing Power of Money*.
>
> There was presented his early work in price-index numbers. There appeared his index of the Volume of Trade and other creations that were then novel, among them his ingenious method of estimating the velocity of money. Also, there was an elaborate attempt at statistical verification of results. All of these pieces of research are among the classics of early econometrics.
>
> It is less easy to show that the book is the most important link between the older theories of money and those of today. As was his habit, he made no claims to originality. The book is dedicated to [Simon] Newcomb, and other predecessors could easily be mentioned. Yet the central chapters, IV, V, and VI represent a contribution that was more than

synthesis. Fisher accepted without question what then was still a new theory of bank credit. He assigned a pivotal role to the lag of the interest rate in the credit cycle. He explicitly recognized the variability of velocity. And he took due account of a host of factors that help to determine purchasing power.

Why was it that friends and foes of *The Purchasing Power of Money* saw nothing in it but another presentation, statistically glorified, of the oldest of old quantity theories—that is, a monument of an obsolescent theory that was to become quite obsolete before long? The answer is simple: because Fisher said so himself—in the Preface and at various strategic points.

All the rich variety of factors that do interact in the monetary process was made to disappear—as "indirect" influences—behind the five factors (quantities of basic money and deposits, their two velocities, and volume of trade) to which he reserved the role of "direct influences" upon the price level which thus became the dependent variable in the famous Equation of Exchange.

And it was this theory which he elaborated with an unsurpassable wealth of illustrations, whereas he shoved all his really valuable insights mercilessly into Chapters IV, V, VI and disposed of them semi-contemptuously as mere disturbances that occur during "transition periods" when indeed the quantity theory is "not strictly true."

In order to get at the core of his performance, one has to scrap the façade which was what mattered to him and both to his admirers and opponents and on which he had lavished his labors.

But why should he have thus spoiled his work? It cannot be urged that much of his or any quantity theory can in fact be salvaged by interpreting it strictly as an equilibrium proposition—valid, as it were, for a sort of Marshallian long-run normal. For, on Fisher's own showing, this equilibrium is not arrived at by a mechanism that could be fully understood in terms of his five factors alone.

I cannot help thinking that the scholar was misled by the crusader. He had pinned high hopes to the Compensated Dollar. His reformer's blood was up. His plan of stabilizing purchasing power had to be simple, in order to convince a recalcitrant humanity, and so had to be its scientific base. This is enough to suggest my own solution for what has always seemed to me an enigma. In this case at least, what did Fisher himself, or economics, or this country, or the world gain by his crusade?

There is no doubt that the author of *The Purchasing Power of Money* considered it merely the first stepping stone in his stabilization program. Further developments in this direction, as well as partial answers to Professor Schumpeter's final question, will be found in later chapters. Meanwhile, attention must be turned to other crusading activities.

10. Crusading Spirit

As his interests widened Father grew less and less content with things as he found them, and devoted an increasing proportion of his "spare time" to a long list of worthy causes, ranging from calendar reform, simplified spelling and the movement to have Esperanto adopted as an international language, to conservation and public health.

Whatever the cause, his participation was wholehearted and his enthusiasm swept co-workers along like surf riders on the crest of a Waikiki comber. Once he was convinced in his own mind, for instance, that such iniquities of civilization as alcohol, tea, coffee, tobacco, refined sugar and bleached white flour were detrimental to health, he was confident that the public could be persuaded to give them up. All that was needed was time and perseverance on the part of the enlighteners. Even those who disagreed with him seldom questioned his sincerity of purpose, however much they might deprecate the "fanaticism" with which he sought to persuade them of the error of their ways.

One of his earliest efforts along these lines was the formation in 1907 of the Committee of One Hundred on National Health, an offshoot of the American Association for the Advancement of Science. Its goal was a National Department of Health. He persuaded Will Eliot to be the organization's West Coast anchor man, and for five years their correspondence dealt almost exclusively with the inner workings of this committee. Its letterhead bore two quotations from Theodore Roosevelt, and the list of vice-presidents included such names as Lyman Abbott, Jane Addams, Felix Adler, James B. Angell, Joseph H. Choate, Charles W. Eliot, Archbishop Ireland and Judge Ben Lindsey.

Speaking as president of this committee, Father addressed the Association of Life Insurance Presidents on February 5, 1909, on the "Economic Aspect of Lengthening Human Life." Holding that it was to the financial interest of the insurance companies to invest money in prolonging human life, he proposed that they underwrite the educational work of his committee to the extent of $200,000 a year. Citing the success of the fire insurance companies in increasing their earnings by educating the public in the prevention of fires, he argued that the life

147

insurance companies could increase their profits by similar tactics. By keeping their policy-holders alive, the companies would receive more premiums and bring about "immeasurable gains of longevity, vitality, efficiency and happiness." One company made a sizable contribution but the others remained unconvinced.

When he testified at Senate Committee hearings on the Owen bill for the establishment of a department of health, the gallery's enthusiasm was so articulate that the chairman of the committee had to "request them to abstain from applause." Eight hundred pages of testimony later, the net gain was merely a change in nomenclature. Thereafter the Public Health and Marine Hospital Bureau of the Treasury Department was renamed the Public Health Service. "The mountain had laboured and brought forth a mouse."

Meanwhile he had been appointed to Theodore Roosevelt's National Conservation Commission, under the chairmanship of Gifford Pinchot. In this position he wrote a one-hundred-and-thirty-page *Report on National Vitality*, which was issued in 1909. In this document he called attention to the need for the conservation of human as well as natural resources. At that time the treatment of longevity from the economic standpoint, and the calculation of the financial waste which resulted from preventable illness and death, seemed epoch-making. In fact, it was given such widespread publicity that its author feared lest the sensation-seekers might do more harm than good by exaggerating "many of the original statements as to possible longevity." Dr. Ditman, a Columbia University pathologist, characterized the report as "the greatest medical step of the century."

In an address delivered before the American Academy of Political and Social Science on January 19, 1911, shortly

before the publication of *The Purchasing Power of Money*,
Father said:

> The idea of conservation has its center of gravity
> in our love for posterity. Civilized man prides himself
> on his foresight as compared with the savage.
>
> Those nations which have attempted to flourish by
> exploiting the present, as Rome attempted to exploit
> those about her, have always committed national sui-
> cide. It is hard for us in America, enjoying the
> present plenty, to realize that we are scattering the
> substance that belongs to future generations.
>
> At first it may seem that Man does not need any
> consideration, that he considers himself, that our vital
> resources perpetuate themselves, and that we have
> ocular evidence of it in the increase of our population.
> But we must realize that the earth and man must
> both be conserved, if there is to be any future for the
> human race.
>
> The health movement aims to spread the idea of
> improving the vitality of the present generation,
> increasing the length of life, decreasing the burden of
> illness, and increasing the power to work. If all the
> preventable deaths could be prevented the average
> duration of human life in this country would be fifteen
> years longer. It is probably forty-five at present, and
> it might be sixty. [It is now close to seventy.]
>
> It has been established that the loss in dollars and
> cents from premature deaths of wage earners and
> from sickness amounts to a billion and a half dollars
> per annum. [In 1955 this figure was approximately
> ten billion dollars.]

He took the whole family to Europe that summer, primarily to visit the International Hygiene Exhibit at Dres-

den. Due to a minor mishap to the ship on which we were originally booked, we were shifted to a small cattle boat which took twelve days for the crossing.

We had expected to cover the Continent first and visit England before sailing home, but the switch in steamers landed us in London three days before the Coronation of George V, so it was quite a scramble to find accommodations for a family of five. From London we went to Wales for a glimpse of the nurse who had taken care of Mother during her bout with typhoid twenty-two years before. Then we paused briefly at Warwick, Chester and Kenilworth en route to Oxford, where Father hobnobbed with Professor Edgeworth and other colleagues.

In Paris we stayed at the same hotel where Margaret had been born, and went to call on an elderly lady who gave us our first taste of wine. I remember that when we walked down the apartment house stairway afterwards the steps seemed to have acquired a peculiar escalator quality, although Mother had diluted our portions liberally with water. I'm still not sure whether she ever confessed this episode to Father.

Soon after we reached Switzerland, she had the misfortune to sprain her ankle, so we stayed in Berne for a month while he went on to Dresden. In his letters to Mother he told of covering the Hygiene Exhibit so thoroughly that he had to hire an English-speaking typist to codify his careful notes. On the whole, the exposition surpassed his expectations, though he was disappointed that the United States was the only civilized country not represented, and that the German authorities had compromised with commercialism to the extent of permitting the brewers to display and sell their wares. To do it up brown he attended a performance of the can-can, but found it merely "revolting." Otherwise nearly every moment not spent at the exhibit was devoted to correcting proof. Here are two of his letters:

Be of good cheer and write me more letters telling me your real feelings. When you leave out the "bad" things, I vaguely know it and feel left out myself. Things are always "wrong" to some extent; but it's all in a lifetime. The central idea of a philosophic spirit is to "accept" things as they really are, which is the basis of James' "religion of healthy-mindedness."

Please don't smile at my sermonizing. Perhaps it is like Carol's pious efforts—actuated by a consciousness of her own shortcomings. Never mind, I'm making progress and you have helped me more than any other human being because you unconsciously taught me the vanity and shallowness of those valuations I used to have—the academic point of view—before I married you and especially before I had my three years enforced vacation.

The changed point of view I experienced after I went to Colorado was due to you. This I can see more clearly now as I look back than when going along day by day I "could not see the woods for the trees" and blamed you for the very criticism which wrought the change in me and accused you of not appreciating my point of view.

It was also true that I didn't appreciate yours and that you had the thankless task of making me do so. I never saw a person, so free from the worldliness all around us as you, my love. You got your point of view unconsciously without knowing that there was any other. It was for this natural ingrained angelicness that I fell in love with you and it has been that which has been my lodestone ever since.

I liked your "pickle" letter, including your "insults!" I'm very sorry if I ever seem "sneering." I don't doubt there must be some basis for you to feel it; but I think you must read much of it into my expression. I see your point about being a health prude and think it is well taken. As you say, it's all wrong to make a burden of Hygiene. True Hygiene means serenity and unconcern. It is my fault very largely that you are so often irritated and my talking hygiene and correcting the children is one of the causes.

I realize the apparent inconsistency in saying everything is all right and then moving heaven and earth to change things. Epictetus, when asked why people should make an effort to do anything if, as he claimed, everything was all right anyway, replied, "That thou may'st have been."

After returning to Yale that fall, he delivered the talk on socialism already mentioned; and the following spring he summarized his personal health credo in an address to the students of Oberlin:

I believe that what we want most of all is a sense of the ideal mode of life, as distinct from the average. You cannot take the average as normal. The average per capita consumption of beer in Germany does not represent what is normal for health, nor the average consumption of whiskey in Scotland, nor the average use of opium in China, nor the average use of hashish in Turkey, nor the average use of tobacco in almost all countries.

But what is the normal use of these things? According to the best light scientifically that has been shed on them, the normal use is none at all, and if that is so those who see it should not be ashamed to live up to their ideal any more than they should be ashamed to live up to the Ten Commandments.

While testifying before a Subcommittee on Excise and Liquor Legislation of the Committee on the District of Columbia in March, 1912, he made these pertinent references to his *Report on National Vitality:*

After making what I believe was a thoroughly disinterested study of the question, being perfectly willing to be convinced that alcohol is a benefit or at any rate not an injury, I came personally very strongly to the conclusion, on the basis of statistics as well as on the basis of physiology that alcohol so far as we can observe its effects, is an evil and no benefit. It is not a stimulant, but a depressant. It is apparently a stimulant, because it puts to sleep the nerves that indicate fatigue.

Last summer I visited the great international hygiene exhibition in Dresden, in which was represented the public health work of all the nations of the world, with the one exception, I am regretful to say, of the United States of America. I was very much surprised to see that in Germany, distinctively a beer-drinking nation, that so much attention was given to the evils of alcohol, and I found that at this exhibit there were a number of interesting and new statistics on the subject.

The method of fighting degenerative diseases is through personal hygiene and the question of the individual taking care of himself, the question of fresh air, sleeping out of doors, living out of doors and taking exercise, questions of attire, and questions of mental attitude. These are the methods by which the degenerative diseases are combatted, and I believe that in personal hygiene one of the most important branches is the use one makes of alcoholic beverages.

When national prohibition was later adopted as a wartime measure, he was jubilant that the illwind of a world war had brought this indirect benefit. But after the Eighteenth Amendment became the law of the land, he soon realized that this sweeping reform had come too soon. He deplored the rise of the bootlegger and racketeer, and the prevalence of disrespect for law even among the "best" people. He did his utmost to fill the educational vacuum in a futile effort to stem the tide which finally swept the Eighteenth Amendment into limbo.

He wrote three books on the subject—*Prohibition at Its Worst* (1926), *Prohibition Still at Its Worst* (1928) and *The Noble Experiment* (1930)—the last two in collaboration with H. B. Brougham. Referring to these books, Professor Ray B. Westerfield said in his memorial article in the September, 1947, issue of the *American Economic Review*, that "it seemed to many he, unconsciously no doubt, selected his data to prove his position." Similarly, Professor G. Findlay Shirras in the British *Economic Journal* asserted that the author's judgment with regard to alcohol "was sometimes a little warped." In particular he criticised Father's dictum that: "A man who has had one beer is one beer drunk." Such slogans were just as much a matter of common sense to Father as that two plus two makes four. No matter how fanatical he may have seemed about alcohol—and the same applied to tobacco—he didn't consider himself intolerant of other people's opinions, but blamed the emotional bias of those who liked to "treat their resolution" for blocking their acceptance of his position.

His sense of proportion on this topic was not entirely lacking, however. Witness the mingled glee and chagrin with which he reported to us the incident which was responsible for defeating the prohibition plank at one of the national nominating conventions. The first speaker in favor of the plank was a gaunt Yankee who began in a high nasal voice: "Me and my wife—" This produced such an uproar that it was several minutes before he could proceed: "Me and my wife—we fought for thirty years in the county jail—" Presumably he meant that they had fought liquor, but the audience would not allow him to continue, and that was the end of the discussion for that year.

Father attended both 1912 conventions to work behind the scenes for the adoption of a suitable public health plank. His letters from Chicago to Mother at Sugar Hill give his impressions of the proceedings, which were dominated by the split between Taft and Roosevelt:

CHICAGO, June 14, 1912

I had a long talk with Mr. Kellogg of California about the Health plank and he is likely to be of much help. This morning he took me to see several newspapermen and got them interested. Just now we want to lie low and avoid attracting the attention of the opponents, who will appear on the scene before long.

I saw Mr. Hilles of the Taft side and Gifford (Pinchot) of the Roosevelt side and both will help about the plank. I also saw Barnes the New York State boss. He is a big factor and not yet very much inclined to put in the plank. But I think I made some impression on him and John Hays Hammond will help.

The Taft–Roosevelt fight is very bitter and the air is full of accusations. The Taft men have a majority

155

in the National Committee, and apparently are deciding contests in a very high-handed way. On the other hand, the Roosevelt men have apparently been buying the Southern Negro delegates. It's a very unsavory mess.

Dr. Evans of the Chicago Tribune called me up and told me that there is a plan on foot for the women's clubs to repudiate their endorsement of the Owen bill, under the influence of the Christian Scientists.

It's very interesting to be in so many fights and to see a big fight *without* being in it. It's amusing to hear Pinchot "cuss" the Taft side and Hammond "cuss" the Roosevelt side and each assume that of course I must see it from their point of view.

CHICAGO, June 15, 1912

About beer. I'd not get it unless Leonard and Patty [Bacon] ask it or unless you want to ask them if you shall. If they think they need it so much they can order it or take it along. They are too young to require us to cater to their notions, especially when they seem silly to us. If they were Mr. & Mrs. Balfour, who are old and foreign, we might yield our ideas for hospitality, but not to Leonard. That's my feeling, but of course you must do as you think best, especially as I'm not there and you are.

Today I had a conference with Dr. Evans and three ladies, two of them doctors, in reference to the meeting in San Francisco in two weeks of the Federation of Women's Clubs at which the Christian Scientists are going to try to rescind the previous action of the federation in endorsing federal health legislation.

I also saw Col. Roosevelt arrive and speak from the balcony to a crowd in the street, of which I was one. It was dramatic. He wore his sombrero and talked of *stealing* and how the receiver (Taft) of stolen goods (delegates) was as bad as the thief.

Chicago, June 16, 1912

I saw Charles Hopkins Clark, Editor of the Hartford Courant, and other Connecticut men. Clark is on the resolutions committee. I saw Chaunc[e]y Depew who will help by seeing Barnes of New York. Tomorrow will be a very critical day. People are interested in nothing except this Taft-Roosevelt fight. It is all very much like Class Reunion (beer, brass bands, etc.). By the time the real sane exercise of judgment is to be made, these people will be in a tired, abnormal and alcohol-soaked condition, unfit for the best work. In such an atmosphere history will be made!

Chicago, June 18, 1912

This was the first convention day, and a red letter day it was. In the first place came good news this morning that the California delegation had already helped in the health plank. A California physician not on the delegation came on with them on purpose to get this right.

He found the strongest man (Rowell) of ten delegates was strongly for it and got him put on the platform committee, although there were five Christian Scientists on the delegation. This was all done on the train. After they got here Senator Works met them and asked to have his plank against the movement put in but his proposal was tabled or rather it was voted to leave the matter to Rowell! So Works is repudiated in his own State and California will work hard for the plank!

Then came the Convention and the Taft victory in electing Root as temporary chairman. I don't know

157

what Roosevelt will do but it looks now as if Taft would get the nomination. It is very exciting. I sat from 11:30 A.M. to nearly 8 P.M. without lunch and never lost a second's attention.

Root made a good speech. Gifford looks broken hearted.

As Father added new irons to his fire, his office staff was correspondingly augmented. At first two or three stenographers were sufficient to handle his correspondence and type his book manuscripts. They were crammed like sardines into a tiny third-floor room, until a flat-roofed extension was built at the rear of Four-sixty during our summer in Europe. These new quarters were a flight below the library on the basement level, but due to the slope of the land they were entirely above ground and opened directly onto the rose garden—to Mother's regret and envy. Before long the enlarged staff became almost as cramped in the three new rooms as they had been on the top floor, and at the peak of the 1929 boom further alterations were made to the tune of $30,000. A modern kitchen wing was added on the main floor level, so that the former kitchen and laundry could be converted into additional office space. The final layout contained ten workrooms, each capable of accommodating two workers. House guests and chance visitors were always amazed to discover this hidden beehive of activity below decks. Also noteworthy were the constant stream of new gadgets which were installed to heighten the staff's efficiency, such as: dictaphones, interconnecting telephones (with glass mouthpieces for easy sterilization), and an ozone machine for adding stimulation to the atmosphere in which he and the staff worked.

Father's predilection for mechanical gadgets increased steadily from the time of his first patent application as a

Yale Freshman, and over the years his inventive bent found expression in such diverse brain children as: a three-legged folding seat for sports or occasional home use; an icosahedral world map for representing our global world on a flat surface with the least possible distortion; and an apparatus for determining mechanically whether or not a certain meal was well balanced. This enlivened many Four-sixty gatherings, when the bountiful Sunday dinner an unsuspecting guest had eaten was subjected to rigid scrutiny, with considerable resultant hilarity over the precise size of the portions he or she had consumed.

For the focal point of the Four-sixty rose garden he designed a semicylindrical sundial, the eastern edge of which cast the shadow in the morning and the western edge in the afternoon. At Sugar Hill, with the help of a local blacksmith, he constructed another type of sundial out of a metal hoop with a rod or gnomon attached to the upper side to cast the shadow. This enabled him to tell time accurately at midday to within a few seconds. Another Sugar Hill project was a Goldberg-like wooden clock, consisting chiefly of two meshed wheels, each the size of the head of a barrel. Stationary arrows at the bottom of each pointed to the revolving numerals, with one wheel registering the hours and the other registering the minutes. A heavy boulder hoisted to the ceiling by pulleys provided the necessary propulsion power. The release mechanism was a grooved board which tilted first one way then the other, as a marble rolled back and forth along the groove. Being constructed almost entirely of wood, changes in the weather naturally interfered with the regularity of its performance, so Father was elated one morning to find that his clock had actually run through the night without stopping. His pleasure was short-lived, however, when the cook complained that the rumbling marble and the click-clack it made at each end of the runway had kept her awake all night.

A decade before his death he applied for patents on a novel bed, which might be considered the culmination of his tuberculosis tent. In the intervening years his notions about fresh air had been considerably revised, so that he finally believed that the circulation of air was just as (if not more) important as its freshness. His bed provided this to the whole body, not merely to the respiratory tract, by surrounding the sleeper with a wooden frame which was attached to the ceiling by pulleys. Strategically-placed light bulbs controlled by thermostats kept the sleeper warm without any encumbering blankets, and caused an imperceptible upward current of air similar to the current of the tent. On the day when this sarcophagus-like contraption was delivered from the model-maker, Mother made a special point of calling on an elderly neighbor, to emphasize that everyone at Four-sixty was hale and hearty, in case she had seen the bed being carried up the front steps and mistaken its import. Father's experiments with this model-T electric blanket continued for many months before he abandoned it.

The only one of his inventions which was commercially successful was the visible card-index system which he devised in 1912. Intended to eliminate the laboriousness of thumbing through a conventional card catalogue in his own office, this device consisted mainly of a simple cut in an ordinary index card, enabling it to be mounted on a metal strip so as to make the first line of each card clearly visible at a glance. By sliding the cards along an aluminum strip, new ones could be inserted or old ones removed just as easily as from a drawer file; and the strips in turn could be mounted vertically along a wall, or in shallow drawers, or—for maximum compactness—on a rotary stand.

160

The idea was so simple and straightforward that Father could not understand why none of the existing office-equipment firms could be persuaded to add it to their lines. Instead he organized his own Index Visible Company to manufacture and promote it, after first securing his basic patents in 1913. Operations commenced in a tiny loft with a total payroll of three people, one of them being his brother Herbert. Then slightly larger quarters were rented over a carpenter shop on the present site of the Yale Law School buildings. In 1919 the firm required a three-story factory—with the rough-diamond Irish carpenter who had made the early working models serving as general manager —and opened sales offices in the Times Building, New York. One of the first large-scale users of the new system was the New York Telephone Company, which supplied miraculously fast information service after installing Index Visible equipment. In the end the small firm struggled out of the red into the black and merged with its chief rival to form the nucleus of what was known as Remington Rand and has since been enlarged into Sperry Rand. Although Father's personal financial gain from this venture was comparatively short-lived, it enabled him to broaden the scope of his crusading activities throughout the booming twenties.

Since he always liked to encourage co operation between his various activities, he saw to it that Index Visible equipment was installed in the New York offices of the Life Extension Institute; and reciprocally the institute's medical examination service was made available on a group basis to the employees of Index Visible. In the course of these negotiations the patience of the latter's general manager was worn thin by the inadvertence of an institute typist. In high dudgeon he wrote: "If you don't quit addressing us as the Index Invisible, we'll henceforth address you as the Life Extinction Institute." This pro-

161

duced the desired effect and incidentally tickled Father no end.

When the life extension program seemed to have reached an important turning point, Father's elation overflowed in this letter to Mother:

> October 18, 1921
>
> Mr. Ley (co-founder of the Institute) tells me most exciting news.
>
> To begin at the beginning, when we started the Life Extension Institute, Mr. Ley, I, Dr. Fisk and a very few others believed that life saving could be made profitable to the Life Insurance companies, that is it would pay them to have their policy holders examined because this would prolong life and give them more premiums.
>
> Before I met Mr. Ley I had addressed the Association of Life Insurance Presidents on these lines, and one company, that of which Dr. Fisk was then Medical Advisor took this seriously. But the others sneered and said that Postal was merely trying to use this absurd claim to lengthen human life as an advertising dodge and after Dr. Fisk published their very favorable experience they said there was something the matter with his statistics.
>
> Then we started the Institute. Year after year I urged Dr. Fisk to get statistics together. We started off with the Metropolitan and were disappointed not to get the New York Life to follow suit. Well, at last, a year ago, after my repeated hammering, Dr. Fisk got Mr. Dublin, Statistician of the Metropolitan, to make a thorough analysis of their six or seven years' experience and six months ago he entirely confirmed what we had always contended.
>
> We were eager to publish these results, but the Metropolitan wouldn't let us. The reason was that

162

the Actuarial Department pooh-poohed it all. Finally it was put up to the President, Haley Fiske. He then said to the Actuarial Department, "If Dublin is wrong, prove he is wrong. I want you to go over all his work carefully and report your own findings."

This was done and though they trimmed down Dublin's figures they still found his main conclusion true. They estimate that for $40,000 paid to the Life Extension Institute, they have had a return amounting to $120,000—a return of 200% on their investment. Dublin had estimated that the return was six fold.

And now they are ready to publish the results. So our faith is vindicated. This will be the rock on which our future work will stand. Health pays. It means a great activity which we have dreamed about but never seen.

Meanwhile events in Europe had precipitated him into the thick of still another crusade—for world peace.

11. First World War

In 1914, when Europe was on the brink of war, Father was optimistically helping Dr. Kellogg organize the first International Race Betterment Congress at Battle Creek. Soon after the outbreak of war, he resurrected and brought up to date his paper on "A League for Peace" which he had delivered before the Yale Political Science Club in 1890. The *New York Times* printed it in full on August 16, 1914, and it was issued as a pamphlet by the Church

Peace Union, with a prefatory letter by Lord Bryce, under the title: "After the War, What?" Here are some excerpts from this fervent proposal for international cooperation:

The universal war fever is but a symptom of a terrible disease of the body politic. . . . It is the fear of losing a fraction of "sovereignty" which keeps political structures unchanged. . . . The Psychology is for each nation to seek military expansion even when it realizes that the net result is a loss to all concerned. . . . There is only one way of avoiding such cut-throat competition—submission to common regulation.

Only by a general agreement can we secure a general disarmament; it is through some such rudiment of international government, that militarism and war can be made to disappear or diminish. In order to have stable peace we must provide machinery to handle the growing volume of questions and controversies, just as the courts handle the numerous quarrels in any civilized community.

We must substitute for the crude idea of the balance of power the idea of the pooling of power. The power pooled must exceed the power of any individual nation. A league of peace without power to keep the peace would be a rope of sand.

The league would in essence be simply a great mutual war insurance company. It would be both cheaper and more effectual to provide against war by paying small insurance premiums to a great league of peace than by maintaining a great army. The league would be in fact a rudimentary super-government. But its powers would be limited to the one function of keeping peace. As President [Theodore] Roosevelt said, "What is needed in International matters is to create a judge and then to put power back of the judge."

Father soon found that other minds were thinking along the same lines, and he subsequently felt that his conversations with Hamilton Holt in the Four-sixty library that fall helped germinate the movement which culminated in President Wilson's proposal for a League of Nations. Then followed four dinner meetings at the Century Club in New York early in 1915, beginning with a nucleus of fifteen or twenty enthusiasts like Theodore Marburg, Edward A. Filene, President Lowell of Harvard and ex-President Taft. Three hundred were present when *The League to Enforce Peace* was organized in Independence Hall that June, and two thousand attended the first assembly of the organization in Washington the following May, when President Wilson first declared himself in favor of a League. But the whole issue was hopelessly bogged down in party politics and the Senate finally rejected Wilson's plan.

Meanwhile the effect of the European war was felt even on Prospect Street. Neighbors gathered regularly in the Four-sixty living room to roll bandages for the Red Cross. Mother knitted innumerable khaki sweaters out of Peace Dale yarn. Madame Vandervelde was a Four-sixty house guest when she lectured in New Haven for Belgian Relief. Another guest was a naturalized Russian who held an impromptu gathering in the living room spellbound with his incredible tales of the Russo-Japanese war. And, with the twenty-four-hour-a-day humming of the nearby Winchester plant constantly in the background, it was inevitable that one incident should contain the elements of a full-scale spy scare.

On that particular evening, Father was working in his library and Mother was writing letters at her desk in the living room bay window. Someone pushed open the door from the back stairs into the front hall and there was a muffled whispering behind the closed portieres. Jumping to the conclusion that a former Scotch maid had dropped in for a visit on her evening off, Mother called out: "Just a minute, Annie, I'll be right with you," and finished what she was writing without any feeling of pressure. But when she reached the hall she was startled to find, instead of Annie, a short thick woman whom she had never seen.

Speaking with a strong Germanic accent, the woman said: "It is so gracious of you to receive me, Madame." Since she had entered unannounced via the basement kitchen and been kept standing in the hall for several minutes, Mother felt that her reception was far from gracious.

The stranger introduced herself as Madame Rosika Schwimmer, the Austrian-born pacifist who subsequently organized Henry Ford's Peace Ship expedition. Appearing without warning or appointment, it was almost as if she had arrived by submarine. Father was summoned from the library and they sat in the music room with their uninvited guest, listening to a rambling dissertation on the advantages of peace. Father suspected that her pacifism was nothing more than a poorly disguised pro-Germanism, and he sensed that she might have hoped to find him sympathetic to the German cause, since he had studied in Berlin.

Had she arrived via the basement kitchen simply because it was the nearest entrance to the Winchester trolley line? Or had she hoped to find a German cook in the kitchen to enlighten her as to where Father stood? No matter how hard he tried, he could not pin her down as to just why she had come or what she expected of him. She finally departed—by the front door—without getting any encouragement from Father, and when he was later invited to join Mr. Ford's quixotic expedition, he declined to have anything whatever to do with it.

My sister Margaret, who had finished her schooling and been presented to society the preceding winter, divided her time between war relief activities and lending a hand in Father's office, where the staff never seemed to be large enough to do all the things which he wanted done. At first the "regulars" were shy about referring to him as "I. F." in Margaret's presence, but it was not long before they accepted her as a full-fledged member of the team.

Socially her schedule was also a busy one, and when her week-end callers considered our supply of dance records inadequate, she more than once conducted them to Father's sanctum to whistle new favorites into his dictaphone. These impromptu recordings lacked volume when played back, but they sufficed for the moment, and on Monday she enjoyed hearing the transcriber's giggles at discovering such unexpected interpolations in a dissertation on money.

Carol and I were both away at boarding school. I was at the Thacher School in California, where one of my first chores had been to help the headmaster and the school blacksmith set up a replica of the Sugar Hill sundial. During the summer of 1915 the whole family used Aunt Caroline's Santa Barbara house as headquarters. From there we made excursions in her chauffeur-driven Cadillac to both the San Diego and the San Francisco expositions, commemorating the opening of the Panama Canal.

The high point of the summer was a chance encounter we had at Paso Robles, on our way north from Santa Barbara to San Francisco. As we approached the rambling resort hotel, Father spied someone who looked surprisingly like Paderewski taking a late afternoon stroll. Inquiry at the main desk revealed that he was a steady customer, since he found that the local sulphur baths relieved his neuritis. Father had once met him at a dinner in New York, so we were all introduced to him in the lobby after our evening meal. When I was presented with the remark that I played the piano a little too, I wished I could sink through the floor. Mr. Paderewski expressed interest and invited me to play for him at eleven o'clock the following morning. We had expected to make an early start for San Francisco, so I thought it would be impossible for me to accept the invitation. But I was finally persuaded not to miss the opportunity, and the chauffeur was dispatched with the car and luggage on schedule, while we arranged to follow by the midday train.

During my half hour at Mr. Paderewski's keyboard, he was the personification of graciousness and much less formidable than I feared. My repertoire consisted of several unpretentious pieces which I had played at school recitals. My chef d'œuvre was the "Funeral March" from Beethoven's *Sonata, Opus 26*. Afterwards he played some passages over for me, to suggest varying interpretations, but I was especially amazed that he seemed to know everything I played, even such an insignificant item as "Enchanted Hour" by H. Mouton. It didn't occur to me until years later that he had played it by ear after one hearing.

He spoke appreciatively of my feeling for the music, but he made it plain that if I expected to make a career out of it, I would have to practice for many hours every day. His most favorable comment was that I showed an unusual facility with the pedal.

At this point, Father, always seeking the rational explanation, asked me, "Have you had any special instruction in the use of the pedal?"

Before I could stammer any reply, Mr. Paderewski interjected with some vehemence: "It *cannot* be taught. One must be born with it!"

A few weeks later we met him again after a unique meeting in an auditorium on the grounds of the San Francisco Exposition, when he spoke eloquently on behalf of Polish Relief for an hour, then played an hour's program of Chopin. Father took me backstage afterwards and Mr. Paderewski caught sight of us as he was preparing to take his final bow. Obviously moved by the occasion and the ovation which the audience was giving him, he embraced me and kissed me in continental fashion. Father shouted that the audience wanted him to play the Polish national anthem. He shook his head, indicating that the ordeal would be too much for him, then went on stage and played the anthem as it has probably never been played before or since. When we rejoined the crowd which was pouring out of the auditorium, our eyes were not the only moist ones.

Equally memorable was the week we spent in the Yosemite and in the Mariposa Grove of big trees, covering the same ground Father had covered alone fourteen years before. During this excursion we were joined by Will Eliot and his son and daughter. More than thirty years had elapsed since Eliot and Fisher had argued against the feasibility of building the Panama Canal, and a like span was destined to pass before death terminated their long-range friendship and correspondence.

At the time of this meeting Will Eliot's daughter Clara was majoring in economics, and three years later she came to New Haven to serve an apprenticeship of several years in Father's office, before proceeding to a distinguished teaching career on the faculty at Barnard College. That is how it happened that the daughter of his St. Louis chum "helped at every stage of the work" in preparing the volume which is to be considered in the next chapter. During her first winter in New Haven she lived at Four-sixty like a member of the family and contributed her share to the home-front activities as well as on the technical level. Once, when the whole family had succumbed to that particular brand of Sunday evening hilarity which Mother believed was the harmless and natural reaction to attending church,

169

Clara remarked half seriously that dedicated men like her father and mine owed it to themselves to kick over the traces in an occasional binge, to maintain a reasonable equilibrium. Father then ejaculated "Oh, Clara!" with an expression of real horror at the enormity of such a suggestion, but laughing so hard that it hurt.

Prior to our California sightseeing in Aunt Caroline's Cadillac our sole means of locomotion in and about New Haven—aside from horse-drawn hacks—had been Mother's electric. Her first one had been an open Babcock, with patent-leather mudguards and matching top which folded back like a buggy when weather permitted. Although it was intended to seat only two, occasionally all five of us squeezed into it. My sisters, garbed in the full length linen dusters of the day, sat on the collapsed top with their feet demurely tucked in between my parents on the seat, while I occupied a precarious perch on the starboard step. Once, when we ventured downtown in this formation on Memorial Day, we were inadvertently caught in the tail end of a parade, and were greeted by rousing cheers as we proceeded along New Haven's main thoroughfare for several blocks before we could disentangle ourselves.

The Babcock was followed by several Detroits, culminating in a super-de luxe closed model, which seated four and resembled a square-sided goldfish bowl with rounded corners. Since the electric had to be recharged every night, Charles the furnace man was taught to operate it, so that he could pilot it to a downtown garage at night and return it to us in the morning. Each electric was equipped with two tillerlike bars which extended horizontally across in front of the operator, one for steering and the other for controlling the speed. When not in use these bars folded up out of the way, so that the driver could step in and out with much more dignity than owners of present-day stream-

170

lined vehicles. There were five speeds forward, and by raising the control lever to an angle of forty-five degrees, these same five speeds could be used in reverse. Fully charged the electric was capable of attaining a top speed of twenty-five miles per hour on the level, but there was no limit to its downhill free-wheeling speed.

Thus a great change was wrought in our lives when Father succumbed to the lure of the open road and bought our first gasoline car in the spring of 1916. It was an open five-passenger Dodge with a "one-man top" which could be folded down in fair weather or completely buttoned in with isinglass curtains when it rained. Father admonished us not to "step on the gas" too vigorously, as the Dodge opened up almost unlimited vistas in comparison with the twenty-five-mile-per-hour top speed of the electric. But he was the one who turned out to be a speed demon. His single-track mind showed in his driving, and when other vehicles popped out unpredictably from side streets or from the curb, he was always indignant at their ignoring his prior claim to the center of the road. Although Mother freely expressed her preference for a driving technique which consisted of gradual crescendos and diminuendos, Father never outgrew his tendency to jam on the brakes and round a corner on two wheels. He seemed to lead a charmed life, however, and seldom suffered more than an occasional dented fender.

Those were the days of leisurely motoring, in comparison with present-day high-speed travel, so that most of our mileage in the Dodge was chalked up on unpaved roads. As far as Mother was concerned, the remoter our route the better she liked it, and it was not long before we were familiar with most of the rural areas of New Haven County. Whenever we came to a fork, one branch of which was known and the other unknown, she always voted for the unknown, and there were frequent halts to admire the view or to gather wild flowers.

The hundred-mile trip to the cottage overlooking Narragansett Bay, in Rhode Island, where we summered from 1916 on, was accomplished more purposefully in a running time of approximately four hours. The house had been built by my grandparents in 1880, and they called it "Whimsy Cot," because grandfather pretended it was only a whim of Grandmother's that there could be any difference in the air between its shore-front location and the site of their year-round home in Peace Dale three miles inland. House guests were always intrigued by the name and often misspelled it by adding a superfluous E before the Y. But the ultimate indignity was to have the New Haven newspaper arrive one year with a stencil reading "Whinney Grot." Mother saw to it that the mistake was promptly corrected, because she didn't want even the postal clerks to labor under the misapprehension that we belonged to the "drinky-polo" set. Originally intended for week-end use, Whimsy Cot "just growed" like Topsy. With each addition, more gingerbread-encrusted gables were added until there were fourteen. From the veranda we looked due east toward Spain. At one side and two steps down was "the But and the Ben" (Scotch for lean-to) which contained the library where Father could work in comparative isolation and where Mr. Lee gave his relaxation lessons. Above this were two guest rooms which absorbed unexpected visitors so hospitably that they were seldom empty.

Father commuted from New Haven for weekends, and it was a rare dispensation when he was induced to linger at Whimsy Cot for as long as a week at a stretch. But during the second summer of the Dodge he joined us for an extended motor trip across New England to Plattsburg on Lake Champlain, where a number of our friends were attending Officers' Training Camp. The details of the last day of that trip are still vivid in my memory. We had spent the night at the gargantuan United States Hotel in Saratoga Springs, and hoped to cover the unprecedented total of one hundred and fifty-four miles to New Haven *all in one day.* Intending to make an early start we found on arising that the shoes we had placed outside our doors to be shined were lost in the lower depths of the hotel, so we marched single file into the elegant nineteenth-century dining room wearing our bedroom slippers. The impeccable Negro waiters never batted an eyelash, although in Father's case, the red plush cross-straps of his wicker sandals made a striking contrast against the white of his summer socks.

When we went to the garage to collect the Dodge, we found that it had suffered a flat tire during the night. Not daring to start off on such a long trip without a spare, we waited to have a new tire brought from the other side of town and did not succeed in leaving the hotel until nearly eleven o'clock. Not to waste any time stopping for meals, Father laid in a plentiful supply of peanuts and bananas, to be consumed in shifts as we took turns driving. He had recently read about a man near Niagara Falls who subsisted for a whole year on an exclusive diet of bananas and peanuts, at a total outlay of thirty-five dollars. It was a well-balanced ration and it certainly sustained us in the emergency, but even Father doubted that he could have stuck to such a "natural" diet for a whole year.

Early in the afternoon we had a blowout and, after switching tires, had to proceed from then on without benefit of spare. Two hours later, as we progressed cautiously along a vicious stretch of old-fashioned corduroy road, the car gave a sudden lurch and a series of agonizing thumps totally unlike anything we had ever experienced. As we limped to a halt, we were amazed to see our left rear tire

173

and rim roll merrily along the road ahead of us and finally topple over into the ditch. Investigation showed that one of the lugs which fasten the rim to the wheel had fallen off, and when the wheel and rim parted company the valve of the inner tube had been sheared off. Thus a new tube had to be installed and inflated by hand. Then, using the three good lugs from the spare and the three others which had the maximum amount of bevel remaining, we proceeded at a snail's pace with frequent halts to inspect the doubtful lugs. It was past midnight before we rolled into the Four-sixty driveway. Our trek of one hundred and fifty-four miles had taken thirteen hours.

Within a few weeks Father entrained for the West Coast to deliver the Hitchcock lectures at the University of California, on "Stabilizing the Dollar." Here are three letters written to Mother during his absence:

ON TRAIN FROM NEW YORK TO CHICAGO
September 24, 1917

To think it is a quarter of a century this morning since you have been mine!

I was wondering why I seemed to feel such a deep satisfaction in having you see me off! But I stupidly hadn't waked up to the date. Were you thinking of it, I wonder? and said nothing?

Well, sweetheart, they have been wonderful years together with all their lights and shades, deep valleys and high mountain tops, wonderful wonderful years.

I wonder if you remember in those first days saying that you had read or heard that love was the life of a woman but only an episode in that of a man and asking me, half jokingly, if that would be so with me. I remember being a little shocked that you could even wonder if that might be so, and telling you that it wouldn't be so with me and then wondering if I could

174

really tell from my own heart, if in millions of other lives it were as your quoted adage claimed.

Well, here we are at the silver anniversary of our engagement and I can say that my heart told me truly as it did in that instantaneous glance through the crack of the door!

Whatever happens in the time to come, we cannot be robbed of these precious years together or of their sweet memory. Even the shadows of sorrow and worry and anger seem hallowed with the rest, because they were ours. And perhaps they too were necessary parts of our total joy as I believe they and all else that happens, even this war, are necessarily parts of some great whole beyond our full understanding.

BERKELEY, CALIFORNIA, September 29, 1917

I'm sorry you find a "big hole" in the house, but I'd be sorrier if you didn't! I seem to feel a new sweet tenderness of love which I wish I could express or picture to you in some way. These serene skies, the hushed air, the stately grandeur of California and a subtle subconscious special association of California with you because, in particular, you were here the winter we were engaged, fills my soul to the brim. What a complex thing love is! It seems so simple and yet it has as many sides as a diamond or colors as a rainbow or mansions as our Father's house.

William James says there are realms of consciousness we seldom or never explore. Though you are a very simple girl of whom I could only say, if I were trying to describe you to a stranger, little else than I could say of many other women, it doesn't seem to me that I have any illusions about you. Yet you are for me the wonder of wonders. Your soul and mine possess each other's keys and I have a mystic feeling, which seems especially intense since I have been here, that you have led and are leading me into a wonderland of soul experience, that, somehow, through your soul as my sanctuary, veils are lifted and I get glimpses of heavenly regions the existence of which I never suspected.

I don't think I ever wrote quite this sort of love letter before, and it seems impossible to really express what I mean. It's all too intangible and yet as real as the depths of a California Canyon. When we met at Dotha Bushnell's I felt I had a glimpse of a new world into which I had never looked through any other girl's eyes. There have been many other new vistas opening along the road.

When either of us is cross, the wonderful spiritual scenery is blotted out and that's one reason we ought not to let ourselves be cross. Then my mind becomes prosaic and dull. Without such interference I feel poetry and music through you, just by hearing your magic voice or even just thinking of you, as I am now.

STANFORD UNIVERSITY, Oct. 19, 1917

Friday night Professor Lauschner called for me and brought me from Berkeley to San Francisco to the University Club for the "Smoker" (!) in honor of Dr. Simon Flexner and myself. We were supposed to have had dinner; but nevertheless we were seated at tables and provided with (1) Steins of Beer (2) salad and meat (3) "hot dogs" and (4) cigars and pipes. I ate salad and bread! Simon Flexner rolled his cigarettes and had whiskey!!

I had been told several days before I would be expected to "say a few words" but on the ferryboat Lauschner let me understand I was expected to make a long speech! I asked him on what subject and he said perhaps Public Health. I was called on first and

176

His father Rev. George W. Fisher

His mother Ella Wescott Fisher

Irving Fisher at thirteen

Margaret Hazard, 1891

Before his engagement to her, 1892

Bridal party, Oakwoods, 1893

Honeymoon couple, London, 1893

His price level mechanism, 1892

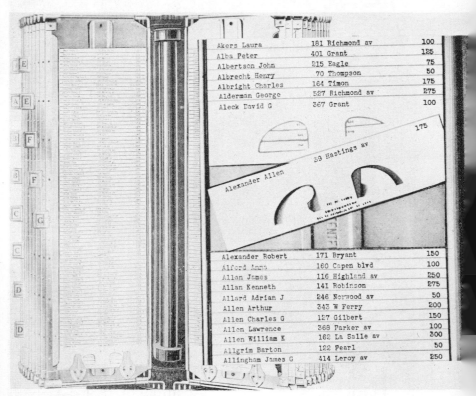

Akers Laura	181 Richmond av	100
Alba Peter	401 Grant	125
Albertson John	215 Eagle	75
Albrecht Henry	70 Thompson	50
Albright Charles	164 Timon	175
Alderman George	527 Richmond av	275
Aleck David G	367 Grant	100
Alexander Allen	39 Hastings av	175
Alexander Robert	171 Bryant	150
Alford Anna	160 Capen blvd	100
Allan James	116 Highland av	250
Allan Kenneth	141 Robinson	275
Allard Adrian J	246 Norwood av	50
Allen Arthur	343 W Ferry	200
Allen Charles G	127 Gilbert	150
Allen Lawrence	368 Parker av	100
Allen William K	162 La Salle av	300
Allgrim Barton	122 Pearl	50
Allingham James G	414 Leroy av	250

His visible index, patented 1913

With family on Four-sixty lawn, 1902

Four-sixty after 1904 fire

Four-sixty living room, 1905

His California sundial
before cementing, 1914

Four-sixty with 1929 additions

Margaret Hazard Fisher, 1918

Irving Fisher
at fifty-three,
1920

On television with
his world map, 1945

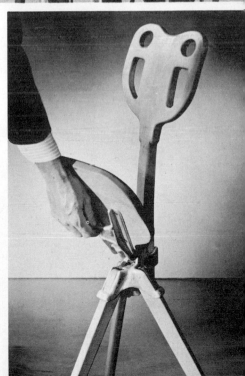

His folding stool,
invented 1945

Edgewood Camp, Sugar Hill, N. H.

Whimsy Cot, Narragansett, R. I.

With Edward A. Filene, Jane Adams &
Hamilton Holt, Rollins College, 1932

Embarking for Europe, 1927

Fortieth wedding anniversary, 1933

spoke on Public Health and the War, pointing out the Eugenic tragedy (killing off the cream of our manhood) and the tragedies of tuberculosis, alcoholism, and syphilis. I was not well prepared and so didn't do half as well as I might have, though it was not bad.

Flexner followed me and made a much better speech as well as much longer. He took his cue from me, backing up all I said and added to it a more optimistic touch. As I thought of these University people, on whom the World depends for its future public health and other reforms, smoking, drinking and stuffing, I was not so optimistic! I had a curious feeling too that these "big" men were not really very big and that, without being conceited, I have a taller moral stature than they.

I had planned to spend the night at the University Club, but Mr. Perrin, Yale '78, Governor of the Federal Reserve Bank of San Francisco button-holed me in regard to standardizing the dollar and we talked to nearly one o'clock. He said he wished I would present it to business men in San Francisco and, as I was delighted, he has arranged a meeting for Tuesday noon.

Yesterday morning I breakfasted with S. S. McClure, who had just returned from Japan. The audience that night at Stanford, where I tried to compress all of my six University of California lectures into one, was largely Professors, not large enough but very intelligent. It went very well indeed and the applause showed it. Perrin seemed much pleased.

Three days later he found himself standing in the pulpit of Will Eliot's Unitarian Church in Portland, Oregon, speaking on Health and Religion. Here are some paragraphs condensed from his impassioned plea for cooperation between science and religion:

The reference your Pastor has made to our lifelong friendship impels me to say that if in any degree I have been a useful citizen, I owe it, in large measure, to Mr. Eliot. His influence on my life has been, I think spiritually at least, second to none except one, and that is the woman who is my life companion.

I make no apology for speaking from a pulpit on Health and Religion, although you may be accustomed to think of science and religion as more or less antithetical to each other. The church history is full of cases where the tradition of the church has collided with a new truth of science. When Darwin brought forward his ideas of evolution they were so strange to the theologians of the day that it took nearly a generation to assimilate them.

Health seems to me, I fear, something quite different from what it seems to you. When I broke down with tuberculosis I was forced to study health as few men outside of the medical profession had studied it and I have become something of a propagandist. . . . The Prayer Book says, "We have done those things that we ought not to have done; we have left undone those things that we ought to have done, and there is no health in us." Most of us, when we hear that mumbled, wonder how it happened that somebody slipped in the word health there. What has doing things we ought not to have done and leaving undone things we ought to have done, to do with our health?

Of course, the writer of those words had a bigger idea of the word health than we have today. We have lost that ideal. The Christian Church in the Middle Ages conceived a notion of asceticism and this medieval attitude of the Christian Church influences us today. The medieval artists pictured their saints as pale and anemic and have handed down to us a picture of the Christ which I have no doubt is a caricature. It is not the face of the Master who drove the money changers out of the Temple.

The greatest problem of all is the problem of bettering the permanent health, that is the innate vitality and sanity of the human race, the problem of eugenics. The marks of this war will be felt a thousand years hence. That is the real tragedy of the war. We are medically selecting the best young men to send them off to war. When this war broke out, having myself studied eugenics, it nearly broke my heart. I live within sound of the Winchester Arms Works, and when through the night I could hear the grinding and groaning of the machinery turning out guns, and realized what it meant for the human race, I could not sleep.

It does not disturb me at all to think of the great tax it is, to think of the economic destruction, to think of cutting off so much wealth, shooting it into the air; that does not bother me. That hole will fill up in a generation. It does not worry me much to think of the destruction of human life. We all have to die sooner or later. It is not the quantity of life; it is the quality of life that disturbs me. If we could only reverse it, if we could only induce our enemies to join with us in setting up on each side, not the best young men but the worst; . . . to get rid of all the degenerates,—I would look upon the war as the best thing that ever happened eugenically.

Most of the men that I know who are studying physiology and biology, and making the big contributions there, are not preachers. They ought not to be asked to go out and tell people how important eugenics is. They ought to be working away in a laboratory, doing their job, making discoveries. But there ought to be some kind of a mechanism connecting their laboratories with those who have the welfare of the human race at heart and whose job it is to take any method that is handed up to them and to make of it an engine to reform and regenerate mankind.

Six months later the war directly affected our household in a way which was especially hard for Father to accept. My sister Margaret, as the eldest child, had absorbed his health philosophy more completely than either of his other offspring. For a number of years she had been an active leader in the Camp Fire Girl movement, and when the United States finally entered the war she volunteered her services in more and more activities. At an open-air bond rally on the New Haven Green, where she was about to make her maiden speech, she was suffering from proverbial butterflies in her midriff, when the master of ceremonies inadvertently restored her sense of proportion by his extravagant introduction: "The celebrated Margaret Fisher, known from coast to coast." She lost all sense of constraint, and spoke so effectively that she was asked to repeat her performance on several other occasions.

In the spring of 1918 she became engaged to George Stewart, who was stationed at Camp Devens prior to being shipped overseas. He had graduated from the Yale Law School the preceding year and subsequently studied for the ministry. By coincidence Will Eliot knew something of George's background, so there was an exchange of telegrams between New Haven and Portland before Father officially approved the match. His own impression of his prospective son-in-law had been entirely favorable, but it was reassuring to have Will Eliot's corroboration. In fact, George fulfilled his expectations so completely that he found himself in the unusual position of urging an immediate marriage, partly because of George's presumed imminent departure for France. Margaret, on the other hand, seemed to require a period of adjustment to the idea of a specific marriage as distinct from marriage in the abstract before she was ready to take the plunge. She enjoyed to the full the flutter of excitement which the announcement of her engagement caused among her contemporaries, but the strain of her inner crisis added to the burden of her home front activities resulted in a complete nervous breakdown.

Although discussion of might-have-beens is seldom fruitful, Carol and I feel that if present-day psychiatric techniques had been available at the time, Margaret's illness need not necessarily have ended in total disaster. She was given the best available treatment in a series of hospitals, and scarcely a week before her eighteen months' illness reached its fatal climax, Father wrote buoyantly that she seemed "much improved." She died at Trenton, New Jersey, on November 7, 1919. Two days later Four-sixty was crowded to overflowing for the only funeral service to be held there during the forty-five years that it was headquarters for the Fisher family. In the spring of the following year the New Haven Camp Fire Girls dedicated an outdoor fireplace to her memory in West Rock Park.

Father could not help reproaching himself for failing to foresee and forestall her breakdown. In retrospect he tried desperately to isolate and explain the underlying physical cause of her death. It was virtually impossible for him to accept that her nervous collapse was the first link in the chain. From the medical standpoint, pleurisy had been the final straw, but he felt sure that there must have been some obscure physical origin of her illness. I'll never forget the fierce determination with which he asserted, shortly after her death, "There aren't going to *be* any more deaths in this family!" And for more than twenty years there weren't.

At the time of Margaret's death, he had been correcting the final proof of *Stabilizing the Dollar*, which will be considered in the next chapter. When the first copy arrived from the publisher, he inscribed it:

> To M. H. F.
> inspirer of all my dreams,
> helper in all my work,
> sharer in all my joys and sorrows.

12. *Commodity Dollar*

In the wake of *The Purchasing Power of Money* he contributed articles on the "burning issue" of stabilization to the British *Economic Journal,* the *American Economic Review* and the *Encyclopaedia Britannica.* In 1915 he published a book: *Why Is the Dollar Shrinking?* Two years later he delivered six lectures on this topic at the University of California in Berkeley. These formed the basis for his longer book, *Stabilizing the Dollar,* which appeared in 1920.

In the preface he acknowledged that "when I first propounded the plan for stabilizing the dollar I supposed that I was the first to do so. It soon appeared, however, that the same thought had occurred independently to" at least nine others. He dedicated the book to Simon Newcomb "and all other anticipators." Here is an outline of the plan, taken from the summary given in his fourth chapter:

Our dollar is now simply a fixed weight of gold— a unit of weight, masquerading as a unit of value. It is almost as absurd to define a unit of value, or general purchasing power, in terms of weight, as to define a unit of length in terms of weight. What we really want to know is whether the dollar *buys* as much as ever. We want a dollar which will always buy the same aggregate quantity of bread, butter, beef, bacon, beans, sugar, clothing, fuel and other essential things for which we spend it.

There used to be a song about a shopkeeper who, being asked the price of a box of socks, replied, "One dollar a box." "I'll take the box," said the customer, handing over his dollar; whereupon the shopkeeper took out the socks and handed over the box. "I sold you the box, not the socks," said he!

Our dollar is somewhat like that box. It keeps its form, but loses its content. The removal, in this case, is not intentional or committed by one of the parties to the contract, but so much the worse!—for the injured party has no recourse. It is as though the buyer of the box of socks were forced to agree in advance to let a bystander remove or insert socks *ad libitum.*

What is needed is to stabilize, or standardize, the dollar just as we have already standardized the yard-stick, the pound weight, the bushel basket, the pint cup, the horsepower, the volt, and indeed all the units of commerce *except* the dollar. Once the yard was defined as the girth of the chieftan of the tribe. Imagine the modern American business man tolerating a yard defined as the girth of the President of the United States! Suppose contracts in yards of cloth

183

to be now fulfilled which had been made in Mr. Taft's administration! . . .

A true standard of value such as we would like our monetary standard to be should not be dependent on one commodity merely, whether that commodity be gold or silver or wheat or any other single sort of goods. Two commodities would be better than one, just as two tipsy men walk more steadily arm in arm than separately. Whenever they tend to lurch in opposite directions they neutralize each other. This is the argument which used to be urged for bimetallism. And the argument applies whenever gold and silver move in opposite directions, as from 1873 to 1896. But an alloy of only two commodities, while steadier than one alone, would not really be very steady.

In order to secure a dollar constant in its purchasing power over goods in general, it should represent a composite of those very goods. We should therefore make our gold dollar correspond in value to an imaginary composite goods-dollar. If we could make our dollar equivalent to such a market-basket dollar, i. e. a composite dollar consisting of a big basket or package containing those goods, that "goods-dollar" would have to be worth a dollar at all times; and the cost of living *could not* rise or fall. That assortment would always cost a dollar simply because a dollar *was* the equivalent of that assortment. In short, it would be just as simple then to keep the price of the composite basketful of commodities invariable, as it is now to keep the price of gold invariable. . . .

By all means, let us keep gold for the attributes it has, but let us correct its instability, so that one dollar of it will at all times buy approximately that composite basketful of goods. Under the plan proposed only the gold dollar, duly corrected, is to be actually handled. The goods-dollar is merely a fiction in terms of which we may statistically test and correct the gold dollar. Money has two great functions. It is a medium of exchange and it is a standard of value. Gold was chosen because it was a good medium, not because it was a good standard. . . .

Yet because our ancestors found a good medium of exchange we now find ourselves saddled with a bad standard of value. What we need to do is to retain gold as a good medium and yet to make it into a good standard—to *make it conform in purchasing power to the composite or goods-dollar.*

When I am asked whether this proposal is not really one to "abandon the gold standard" I like to answer: "No! It is to put the standard into the gold standard!" But abandon the *present* gold standard it certainly does, by converting or rectifying it into conformity with the composite standard.

But how can we rectify the gold standard? In brief: *by varying, suitably, the weight of the gold dollar.* The gold dollar is now fixed in weight and therefore variable in purchasing power. What we need is a gold dollar fixed in purchasing power and *therefore variable in weight.* By adding new grains of gold to the dollar just fast enough to compensate for a loss in the purchasing power of each grain (and reversely) we can secure a stationary instead of a fluctuating dollar, in terms of purchasing power.

Is it practicable to vary the gold dollar's weight periodically?—We have changed the weight of our gold dollar in 1834 and again in 1837. If we can change the weight of a monetary unit once or twice a century, we can change it once or twice a month, without changing, in the least, the nature of the mechanism by which the gold standard now operates.

What criterion is to guide the Government in making these changes in the dollar's weight? Am I proposing that some Government official should be authorized to mark the dollar up or down according to his own caprice? Most certainly not. A definite and simple criterion for the required adjustments is at hand—the now familiar "index number" of prices. ... For every one per cent of deviation of the index number above or below par at any adjustment date, we would increase or decrease the dollar's weight by one per cent.—In other words, to keep the price level of other things from rising or falling we make the price of gold fall or rise.

Will the above rule for varying the dollar's weight really stabilize the dollar? We do not know, any more than we know, when the steering wheel of an automobile is turned, that it will prove to have been turned *just* enough and not too much. If the correction is not enough or if it is too much, the index number, when next computed, will tell the story. There is always a slight deviation, but this is always in process of being corrected. The stabilization machinery, while it cannot absolutely prevent slight aberrations from par, will persistently tend to reduce toward zero every deviation which comes along. It might be compared to the automatic regulation of the "governor" on a steam engine. Every aberration brings its own correction.

And so we conform our gold dollar, approximately, to the imaginary "goods-dollar." We would then be substantially rid of a fluctuating price level with its long train of bad consequences. The monetary yardstick would be standardized.

An indication of the time and effort which he devoted to his plan for a compensated dollar is given in the following paragraphs, which have been condensed from an autobiographical appendix to *Stable Money, a History of the*

Movement, written with the assistance of Hans R. L. Cohrssen and published in 1934:

My own interest in the problem of stabilizing the purchasing power of money began almost as soon as my economic studies began—about 1892. But my attitude at that time was very different from what it subsequently became. . . .

Having the substantial faith which the young and inexperienced often do have in things as they find them, I felt scandalized, when attending the meeting of the American Economic Association at Indianapolis in 1895, at what seemed to me to be the too light-hearted way in which Professor E. A. Ross and others were willing to "tamper with the currency."

I took part in the "Sound Money" campaign against Bryan in 1896. Had that campaign occurred at the present time, I would not have been so strenuous an opponent of Mr. Bryan; for I now know that the evil of which he complained was more real than I then thought. His proposed remedy—bimetallism at 16 to 1—was, I still think, far from good. . . .

Beginning about 1905, the subject of a better standard of value was considered in my class room for many years. The first solution offered by me was in 1911 (in *The Purchasing Power of Money*). I then avoided any attempt to state my proposal in popular language because it is easy to laugh out of court anything as new about money as stabilization seemed to be at that time. The thought was to try out the idea first in academic circles and, after a few years, to consider the possibility of popularizing it.

This program would have been followed out literally had it not been for an invitation, from Professor Taussig of Harvard, to present a paper on the proposal before the International Congress of Chambers of Commerce, meeting in Boston in 1912. This seemed too good an opportunity to lose.

Within five minutes after reading my paper, entitled *An International Conference Regarding the Cost of Living,* a business leader of Chicago asked for the floor and made a fervent speech against the plan. He had taken alarm at the idea of even hinting that anything could be wrong with our dollar, or of allowing "labor" to think that the "high cost of living" could be cited as a proper cause for complaint or as a reason for adjusting money wages. The gentleman's alarm amused Professor Taussig, who replied that there was no thought at that meeting of endorsing the proposal but merely a desire to give it a hearing.

Meantime, Hamilton Holt, then editor of the "Independent," had offered to print the substance of my address in his magazine and to supply a reprint for wide distribution. "The fat was now in the fire."

Up to that time plans for stabilization had been thought of as "academic playthings" rather than practical proposals to be taken seriously. It was not long before the Commercial and Financial Chronicle (in 1912) had a series of editorials ridiculing the idea and asseverating that our gold dollar is "the Rock of Gibraltar"—the one thing that never varies!

One result of this and other controversies was to stimulate me, from that time forth, to write and speak in defense of stabilization and in answer to criticism. My secretary counts up, since then, 99 addresses, besides 37 letters to the press, and 161 special articles, as well as 9 testimonies at hearings held by government bodies and 12 privately printed circulars, together with 13 books bearing on the subject.

The phrases "compensated dollar" and "stabilizing the dollar," suggested by me, have come into general use. I had also tried several other phrases, such as "standardizing the dollar" and "an unshrinkable dollar." All these have been largely replaced by the phrase "commodity dollar," as more nearly self-explanatory. I had supposed that I was the first to think of this plan, but I found anticipators in almost every particular. All nine known anticipators are mentioned in the preface to *Stabilizing the Dollar*.

While preparing *The Purchasing Power of Money*, I had conceived the idea of an international commission to study the money problem, with special reference to the "High Cost of Living," and had secured the adherence of a hundred or more influential people. President Taft sent a special message to Congress on February 2, 1912, favoring an appropriation for such a Conference. The wording of this message was prepared by me in cooperation with his Assistant Secretary of State, Huntington Wilson. The bill passed the Senate under suspension of the rules. In the house it was never reached on the calendar.

Soon after Woodrow Wilson's nomination for the Presidency, in 1912, I visited him in Trenton. He said: "I think we might curb rising prices by increasing the weight of the gold dollar." He was surprised to find that I had advocated something similar and took with him on his vacation trip to Bermuda, before inauguration, a typed copy of what eventually became *Stabilizing the Dollar*. After his inauguration, consideration of the money problem was elbowed aside in the rush of more pressing questions. . . .

On March 8, 1920, Mr. Frank A. Vanderlip gave me a dinner to which he invited the leading presidents of banks of New York City. I addressed them on the subject of my book *Stabilizing the Dollar*, copies of which he had sent them in advance. The criticisms were mostly adverse, although President Hadley of Yale, who had from the first approved my proposal, spoke in its favor. Afterward he commented caustically to the effect that the bankers present "seemed merely to be thinking in terms of three to six months ahead."

On publishing *Stabilizing the Dollar* in January, 1920, I had asked the publishers to insert a post card in each copy, with a request that the reader mail it to me in case he was interested in the formation of an organization devoted to stabilization. On December 31, 1920, at the new Willard Hotel in Washington, a dinner was held for discussing the advisability of forming a "Stable Money League." There were twenty-five present, and I was able to announce that I had names of about 1,000 other persons interested in the project. The meeting ended with a midnight visit by many of us to the Washington Monument where we ushered in the New Year by dedicating ourselves to the new movement. The organization meeting was called for May 28, 1921, at Washington.

Up to that time I had been almost the only active proponent. Now the lead was passed on to others. Although urged to accept the presidency of the League and to try to commit it to the "compensated dollar plan," I declined both suggestions. I had never believed that the compensated dollar plan was the only possible plan, nor even ideally the best. I had offered it as requiring the least radical change from the existing gold standard, and therefore perhaps politically the most feasible.

If the gold standard is to be retained, the compensated dollar plan is almost necessary. I am still in favor of it for America, although, for simplicity, the method recently adopted by Sweden (a managed currency independent of gold) seems better. But when *Stabilizing the Dollar* was written, any proposal to "go off gold" completely, as Sweden has done, would have been hooted down; and even more preposterous at that time would it have seemed to advocate a purely discretionary "managed money."

One of the greatest obstacles then standing in the way of stabilization was a prevalent idea that index numbers were unreliable. To do my bit toward solving this problem, I wrote *The Making of Index Numbers*, a work requiring several years of costly calculations, partly financed by the Pollak Foundation for Economic Research. It was published in 1922.

In January, 1923, I began the publication in the newspapers of a weekly Index Number of Wholesale Prices. This was the first *weekly* index ever published, being made possible by certain short-cuts in calculation. This index series now (1934) appears in several countries and in various official publications of the United States and other Governments.

The chief purpose of this newspaper publication was to invert the ordinary index number representing the price level, thereby obtaining an index number representing the purchasing power of the dollar, the idea being to accustom the public to the thought that the dollar is not a constant but a variable.

It had taken a long time for me to realize the need for this sort of public education and to perceive that there was what I came to describe as "The Money Illusion." In 1922 Professor Frederick W. Roman and I visited Germany to find out if the ordinary German realized that the mark had lost 98% of the purchasing power it possessed before the War. We found that at least 19 out of 20 had no idea that anything had happened to their mark. They all knew that prices had risen, just as we all "know" that the sun "rises." To them the dollar had risen, and commodities had risen; but the mark had not fallen! . . .

Forecasting is one of three ways of escaping or mitigating the baleful consequences of the unstable dollar, the other two being: (1) to stabilize the dollar, and (2) to frame contracts in terms of index numbers—that is, to use the tabular standard.

Regarding the last, I was apparently the first in this country to introduce the index wage for the purpose of offsetting the rising cost of living in the World War. This method was used in my personal office, in the office of the American Association for Labor Legislation, of which I was then President, and in a commercial business of mine—the Index Visible.

During the war millions of laborers worked under such wage agreements, but they were almost invariably dropped when prices fell, because the wage earner objected to a cut in money wages. As long as the cost of living was getting higher, the Index Visible employees welcomed the swelling contents of their "High Cost of Living" pay envelopes. They thought their wages were increasing, though it was carefully explained to them that their real wages were merely standing still. But as soon as the cost of living fell they resented the "reduction" in wages.

Such experiences afford proof of the practical omnipresence of the "money illusion" and of the impracticability of index wages as a general solution of the great problem of unstable money. The only general solution must come, not from mending or patching the dollar from outside, but from truing it up inside.

It seems to me as inevitable as anything human can be that some day the money illusion will be conquered; that stabilizing or standardizing money will be as much a matter of course as standardizing the yard or the ounce; that the world will wonder why so simple a project as stable money should ever have met any opposition.

He persuaded Frederick A. Delano to accept the presidency of the Stable Money Association and the roster of honorary vice-presidents included such notables as Sir Josiah Stamp (governor of the Bank of England) Elihu Root and Nicholas Murray Butler. Dr. Royal Meeker's enthusiasm for the plan is suggested by the quotation from his 1947 appreciation given in the foreword. Some of his other colleagues, however, agreed with Professor Schumpeter that "the scholar was misled by the crusader." In a memorial article in the *American Economic Review* for September, 1947, Professor Ray B. Westerfield of Yale wrote:

> Fisher was never content to stop with scientific research; he was imbued with an irresistible urge to reform, along lines indicated by his studies. For example, having seen and felt the evils of unstable money and having discovered the causes and cures, he was determined to do all he could to make it stable.
>
> Unfortunately his eagerness to promote his cause sometimes had a bad influence on his scientific attitude. It distorted his judgement; for example, he was carried away by his "new economic era" ideas in the late 1920's and lost his fortune. . . . He relied upon concomitancy too much in his belief that the stability of the price level from 1925 to 1929 was due to Federal Reserve action and refused to give due recognition to other factors at work.

In the corresponding issue of the British *Economic Journal*, Professor G. Findlay Shirras reached similar conclusions:

> The drawback to a completely rational mind is that it is very apt to assume that what is flawless in

logic is therefore practicable. "Very pretty," as Lord Milner used to say, "but it won't work."

Irving Fisher, however, did a great service in destroying the illusion that the gold standard brought a steady level of prices and in opposing so resolutely every form of inflation, and when values had fallen of putting forward a system of "reflation" to restore previously existing standards.

He himself has already stated that his efforts to popularize monetary stabilization led him to write *The Making of Index Numbers,* a work of pure and unadulterated scholarship, which was undertaken to dispel "the prevalent idea that index numbers were unreliable." Inasmuch as this book required "several years of costly calculations" before it was ready for publication in 1922, the preliminary spade work was in progress long before the release of *Stabilizing the Dollar.* He had given a preview of his ideas on index numbers in a paper which he read in December, 1920, at the Atlantic City meeting of the American Statistical Association, and before the American Academy of Arts and Sciences at Boston in April, 1921.

Dealing as it did with a highly specialized subject, *The Making of Index Numbers* was one of his longest and most technical books—covering more than five hundred pages. It contained sixty-eight charts and nearly as many tables, not to mention the innumerable mathematical formulae in the body of the text. The preface stated: "This book is primarily an inductive rather than a deductive study. In this respect it differs from the Appendix to Chapter X of *The Purchasing Power of Money,* in which I sought deductively to compare the merits of 44 different formulae. The present book had its origin in the desire to put these deductive conclusions to an inductive test by means of calculations from actual historical data. But before I had gone far in such testing of my original conclusions, I found to my surprise, that the results of actual calculations constantly suggested further deduction until, in the end, I had completely revised both my conclusions and my theoretical foundations. . . ."

Methodically he tested several thousand index number formulae, comparing each by plotting their curves, covering the same series of statistics for the period from 1913 to 1918, to see how closely they conformed. He stated that "an index number of prices is intended to measure such magnitudes as the price level." Moreover, in the period under scrutiny "the dispersion of the price relatives" of the various items which entered into the calculation of the index numbers was especially great. For example, "the price of wool in 1918 (relative to 1913) was 282 per cent and that of rubber, 68 per cent. Their average or index number (reckoned arithmetically) was 175 per cent."

Index number formulae were divided into six main types, and each could be "weighted" in six different ways. To illustrate: wool might be counted twice, compared with rubber, if the value of the wool sold during the base year was twice that of rubber. Similarly, other systems of weighting might be used to suit other circumstances. Some of the formulae tested showed definite "freakishness" and were unceremoniously discarded. Others—including several which had been in general use up to that time—showed either an upward or a downward "bias," and to varying degrees.

He admitted that "we can never say with *certainty* how far wrong any one index number may be. Nevertheless we can, on ground of probability, narrow down the fringe of doubt until it is practically negligible." He asserted that "besides the cases of bias lurking in *types* of index numbers, there is another sort of bias pertaining to certain systems of *weighting.*" Also, that "a formula of unbiased *type,* needs also to have unbiased *weighting.* A biased type, however, can be remedied by the use of an oppositely biased weighting, or *vice versa.* Some formulae have both type bias and weight bias."

When all freakish formulae were discarded, those remaining were superimposed on each other in one graph. The resultant picture resembled a five-tined fork. Those formulae which fell along the middle tine showed no bias, while the two nearest tines represented formulae "having a single dose of bias" and the two outer tines portrayed the formulae "having a double dose of bias." Out of the original total of formulae tested, forty-seven remained on the middle tine. Of these forty-seven, thirteen agreed "with one another still better." This total was then further reduced to eight, which were considered "the only ones which ever *need* to be used, although not by any means the only ones which *may* be used." One formula in particular was labeled "ideal" since it seemed to be "slightly superior in accuracy to any of the others," and was "demonstrably correct within less than one eighth of one percent." But he refrained from claiming that this ideal formula should be regarded as "the one and only." On the contrary, he asserted that "all index numbers which are not freakish or biased practically agree with each other."

His conclusions departed "from previous thought and practice" since "hitherto writers have been debating the 'best type' (whether arithmetic, geometric, or median) by itself, the 'best weighting' by itself. . . . But from our study it should be clear that it makes little difference what type we start with, or what the weighting is (so long as it is systematic), or what the distribution of price relatives may be so long as we 'rectify' the formulae and so eliminate all

196

these sources of distortion or onesidedness. . . . The chief
practical restriction on the use of the many fairly good
formulae is imposed by the time required to calculate
them." His investigations "largely confirmed and supported" the work of his predecessors "yet many of the
conclusions are new" and "some of the methods of calculating index numbers now most in vogue should be discontinued."

Much to his surprise a second edition of this technical
work was needed within five months of its first publication.
In the interval it had caused "much comment, favorable
and unfavorable," but the author declared in the third edition, which appeared five years later, that if he were to
rewrite the book he would only elaborate two technical
points, which in the light of criticism had not been sufficiently stressed. The appendix to the third edition listed
thirty-four critical articles which discussed the subject in
various technical journals, as well as five rebuttal articles
by the author.

Toward the end of 1921, while this book was still in
preparation, he went to Europe to lecture on "Business
Depression and Instability of Money" at the London School
of Economics, and incidentally to observe Germany's run-
away inflation at first hand. In his London lectures as
printed in the *Banker's Magazine,* he asserted that "the
only solution, at once just and practicable, is that the cur-
rencies of Continental Europe shall be stabilized at greatly
reduced valuations as compared with pre-war values." He
would even have preferred to have the British face the facts
and start with a clean slate instead of perpetuating the
elaborate fiction that the Bank of England redeemed its
paper money in gold, when everyone knew that for all
intents and purposes specie payment had been discontinued.

To find out for himself to what lengths the authorities

went in this matter, he visited the Bank of England and tried to redeem a five-pound note. He was referred from one person to another until he reached an official in a private office who greeted him with "most excruciating politeness and patience" and asked why he wanted the note redeemed.

Father answered the question by asking another: "Does it make any difference?"

"Oh, yes," said the official. "We are clothed with full powers to ask particulars as to the purpose."

"Well, I want it for a Christmas present for my wife."

"But, my dear sir, your wife can get along just as well with paper. It is really more convenient. It is just as good as gold if you have enough of it. I hope you will not insist. Of course, if you were to insist—"

"I do insist."

"Oh, well, I am sorry, but the purpose for which you wish this gold is not sufficiently important."

"Then you refuse?"

"No, but I could not let you have it for the purpose you mention."

"For what purpose would you let me have it?"

"Oh, my dear sir, I could not attempt to answer that question."

"Then may I go out and say that the Bank of England refuses to redeem its notes?"

"No, indeed; of course we redeem. Here is the list of those who have received gold for their notes, but—"

"Redemption with if's and but's is no genuine redemption. Why don't you post a notice that you have suspended specie payments?"

"But we do redeem—"

"Then redeem this note."

"I'm sorry indeed, sir, but not for the purpose you mention."

So Father departed without the gold. But at his next lecture he was amused to spot the Bank of England official seated in the audience, obviously worried that Father would let the cat out of the bag. A girl economic student told him that when she had mentioned a similar experience in her thesis, her professor would not allow her to include the incident because she had had no witness; and when she returned to the bank accompanied by a witness she was ceremoniously given the gold.

Soon after his return from Europe, Father wrote a letter to Mother who was visiting my sister Carol in Ohio, which gives a capsule impression of one hectic but not entirely exceptional Four-sixty day. The book mentioned was *The Making of Index Numbers:*

HOTEL TAFT, NEW HAVEN, March 30, 1922

I'm sorry I missed the mail last night, for this may just miss you in Cleveland. I've been in a whirl with my book and so many other things. *But the book is now really off!* I took it down to the station and sent it myself, insured for $1,000! It seems too good to be true.

Today has been a weird day. It has snowed and slushed for one thing. My book kept me from supper for another—finishing it up. Miss Dietel and Miss Gutekunst stayed to the bitter end but wouldn't come upstairs for supper. I felt between the upper and the nether millstone, trying to get the book off before I took Mamma and Bert to the Lawn Club to hear the wireless entertainment. As it was, the book got done but the Express office was closed, so I took Mamma and Bert to the Lawn Club first.

Then was the weirdest part. For I had been asked to go down to A. C. Gilbert's factory and speak for the Lawn Club entertainment and was told I'd be

199

heard by thousands. At the appointed time, nine o'clock, I was on hand, sat in a bare room on a wooden kitchen chair with a factory employee. On the second of nine he "threw in" the apparatus and introduced "Prof. Irving Fisher of Yale" to perhaps the largest audience I ever addressed—an audience I couldn't see or hear or quite believe existed.

I talked fifteen minutes on my trip to Europe. I began by speaking of how wonderful it was that last week the voice of America had for the first time carried the Atlantic. This makes the whole world a neighborhood and the U. S. must play the neighbor to Europe. I talked into a phone piece, but there was no ear piece and I had to talk on faith. Then I went back to the club and found I had been heard very well, though five per cent or so was missed on account of "static."

It seemed terribly strange to me as to the audience. Then I took Mamma and Bert home, called up the Railway Express, found they were open at the Station, went there, sent off the manuscript, went to the Post Office and mailed letters, found I had nothing to write on so came here to write you. And now I'm going to get a sleep I sorely need.

I thought of telegraphing you to listen in but was told that Cleveland was too far for this station. Mama wants a wireless set. So, I've ordered one for her and one for us, $25 each plus accessories of about the same. It is estimated that $35,000 worth of sets have been paid for in the last six months.

He was like a juggler keeping half a dozen objects twirling in the air at the same time. While he was thus devoting his energies to the commodity dollar plan and his book on index numbers, he was also heavily embroiled in politics— the topic which comes up for discussion in the next chapter.

13. *Political Activity*

Father never enrolled as a member of either political party, because he could not stomach the type of loyalty which is implied by the phrase: "My party, right or wrong." He considered it better citizenship to be loyal to one's country first, then support whichever major candidate seemed to him to fit the country's need better. He was convinced that it was the small body of independent voters like himself who were the deciding factor in most elections. During his first thirty years of voting he could boast that every presidential candidate for whom he had voted had also been elected.

Without any premeditation on his part he developed a technique for making his own choice at election time, which might have been considered perilously close to ambulance-chasing, if his motives had not been so patently unselfish. In spite of his crowded schedule he usually managed to attend both nominating conventions, and as already indicated he often participated in the jockeying behind the scenes. Then after both candidates were named, he sought and was usually granted interviews with each of them, not to ask for any personal favors but simply to form his own first-hand opinions and to offer each prospective White House incumbent his counsel on the issues which were closest to his heart. These preliminary meetings were frequently followed up by conferences with the winning candidate before and after inauguration.

In addition to campaigning for public health planks at the 1912 conventions, he had a personal reason for attending the Democratic Convention that year, in order to hear his uncle Judge John W. Wescott make the speech which nominated Woodrow Wilson. The time for his uncle to mount the rostrum did not come until the small hours of the morning, after a marathon day-and-night session. At the first mention of Wilson's name organized pandemonium broke loose. Realizing that the demonstration would be synthetically prolonged for at least an hour, Father philosophically closed his eyes and tried to relax until his uncle was permitted to proceed. As the demonstrators surged past his aisle seat, an impudent participant placed his megaphone against Father's ear and shouted in stentorian tones: "WE WANT WILSON!" In retrospect, Father was amazed at the speed and precision of his instinctive reaction. Without time to think what he was doing or why, he sprang to his feet and his fist connected hard with the demonstrator's shoulder. There was no chance for any verbal exchange. The man with the megaphone was swept irresistibly along on the human tide. All Father could do was to point to his own WILSON button to indicate that he harbored no permanent ill feeling.

An indirect result of his post-election interview with Wilson, mentioned in the autobiographical appendix to *Stable Money*, was the unfounded rumor that Father was to be offered a cabinet post. He remained a staunch Wilson supporter throughout both terms, although he appreciated as keenly as anyone the tragedy of Wilson's tactless handling of the irreconcilable Senators with regard to the League of Nations. In view of all the careful groundwork which had been done by the League to Enforce Peace, the squelching of Wilson's dream was a bitter personal blow to Father. He always felt that if, instead of repudiating the League of Nations in 1919, the United States had participated in it and helped it grow into an effective instrument for Peace, there might not have been any second World War.

It was the League issue which aroused him to participate actively in the first postwar political campaign. After attending the opening sessions of the Republican Convention in Chicago, he interviewed both nominees at their respective homes, then went to Murray Bay to confer with ex-President Taft, before finally charting his course. The series of letters written to Mother during this period give some sidelights on the current political scene, and enumerate the considerations which led him to back Cox instead of Harding:

ON TRAIN TO ALBANY, June 5, 1920

By my usual good luck this is the special train taking the Connecticut delegation to Chicago. The fourteen delegates, alternates and guests have three cars to themselves. As I entered car No. 1, I found several cases of ginger ale and other bottles and a very "rummy" smell. The first compartment contained Prof. Bakewell, Mr. Roraback, the National Committeeman and chief Republican politician of Connecticut and Mr. Hopkins Clark the power behind the throne, owner of the Hartford Courant, Bones man, but a rapscalion, and a few others.

Bakewell greeted me very effusively and introduced me around. I asked jokingly, if they were preparing a prohibition plank for the Republican platform; and they jokingly replied that they were and were drinking a non-alcoholic beverage. But they didn't offer me any and I *think* it was whiskey.

I asked Roraback who from Connecticut was on the Platform Committee. He said Ullman. Good luck again! Ullman was President of the New Haven Chamber of Commerce when I spoke on Stabilizing the Dollar. I found him and showed him my prepared plank which he approved. He advised me to see Senator Wadsworth of New York and some others about it and attend the Platform Committee Tuesday night.

ON TRAIN FROM CHICAGO, June 8, 1920

I found where the platform committee met and got my hearing. I spoke about ten or fifteen minutes and got good attention. I do not expect any result but Ullman, who was made Secretary of the Committee said he would push it. Of course I think he wanted to please me and that he won't really fight for it. Nevertheless I'm glad I spoke.

ON TRAIN FROM BATTLE CREEK, June 12, 1920

Did you ever see anything sillier than the plank in the Republican platform on the League of Nations? I think any self-respecting ostrich would feel ashamed if he couldn't bury his head in the sand to better effect than these Republican ostriches.

A plank to suit Johnson and make believe suit Lodge won't suit Mr. Voter who doesn't know what it means or knows it means nothing. And they are probably going to mess it up more by nominating a candidate who disagrees with Johnson. Almost everyone thinks the Republicans are going to win but I am just now inclined to bet on the Democrats, if they use ordinary common sense and make use of their opportunity.

DAYTON, OHIO, July 30, 1920

Governor Cox sent his machine for me which took me to "Trail's End," his beautiful Estate in the country. I had to wait an hour, as Mr. Cox was putting the finishing touches on his speech of acceptance. Then I had about an hour and a half with him including lunch with Mrs. Cox and his two secretaries.

I do not take him to be a great man in the class of Roosevelt, Taft or Wilson. But I should take him to be a big man, who has not been spoiled and who doesn't pretend to know it all. He promised to read *Stabilizing the Dollar.* I told him of my tentative plan to organize a Cox Independent League from enthusiasts in the League to Enforce Peace and he was delighted.

In the afternoon I went to his newspaper office and read the galleys of his speech as they were set up. I have 150 copies in my bag to use with the list of the League to Enforce Peace men. It's a great speech.

I have an appointment to see Mr. Harding Monday morning. I thought it best, especially when I found how close the two places are, to see both while I'm at it, not only for my satisfaction but to satisfy others whom I will try to influence. But I can't see how I can vote for Harding. I'm sorry for Mr. Taft. Wouldn't it be dramatic if *he* should bolt!

TOLEDO, OHIO, August 2, 1920

I left Marion this morning after half an hour with Harding. I asked him how a new "association" of nations could be formed in view of the existence of the present League. He said that his statement on that subject was for the purpose of securing harmony in the party. I said, "Why not be public about it all? Why allow any doubt but that we are to enter the present League?"

He said, "Before the campaign is over we shall have to be more specific. I will tell you confidentially —or rather personally—what we have up our sleeve. If next March the present situation still exists, I'll try to negotiate a modification in the present League, so that, in effect, the Lodge Reservations will be incorporated as amendments applying to all the other nations as well as the United States. They all want us in and will do anything to get us in. I want a League as much as you do."

He gave me the impression of sincerity and yet a liking for finesse and indirection. He seemed to be enjoying the joke of puzzling the enemy and having some clever tricks to spring. The supreme issue to him is, I think, the success of the Republican party rather than of any particular idea it stands for. It was not quite what I expected. I expected evasion and discomfiture in explaining away his words and the platform. But he seemed to know what he was after and to like to show off by telling me all about it "confidentially, or rather personally," as he ex-pressed it.

My own feeling is that while Harding's "strategy" may keep harmony among Republican politicians, it won't please the rank and file nor the independent voters. They will prefer the directness of Cox. I'm relieved to know that Harding favors or thinks he favors or says he favors a League of Nations. But it is hard for me to imagine the Lodge, Penrose, Brande-gee, Johnson and Harding crowd trying for a League in a spirit of friendship after all they have done to slap the rest of the world in the face. And a League not sought in the spirit of friendship seems to me impracticable.

ON TRAIN FOR QUEBEC, August 6, 1920

I arrived at Murray Bay at three; phoned Mr. Taft and made my appointment at five. He said he had wired me *not* to come, to save me the trouble and not realizing that I was wanting to ask him questions but thinking I wanted to inform him about my visits with Harding and Cox.

In our talk, Mr. Taft read me one of his editorials in the Philadelphia Ledger explaining why he would not desert his party, though Cox's stand on the League agreed with his and Harding's did not. The excuse he gave was that if Cox insisted as Wilson had on no compromise he would be blocked by the irreconcilables in the Senate who will constitute over a third, so that the program Taft and Cox both want theoretically, can't be had practically.

He had me stay to dinner with himself, Mrs. Taft and Miss Herron. He was much pleased to get an advance copy of Cox's speech which I gave him. He wasn't surprised at the program proposed by Harding. He is very sore at Mr. Wilson for not compromising when he had the chance.

In the final weeks of the campaign, he organized some of the former members of the League to Enforce Peace into a new group called the Pro-League Independents, and chartered a private railroad car for a trans-continental stump-speaking tour in support of the Democratic ticket. Financial support for this venture was secured from such League enthusiasts as Mrs. Emmons Blaine and Bernard Baruch. Father's letters, written to Mother during his absence, complete the record of his part in the 1920 campaign:

ON PRO-LEAGUE INDEPENDENT CAR, NEAR-ING INDIANAPOLIS, October 20, 1920

I got to Penn Station (in New York) before anyone else and had to wait until the gates were opened to get to the private car. It is new and spic and span consisting entirely of compartments. I took the rearmost. Soon Mr. Morgenthau and Mr. Paulding came and we laid out the rest. One by one the party appeared, Mr. George Foster Peabody bringing Secretary Baker. A camera man came and took some stills. Capt. Chamberlain asked him if he was going to take all of us and he said "Oh, No! Only the important ones!" which set us all laughing.

We started off at 12:30 A.M. Our party consists of I. F., Sec'y Baker next, then his Secretary with Capt. Chamberlain, then Col. Whittlesey, Mr. Parsons, Miss Prentiss (I. F.'s secretary) with Miss Cobey, Mrs. Mead, Miss McIlvane, Capt. Gillen with Mr. Woods (publicity man), leaving the other end compartment for a work room. There are four typewriters aboard, usually going.

I slept remarkably well, feeling a relief in getting started in perfect order. In the morning we conferred among us. I'm in charge (the Secretary of War being under me!). Gillen is bursar and renders me a report every morning.

Our first stop was in Pittsburgh. Some local members of the Pro-League Independents got it up on the spur of the moment. They had an informal reception, a theatre meeting at noon (with over 2,000 people) and a luncheon. The speakers were I. F., Mrs. Mead, Col. Whittlesey, Capt. Chamberlain and Mr. Parsons. We each took ten minutes. Sec'y Baker said afterwards it was perfect, not a word which he would have changed.

At the end I sprang to my feet and asked all Republicans to hold up their hands. Three fourths of the audience did so. Then I shouted: "All who are going to vote for Cox stand up and be counted!" and three fourths of the audience arose and applauded. Several present who knew the town mentioned the people they saw—prominent Republicans—who were there saying they would bolt.

In Cleveland we were whisked to the Statler, ate in a hurry, as we were late for our six meetings, two in tents, which were regarded as a great success. We got back to our car at near midnight and made our next "hop" to Louisville. If I were to believe all I was told about myself in Louisville, I'd be a terribly conceited man.

We are due at 8:30 in Indianapolis, where we have three meetings tonight. We reach St. Louis tomorrow morning. Everybody seems pleased with the way the trip is going and the impression the speeches are making. But my questions to the audience show that the converted come to listen. Mrs. Emmons Blaine may join us for one meeting at Omaha. She's a bolter from the Blaines and from her own family the Mc-Cormicks.

I don't expect to win. But I'm glad I'm doing my bit and believe it's worth while, if only to show Harding that there is real sentiment for the League.

EN ROUTE DES MOINES TO OMAHA [undated]

I'm very much elated. Everyone sees the tide has turned. It's simply a race against time and good observers think there is still enough time. At Des Moines at 10 A.M. the Theatre holding 2,500 was full so that an overflow meeting was held across the street. I was "heckled" a little but the result only added to the enthusiasm, as my answers satisfied the audience. Altogether I must have spoken three hours.

We left at 7:30. At the station I met Mr. Taft. He said "Hello, Irving." I said, "We invite you to join us!" He said, "I fear that is an invitation meant to be declined." I denied it. It was a very pleasant meeting.

NEARING RENO, October 26, 1920

Arrived in Salt Lake at noon and discovered that Mr. Taft was in town at another Hotel and was to speak in the Tabernacle the same evening. We remembered his saying jokingly in St. Louis that perhaps he and I could debate in the Tabernacle and we all got ambitious to try to get something of that sort arranged. The final form was to ask him if I could follow him when he was through and speak to any one who chose to remain, and to offer him the same opportunity to follow me at the theatre.

So I went to see him with Merrill and other local people. When I presented the proposition I must have bungled it, for he flew into something of a rage for a few minutes, and he said he would not have thought it of me. He soon cooled off and said if he had hurt my feelings he would take it all back, etc. We parted good friends and I wrote him a note apologizing for annoying him. I was probably pretty "cheeky" to approach him at all. But the rest think I was putting up a fair proposal and that Mr. Taft had no need to lose his temper. I learned that while he filled the Tabernacle he didn't hold his audience and that he wouldn't talk much on the League, only on the sins of Mr. Wilson. Whenever he mentioned Wilson's name he had to stop, they cheered so much!

I have spent some of the time today in the sunshine on the rear platform just gazing at the mountains and plains and wishing my lady-love were with me. There is a fascination about this sunlit country which makes me want to get out of the car and lie down in the sand. I felt I was holding communion with the Universe and feeling the mystery of creation. It was a sort of silent prayer, not thinking but feeling.

SAN FRANCISCO, October 29, 1920
ALL GOING WELL EXCEPT IMPOSSIBLE TO GET HALLS NEEDED. SAID TO BE BECAUSE ALL HALLS BOUGHT UP AND CLOSED BY REPUBLICANS.

AFTER PASSING SANTA BARBARA
October 31, 1920
On arrival at Reno we found transparencies stating that Professor I. F. "President of Yale" and others

would speak! The theatre was full. The people were rather stolid but woke up and responded in good shape before we were through. Afterwards in San Francisco Senator Pitman told me that we had performed a miracle in Reno. He believes we have turned the State from Harding to Cox. You know there are fewer people in Nevada than in New Haven. So one meeting can reach a large fraction of the population.

At Berkeley I spoke in the same Hall where almost exactly three years before I had given the Hitchcock lectures on Stabilizing the Dollar. On the 29th I spoke at a Luncheon at the St. Francis Hotel in San Francisco, a non-partisan Civic Center women's club meeting to hear Senator Phelan, candidate for re-election to the Senate. I sat next but one to him and had a talk with him which with sundry stray hints I had already had gave me the impression that *he* was opposing secretly our speaking in S. F.!

To make a long story short, Gillen and I believe though we have only circumstantial evidence that Senator Phelan is secretly sacrificing the Cox campaign to save his own skin. He is trading votes for Harding in return for votes for himself. He is getting support from Republican leaders. Probably California will go for Harding and yet Phelan will get elected to the Senate. We believe that Phelan controls the halls in S. F. and blocked us getting them.

At four I went to the Civic Auditorium. The chauffeur did not take me to the entrance but to the outdoor speaking place across the street. There I found Supervisor Hayden, the man who had originally promised the Hall, who volubly explained that if I really wanted the hall, of course, I could have it, but that the outdoor audience was right there and he would advise me to address it. So I did. President

211

Wheeler (U. of C.) was there and told me it was the best speech on the League he had ever heard.

After it was over, Mr. Hayden having realized that I might make trouble for Phelan and wishing to placate me, said he could supply me a hall for the evening if I wished, so that the outdoor meeting advertised for 7:30 could be taken indoors across the street. We went into the Civic Auditorium building and he showed me "Hall C" which was perfectly empty and could have been had that afternoon. I said I would take it for the evening.

Hayden said, "So tonight, if it's cold outdoors, you can come in."

I said, "I understand we can come in anyway."

"Yes," he said, "if you wish, but—"

I said, "I do wish."

I could see that he was preparing to do the same thing in the evening as in the afternoon, i. e. to try to induce me to stay outdoors. I made up my mind we'd actually get into the hall this time!

In the evening we started the meeting outdoors as advertised then shooed the crowd of 500 across the street into the Hall, then the Band played and a new crowd gathered, which we shooed in in the same way. We had nearly a thousand before we got through. It was like going out into the hedges and byways and compelling them to come in. My only regret was that Senator Phelan was not there to see that we actually got a hall at last.

EN ROUTE FROM LOS ANGELES TO CHICAGO
November 3, 1920

TERRIBLY DISAPPOINTED OVER ELECTION. AM WIRING TAFT OFFERING OUR COOPERATION WITH HIM IN HIS EFFORTS TO SECURE ENTRANCE TO LEAGUE THROUGH REPUBLICAN PARTY.

Since Connecticut had no provisions for absentee voting, his own vote did not count that year and, if he had chosen to quibble, he might still have boasted that no Presidential candidate for whom he had voted had ever been defeated.

He was one of the many who submitted World Peace proposals in the $25,000 Bok Contest, but when his particular blueprint did not win the award, he summarized his arguments for joining the League in his 1923 book *League or War?*, which he dedicated "To the Memory of my daughter Margaret, one of the many million radiant young souls torn from this earth by the World War." A year later this book was condensed and reissued under the title *America's Interest in World Peace.*

With another presidential election coming up, he took a half year's leave of absence from Yale to stump the country again on behalf of the League, occasionally interspersing talks on Health or Eugenics for the sake of variety. When both candidates had been named, he supported John W. Davis rather than President Coolidge, because he thought that the Democratic ticket offered the best chance of getting the United States into the League. He himself was mentioned as a possible candidate for governor of Connecticut on the Democratic ticket, but he was relieved that nothing came of this suggestion, because he felt he could be more useful by continuing his free-lance activities. Here are some excerpts from a few of his 1924 letters:

SAN FRANCISCO, July 12, 1924

It troubles me to be away from you so much, especially as I know you need me and find it hard to reconcile yourself to my idea. If it was a selfish indulgence, I'd fly to your side this minute and cancel everything. Perhaps I'm a Don Quixote, but I'm trying to be a Paul Revere.

213

Had it not been for those long years in **Saranac**, Colorado Springs and Santa Barbara, I wouldn't be on these missions but would be the regular college professor, interested in my mathematical economics exclusively. But that illness and your sweet unselfishness aroused the latent altruism which my preacher Father, I suppose, transmitted to me and from that time forth I have felt the urge of the preacher and have wanted to make up for the waste spaces in my own life, by preventing some of the needless waste of this wastrel world. First the tuberculosis fight, then Hygiene in general and the Life Extension Institute, and now the Eugenics and Peace Movements.

It's not the conventional college professor's attitude and it's just because others are not seeing these big things that I'm championing them. What is everybody's business is nobody's business and so I'm making it my business!

It is the same thing that has taken hold of thousands of the world's reformers from the giants like Christ and Socrates and Buddha down through the John Browns, Garrisons, and Cobdens to the social workers in the Salvation Army. I don't know where I belong in the scale, but I do want before I die to leave behind something more than a book on Index Numbers, much as I love my strictly professional work.

And I feel as though I have found a niche in applying my scientific training. Stable money is coming forward by leaps and bounds, and that is largely the fruit of my individual efforts. And in this battle for a warless world I feel that I am needed. The danger of a world war is still with us. We lost our first born through the last war and we may lose our baby [grandson] through the next. Isn't it worth a **big** effort to prevent such tragedies, not simply for you and me but for millions of others?

MINNEAPOLIS, September 27, 1924

I've been reading the life of Frederick Taylor and I felt throughout as though I were reading my own biography. I don't mean the events are alike but the character, ideals and methods of thought and work seem so much like mine that though the book makes the reader greatly admire Taylor, I see his faults more clearly than the biographer intends, because they are mine. Of course I also like to see my own ideals and so I have a mixed feeling of attraction and repulsion. He really did a great work.

CHICAGO, October 2, 1924

I didn't write last night as it was midnight when I got in. I had no idea what I was in for when Judge [Harry] Olsen arranged to have me speak at the house of Dr. Louis Schmidt. About thirty men were there, a group of people who run things in Chicago, including the present Health Commissioner and three of his predecessors, several judges and lawyers, including Crome who prosecuted the Leopold-Loeb case.

The dinner was supposed to begin at seven but we didn't sit down till eight. Cocktails were served first, and wine after we were at table. The dinner was a regular gorge. Afterwards we went upstairs and Judge Olsen introduced me. I spoke forty minutes on the Eugenic Movement, then a dozen others commented, agreeing with all I said but adding a lot. The object of my speaking was to raise money for the movement, but there was no solicitation there. Several wealthy people were there. One of them a wealthy Jew brought three of my books, which he wanted me to autograph.

215

These eight long hard months which I intended as a sort of sacrificial offering in the cause of Peace has been no net sacrifice to me. I have missed you terribly and longed to be doing my research work. But the experience and discipline have been worth all they cost. You may never observe it but I *feel* it. I am a bigger and better man in consequence, that in some way I can't formulate or really understand I have found my soul by losing it.

I feel a curious sense of the shortness of life or rather of the length of my country's life in comparison with mine, however long mine may be. And I have projected my interest beyond my own little life with a more definite realization than ever before. I suppose this feeling is due to the daily self-suggestion from some five hundred speeches earnestly emphasizing the need of ridding this world of war for all time as well as the daily self-suggestion that I am dedicating these months, as a sort of ascetic, for a great cause.

It has turned out that the League is not in the campaign much, and if Davis is not elected, I'm glad the League has not been tied to the Democratic Party too much, glad I had a part in getting the pro-World Court plank into the Republican platform and the Referendum plank into the Democratic platform. I feel sure my efforts, with those of others will ultimately bear fruit.

A week before this letter was written he went to Manistee, Michigan, with Judge Harry Olsen of Chicago to visit an eccentric octogenarian named Ruggles, who had made a fortune in lumber and who lived like a hermit, with a boy coming in by the day to do odd chores. Here is his account

216

of this visit, which was planned with the frankly ulterior
motive of securing backing for the eugenic movement:

October 27, 1924

Mr. Ruggles is seventy-eight years old and is
"worth" between fifty and a hundred millions. He
lives in a shabby wooden house which is occupied on
the first floor by his offices. It was his mother's house
and he has much sentiment about it. He has been
chided for not building a grand house instead of keeping this old "shack" but he is reluctant to change his
way of living. He was shabbily dressed in a dirty suit,
stained with salt from his salt works. He is short and
bent and has a bushy gray beard.

He has only had three grades in common school
but speaks grammatically and expressed himself almost with the simplicity of Abraham Lincoln. His
father, he said, had been the richest man in Oshkosh
and lost his fortune through mis-management. When
he was fourteen years old he took a job in a match
factory at fifty cents a day. He has gotten rich because of being so saving and so farsighted. He now
owns the most valuable timber tract in the world—
the Calaveras forest, near Stockton, California.

Saturday afternon he took us to see his salt works.
He has put some five million dollars into it and it is
full of automatic machinery. Then we went back to
his "shack." There I met his bookkeeper, Mr. Rademaker, who has been with Ruggles since a boy. Ruggles has made him a millionaire, but he is still his
bookkeeper. He cooked an oyster stew, using Rademaker as chore boy. When we sat down to supper,
Rademaker went home to his family, though he evidently wanted to stay.

After hours of talk in which he showed me his many
ingenious but home-made office contraptions he sud-

217

denly said "I'm telling you all this because I suppose this is what you came for, isn't it?" I simply looked at him and he went on. He tested me with his stock questionaire, a little like Edison's, which he uses for applicants to positions. I seemed to pass my examination fairly well. At any rate, he suddenly said "I rather like you!"

He says Olsen is his best friend in this world. Once when Olsen had been maligned by the Chicago Tribune, Ruggles said "What is the Tribune worth?"— "About five million, I suppose," said Olsen. "Well," said Ruggles, "let's buy it and throw it in the lake, and put a sign over the ruins: THIS IS WHAT HAPPENS TO A NEWSPAPER THAT ATTACKS AN HONEST MAN."

Ruggles has had many lawsuits and family quarrels, the worst being with an Englishman who married his sister. It was the bankruptcy of this brother-in-law which threw the salt enterprise into his hands, and brought Judge Olsen into contact with him.

Through Olsen he gave $100,000 to the American Judicature Society, which is responsible for starting important law reforms in seventeen cities. Taft has some credit for this in the eyes of the legal profession. But all he did was to give it his blessing. The real credit belongs to Ruggles, Olsen and Harley, a Professor of Law at North Western University. I am going to try to get Mr. Taft to write Ruggles a letter of appreciation, so that Ruggles can get some recognition which he has never had nor sought.

Of course Olsen's thought and mine in this is not altogether disinterested, for we hope it will help encourage him to do for Eugenics what he has done for Law. No one knows what his plans are as to leaving his fortune. We did not ask him to help the Society this time. He is a little like Hetty Green in being so accumulative, penurious, subject to intrigues of

218

unworthy people (not to say worthy!) and consequently suspicious. He told me he had no relatives
to whom he would leave more than five dollars each
and he told Olsen he had given Rademaker all he was
going to give him.

He is incensed against the Government for taxing
forests before they are cut and for "robbing you
after you are dead," by the inheritance tax. He is
right about the first but wrong about the second.
He seems to ignore the *income* from that capital after
he leaves it. He could do wonderful work in reforms
if he got the fever as Rockefeller and Carnegie did.
So Olsen and I are hoping to interest him in some of
our pet schemes for bettering mankind.

The following month Father was elated to have this
rough diamond come to visit us at Four-sixty—perhaps
the most unusual house guest ever to sign in Mother's guest
book. Mr. Rademaker came along as courier, taking time
off from his duties as mayor of Manistee.

Our guests had been seated in the living room less than
ten minutes, when Mr. Ruggles looked down at himself a
little self-consciously and remarked: "No one has noticed
my new suit!" Mother rose nobly to the occasion and com-
plimented him on his sartorial appearance. Visibly pleased
that she considered his plain black suit becoming, he raised
his beard to reveal a matching flannel shirt, but no tie,
with the explanation: "Why wear a tie when no one can
see it?"

At the supper table, after stirring his tea abstractedly
with the delicately-wrought teaspoon which had belonged
to my grandmother, he raised the spoon, examined it
critically, licked it dry and replaced it on the table, remarking: "I think I like this one better!" Suiting the action

219

to the word, he brought forth from his breast pocket an ordinary but admittedly more robust implement marked PALMER HOUSE, and resumed stirring his tea.

After supper Father ushered his guests into the Library to show off some of his own time-saving gadgets and to expatiate on his pet schemes for bettering mankind. But his efforts to convince the visitor of the importance of the eugenic movement came to naught. When Mr. Ruggles died a decade later he left no will and his fortune was largely dissipated in protracted litigation instigated by self-seeking relatives.

During the course of his stay at Four-sixty he happened to mention that for many years at Christmas time he had cooked up large batches of old-fashioned hard candy for distribution among the children of Manistee, because he was convinced that present-day candy manufacturers were seriously undermining the health of the current generation with their criminally impure products. A few weeks after his visit, Mother received from him a typed list of half a dozen flavors of hard candy, such as clove, anise, cinnamon, etc. with the request that she indicate which were her favorites. She checked two flavors and returned the list to Manistee. A few days after Christmas she was non-plussed to receive notice of the arrival of a freight shipment weighing sixty-five pounds. Mr. Ruggles had sent ten pounds of each variety. This hefty bread-and-butter present lasted many months, although it did not take long for the news of its arrival to spread among the neighborhood children.

Six months later Father had the satisfaction of consummating the merger of his Index Visible venture with the Rand organization. The letter which he wrote to me at the

time reveals the basic philanthropic attitude which moti-
vated all his financial ambitions:

NEW HAVEN, June 17, 1925

I have tried to get time to write you a special letter
ever since coming here Sunday the 14th, but have had
to write and wire at length following up the Kardex
deal on Saturday the 13th.

Mother's and my share will be $660,000 par value
of common stock; preferred stock and bonds of the
Kardex Rand Co. of which part represents $148,000
invested of Mother's money during ten years with 8%
accumulated dividends, and the rest represents my
patent. So Index Visible's "income invisible" becomes
visible all of a sudden, the dividends beginning October 1st next.

I hope you can solve this fall and winter your life
work problem. Irrespective of self expression in your
work, you will find a deep satisfaction in paying your
own way. This has become one of my own "suppressed
desires" ever since I was married and until last Saturday when the desire was satisfied at last.

Naturally I never discussed this with you before.
But having paid my way and supported others going
through college and then entering a profession which
scarcely pays a living wage, I have felt ever since
I married, despite all Mother's sweet wishes that "all
mine shall be thine" and despite every effort to be
sensible about it, that I was not enjoying our joint
income as I would if I contributed a larger part of it.

That feeling, as much as anything, was the reason
I turned to inventing as a chance to make money.
I felt it would be foolish and quixotic to go into business or try to make money by work and so sacrifice
the professional work, ambitions and usefulness to

221

gratify what seemed even to me a foolish but irrepressible whim. Inventing offered the one chance I saw of making money without a great sacrifice of time.

And at last my dream has come true and I am happy on that score.

The money itself is not needed greatly for added personal comforts and neither Mother nor I want it for swelling around. So it is dedicated primarily to the causes in which Mother and I are interested. So I'm getting double satisfaction. For there is nothing more satisfying than having a part in an enterprise greater and longer than one's own life. This added income will enable me to further the four chief causes which we have at heart, the abolition of war, disease, degeneracy, and instability in money.

If God grant me a long life I am confident that, by dedicating much of my thought and time to these causes, far more headway will be made in the next few years than would otherwise be possible. So my dreams now are of (1) getting America into the League of Nations, (2) expanding the Life Extension Institute, (3) developing the Eugenics Society and (4) Stabilizing the Dollar, besides, of course, adding professional contributions to knowledge. It looks as though I had my chance now if any man ever did.

P. S. Please help me get Mother (as a surprise) the last word in Electrics, i. e. hunt around for the best type. Probably she will have to be consulted before we actually buy.

The next chapter will be devoted to his further efforts on behalf of point four of this ambitious personal program.

14. *Money Illusion*

Instead of buying a new electric in 1925, Father invested in a chauffeur-driven Lincoln, though Mother still clung to the independence of her old electric for several more years. Within four years after the merger of Index Visible with the Rand organization, the value of Father's stock holdings in the new company increased tenfold. The office hummed more efficiently than ever. The Stable Money Association was booming. The Index Number Institute sent out its figures to newspapers throughout the world every Saturday. There were new editions of *The Making of Index Numbers, How to Live,* and *America's Interest in World Peace.* He wrote the first of his three prohibition books, and presided over the destinies of the American Eugenic Society. These activities left little leeway for making "professional contributions to knowledge," and his teaching schedule was placed permanently on a half-year basis.

As his extracurricular interests multiplied, the number of students who came directly under his influence grew smaller and smaller. For many years he had taught only graduate courses, and when he finally whittled his schedule down to one half-year course, only a handful of special students took it. In the earlier days, when a new book was in the works, it was his custom to offer a course on that topic, and he often employed one or more of his best pupils to help him whip the manuscript into final shape. In this way a succession of advanced students enjoyed the advantages of an unusually close teacher-pupil relationship. Commenting on the atmosphere of these advanced classes, Professor Ray B. Westerfield of Yale stated in a memorial article in the *American Economic Review* for September, 1947: "Fisher was always very respectful of student opinion and logic, tolerant of their errors and immaturity, and courteous in argument."

Among the other pupils who found niches at Yale were: Fred R. Fairchild, the expert on taxation; Edgar S. Furniss, who became Provost of the University; and Norman S. Buck, now Dean of Freshmen. Richard A. Lester and one or two others joined the Princeton faculty, but James Harvey Rogers, who taught at Cornell before returning to Yale, was probably more sympathetic to Father's economic viewpoint than any of his other outstanding pupils. His death in a 1939 South American airplane crash was a body blow to Father, personally as well as from the standpoint of economic theory.

The improvement in his financial status increased the productivity of his office and swelled the number of personnel on his staff. Sometimes, to vary the monotony of their sandwich lunches, Mother would invite them to join the family for the midday meal. On one of these occasions, after all the plans had been made, she suddenly remembered that she had accepted an invitation to lunch elsewhere. There was nothing for it. Father had to entertain eight or ten assorted females, without the moral support of Mother's presiding genius at the opposite end of the table. The silence which followed his pronouncement of grace was broken by a comparatively new recruit, who glanced shyly around the table and remarked with a giggle: "It's sort of like a harem, isn't it?"

It seemed less so as the boom approached its peak, because a full-time draughtsman was engaged to produce the charts which illustrated all the books and articles; Dr.

Max Sasuly was placed in charge of making the necessary statistical calculations; and Benjamin P. Whitaker was a "regular" until he was appointed comptroller of Union College at Schenectady. And when Ragnar Frisch of the University of Oslo lectured at Yale for a year, his "free time" was spent by prearrangement in Father's office. Their particular bond in common was their admiration for and use of J. Willard Gibbs's vector analysis in the mathematical thinking behind their economic theories. Franklin L. Ho contributed still another international element when he worked for Father part time while studying for his Ph.D., and continued for another year on full time before he returned to China. There he made translations of *The Making of Index Numbers* and the radio series, *Short Stories on Wealth*. The latter appeared weekly in *Ta Ku Pao*, commencing in August, 1930. In World War II he filled a post in the Chunking Government, then served on the staff of the United Nations in New York, and now commutes from New Haven to teach at Columbia University. The most distinguished addition to the Four-sixty staff was Dr. Royal Meeker, who taught economics at Princeton, was Commissioner of Labor Statistics under President Wilson, then worked in the International Labor office at Geneva and as a member of the Commission on Social Research in China. He came to New Haven to shoulder the responsibilities of chief economic consultant in Father's office. He also took over the Presidency of the Index Number Institute, and, as previously noted, played a key role in making the 1930 revision of *The Rate of Interest*.

To maintain his own efficiency at concert pitch, Father engaged Dr. Luther A. Tarbell of Battle Creek to be his personal physician and trainer. Dr. Tarbell brought us up to date on current Sanitarium techniques, introduced us to the mysteries of diathermy, and incidentally married Miss Ashton, Father's head administrative secretary. He solved the exercise problem by evolving a new version of volley ball, which could be played by any number, as long as there was at least one player on each side of the net. Father christened it "Battle Ball" and had a cement court built behind the rose garden, where he ran the male members of his staff ragged at midmorning and midafternoon workouts. Unwary chance visitors were sometimes induced to be his temporary sparring partners, so that these Olympiads took on a truly cosmopolitan aspect, since the Irish chauffeur was always ready and eager to participate when an extra was needed to even up the sides.

In the summer of 1927 Father accepted an invitation to lecture at the School of International Studies at Geneva. While in Europe he hoped also to beard the Italian dictator in his den in an effort to bring about his cherished plan for a World Monetary Conference. Mother stayed at Whimsy Cot, knowing from past experience that she could not maintain Father's pace. His benefits from the Remington Rand merger were rapidly multiplying, so I was taken along for the ride.

There is a photo of us on the deck of the old Mauretania just before we embarked. Our impedimenta included a case of Walker Gordon acidophilus milk for the voyage. Aside from meals and twice-daily games of shuffleboard, Father devoted most of his shipboard time to revising the manuscript of his Geneva lectures, which had been freshly typed before we left home. It was soon covered with so many hen tracks that he realized it would have to be retyped before it would be legible enough for him to read on the platform. Since no typists were available on the ship, he radioed the Paris Remington Rand office, stating that he was a director of the company and instructing the manager to find ten English-speaking typists to copy "a long complicated technical manuscript," during our three-day stopover in Paris. If no such typists were available there, the manager was authorized to import them by air from London.

At Cherbourg we were met by Herman Scheibler, an Austrian admirer of Father's, who was to act as his secretary during the trip. He was briefed on the manuscript problem and told that his first assignment would be to supervise its retyping. On reaching Paris we found that ten typists had flown over from London, and at the last minute one more was located in Paris, making eleven in all. The typewriters had been converted from the French to the English keyboard, and everything was in readiness for the marathon task.

The typists covered a gratifying amount of ground that first morning, and at noon they all went out to lunch, leaving Father and Mr. Scheibler to lay out the work for the afternoon. Half an hour later, when they were ready to go to lunch themselves, they found that they were alone in the hermetically sealed six-story building. Fortunately, the concierge had heard Father mention a one o'clock luncheon appointment, so he returned to release them at that time. Otherwise the building would not have been unlocked until two o'clock. Father reached our nearby hotel only a few minutes late for his appointment with James Harvey Rogers, who incidentally gave us a vivid eyewitness account of Lindbergh's landing at Le Bourget six weeks before.

When Father returned to the Remington Rand office in midafternoon, the work seemed to have slowed down to a snail's pace, and he wondered if the girls' efficiency had been impaired by too much wine at lunch. Instead they finally confessed that they were pining for their afternoon tea.

Scheibler quickly arranged to have a reasonable facsimile brought in from a nearby cafe, and thereafter production zoomed. The whole job was completed in two and a half days, so that the London girls had a little time for sightseeing before they flew home.

At Geneva the lectures were successfully delivered on schedule. Then I flew to England for a week of golf at St. Andrews, while Father and Mr. Scheibler went to Rome for the appointment with Mussolini, which had been arranged through the Italian Embassy in Washington. Here is Father's own account of this meeting, written in a letter to Mother:

ROME, September 2, 1927

I have spent the day preparing for my 5:30 P.M. appointment with Mussolini. I knew Scheibler was dying to go along but he did not expect to be allowed. I found, though he had never been mentioned in the correspondence and though at the Palace Chigi they are very vigilant in excluding people, his going along as my Secretary was taken for granted. He says he'll never forget this day!

The engagement was at 5:30; but I intended to see the Chief of Cabinet (Mameli) first, as he was the one with whom all the negotiations had been made. So we were there at 5:10.

At the entrance to the "Palace" which is a big dingy Government Office building, though highly decorated inside, we were first stopped by one of several policemen. I asked for Mameli and was shown to a little office just inside the entrance where a young official looked at my letter from the Italian Ambassador at Washington in English, and my letter from the Italian Consul in Geneva which was in French. I gathered that he did not understand either letter. But, with great labor and pains he filled out a blank form and sent it upstairs.

228

In ten minutes he informed us we were to go up-stairs. We did and "cooled our heels" about an hour while we saw others let in ahead of us—a delegation of students, one of athletes in running costume and one of about 100 very young cadets. When 5:30 arrived I again spoke to the guard, who assured me he under-stood. Finally my name was called and we were ushered into a large room and the door closed. At the diagonally opposite corner at a desk facing us was a man, whether Mameli or Mussolini I did not know.

I had intended to see Mameli first. But this man came from behind his desk and stepped forward say-ing, "Is this Professor Fisher?" and I said, "Yes, is this Mr. Mussolini?"

He was a little taken aback and said, "Yes. You do not speak English?" Whether he meant to say, "You do not speak Italian?" or "Do you need to speak English?" will never be known.

I explained that I could not speak Italian and he said that he could understand English if I spoke slowly. By that time he had got behind his desk, put one *knee* on his chair, the other foot on the floor, and both elbows on the desk, staring at me with his pierc-ing bulging black eyes, and listening intently.

Scheibler afterward told me there was no wall behind Mussolini but a curtain and he tried to see if he could see any eyes piercing it from the other side, but couldn't. He is sure there were soldiers there ready with revolvers. I was too intent on my message and watching that inscrutable face. I had expected an atmosphere of hurry, but here I was alone with M. and M. apparently with all the time in the world. I had over half an hour with him.

I began by saying, "You are one of the few great men in the world who are interested in the subject of inflation and deflation, unstable money and stabiliza-tion."

229

"Ah!" he said, "Stabilization! And you have made a special study of this?"

"Yes," I said, "for twenty years. I wrote you in April for this appointment. Meanwhile you have already done one thing I wanted to suggest—stop your deflation. I think that was wise. I am glad you have stopped. But there are other suggestions I would like to make. First of all I will introduce myself. I am Professor at Yale University, a friend of Pantaleoni—"

"You a friend of Pantaleoni!" he exclaimed. "Ah! He was a great man."

"Also of Pareto," I said.

"Ah! Pareto? Yes."

"Pareto was a mathematical economist and I am a mathematical economist."

"Ah!" he said. "You have originated some mathematical economics?"

I said, "I have also had some business experience. I am spending $15,000 to $20,000 a year on propaganda for stable money. I have just had three lectures at Geneva on this subject."

"Have you those with you?" he asked.

"Yes, I have brought you a copy especially prepared for you." Scheibler handed him the copy. "I came from Geneva especially to see you. But all I want you to do now is to sign a letter to me such as the suggested form I have prepared. Theodore Roosevelt used to like to have me prepare things for him to sign. If he didn't like them he would change them." Then I handed him the letter which he read carefully. He objected to one sentence.

I outlined the program I proposed, viz. to sign the letter, after he had modified it, requesting me to gather opinions from authorities on stabilization and digest them, with a definite recommendation as to how

260

to solve the problem. He would then accept, reject or modify my recommendation and, when he had decided on what plan to adopt, propose it to the League of Nations for consideration, adoption, rejection or modification by a League Committee.

He said he would send me the letter after modification, after he had read my lectures which he would have translated into Italian. Merely to get him to read the lectures was worth my trip to Europe. I had commented severely on his disastrous deflation policy in one of my weekly articles and included quotations from this article in my typed Mss. I had considered whether to soften this; but decided to let him see exactly what I had said.

I told him I thought stabilization the most important economic problem in the world as to justice between creditor and debtor, business ups and downs, unemployment, social discontent and the stability of government. I said now was a golden opportunity to solve the problem because the war had aroused attention to it of more people than ever before, that it was a hard problem for the average man even to conceive, because of what I called "the money illusion." I feel sure he will read the lectures and write me something. Those were my objects.

I bade him goodbye and he started to walk with me across the room. Then he said, "What do you think of the situation in Italy? Do you think it urgent that the lira should remain stabilized?"

I said, with much emphasis that I did, that I had written about it last September and he would find my comments in the manuscript, that I had predicted that the deflation policy would prove disastrous and said if it were persisted in it might upset the government. He looked displeased, but I'm sure it made the impression intended. I said in the manuscript that it might mean his political, or even physical death! He will want to see what I did say and so will read the manuscript.

He repeated his question, "That is your opinion?" I said, it certainly was. I think he was impressed.

He then asked for my addresses in Europe and we walked back to the desk and he asked me to write them on the letter I had prepared. So, I did, while he waited. I then apologized for taking his time and he very courteously said it was all right. Then he shook my hand very warmly across the table, bowed to Scheibler, and we left him behind the desk and walked across the big room.

When we reached the door, it opened from the other side. I don't know whether we had been watched from there too or whether M. had pressed a button. When we descended to the street, we found it filled with people waiting to see him come out.

Soon after the Mussolini interview, Father, Carol and I converged on London for a brief reunion before he and I were scheduled to sail for home. To take advantage of the newly-inaugurated transatlantic telephone service, he arranged a complicated nine-minute hookup, so that we spoke for three minutes each with Mother in Rhode Island, Grandmother in New Jersey and Carol's family in Ohio. Throughout these conversations, Father kept his eye on the second hand of his watch to be sure that no one used more than his or her fair share of the allotted time. Thus the conversation consisted mostly of hellos and goodbyes repeated three times over, for each of the separate connections. Before we could regain our equilibrium after this dizzying experience, an assistant cashier of the Hotel knocked on the door to dun Father politely for the equivalent of $225 for the nine-minute hookup.

When we reached New York, his head secretary met us on the dock and I recall the troubled expression which passed across Father's face when she told him that there had been enough of a slump in the stock market during our absence to require her to use the full hundred thousand dollars in her agent's account to reduce bank loans. He had paid little attention to market movements during the crowded four-week trip, and he was rather provoked that she had not cabled him while we were still in London. She had reasoned that a few days one way or the other could scarcely matter, and she had not wanted to spoil his holiday. This minor financial setback was the first hint to me of worse to come, but it was more than five years before I had even a glimmering of his complicated financial position.

His Geneva lectures were published in 1928 under the title, *The Money Illusion*, which was his most ambitious effort to popularize the stabilization theme. In contrast to his strictly professional books, its main text covered less than one hundred and eighty pages in large type, while the supplementary material at the back of the book added scarcely fifty additional pages. But he rated it as an even more vital link in his educational campaign than *The Making of Index Numbers*. Unlike the latter, which was intended for specialists, *The Money Illusion* was designed for the widest possible audience, and required a degree of painstaking scrutiny and revision which seemed out of proportion to its brevity. The preface listed sixty-nine individuals as having read mimeographed copies and contributed helpful suggestions. Even my name was included, along with such worthies as Royal Meeker, Carl Snyder, E. W. Kemmerer, Willford I. King, Paul H. Douglas, and Wesley C. Mitchell.

Besides reiterating the damage done by unstable money and mentioning the various possible remedies, the book was beamed especially at "the business reader" in the hope that an enlightened public opinion would some day bring pressure to bear on legislators throughout the world so that something constructive might be done about the problem. He was disappointed that the book did not attract a wider audience at home, although it was translated into fifteen foreign languages—more than in the case of any of his other works.

In a foreword to the British edition, Sir Josiah Stamp wrote:

> Money as a physical medium of exchange, made a diversified civilization possible. And yet it is money, in its mechanical more than in its spiritual effects, which may well, having brought us to the present level, actually destroy society.
>
> In this work Professor Fisher excels himself in practical and illustrative exposition, and he sets forth clearly, but with no undue or pontifical seriousness, the problem before us, and with admirable impartiality some of the lines of possible solution.
>
> The number of thinking men who appreciate the facts of monetary fluctuation is now not small, but the proportion who carry that appreciation into the other fields of thought as a persistent element in them all, is singularly few. It needs the same kind of effort of mind as the realisation of terrestrial and astronomical motion.
>
> Whether our monetary standard is to be of pure and visible gold, or an unseen one managed by a golden handle, or whether gold is to have no more effect upon the price level than the mercury in the

thermometer has upon the temperature, the next decade will more clearly show.

Meanwhile, to unveil the real cause of economic evils, and to create a public interest in a problem to be solved, are urgent tasks towards which Professor Fisher has done his share.

As mentioned in the passage quoted from his autobiographical appendix to *Stable Money,* the author visited Germany in 1922 to study at first hand that country's postwar inflation. He described the omnipresence of "the money illusion" in Germany in this passage from a speech delivered before the Pacific Coast Conference of Sales Executives in Los Angeles on April 4, 1941:

When I visited Germany in 1922, I found that the people realized that the cost of living was high, that prices were high, but they had no notion that anything had happened to the mark. I visited Germany expressly to find out if these people had the illusion that a mark was still a mark. I call it the money illusion. Nineteen out of twenty of them thought that the mark by which they measured business was just the same as it was before.

Professor Roman and I spent over an hour talking with two very intelligent women who ran a shop in Steglitz, one of the suburbs of Berlin, and we bought a number of things, which in terms of our money—the dollar—were very cheap. But these women would have thought we were sarcastic if we asked why things were so cheap, and with our tongues in our cheeks we asked why the prices were so high—thousands of marks. One of these women immediately was on the defensive, saying "Well, we're not profiteers, it's not our fault," thinking that I was blaming her for the

235

high prices, because that's the first thing the consumer does.

They were doing it in Germany, just as in this country, when there was a high cost of living from inflation, people were complaining at the corner grocer. The housewives were disgusted, they had to pay more for their bread, at least they thought it was more. And it *was* more in terms of cents, so they broke the windows of these grocerymen and said they were profiteers. The businessman gets the blame for what is merely a change in an inanimate object—the dollar—by which he measures his business.

Well, these women had no notion that the mark had fallen. They knew prices had risen, but they didn't identify the two things. I said, "Why are prices so high?"

She said, "I don't know. I suppose the blockade of the allies has made goods scarce in Germany."

There was a grain of truth in that. That might have explained a ten or twenty per cent rise in prices, but it wouldn't explain a fifty fold rise in prices. I said, "What else?"

"Well, the labor unions, they make a higher cost of production."

That might make another few per cent—"What else?"

"Well, freight rates are high."

That's just explaining one price by another. Why are freight rates high?—and so it went on, "Has the government anything to do with it?"

She said, "Well, they're very extravagant, and inefficient. I suppose that has something to do with it."

I tried to give her a chance, if she had it in her head to say something about inflation. She did not. Finally I said, "May it not be true that the government is paying debts by running a printing press and putting a great many more marks in circulation?"

That was an entirely new idea to her. She knitted her brow and said, "Why yes, perhaps—Why shouldn't they?" She was entirely ignorant of this tremendous cause which was making all her troubles.

And then to prove she was not a profiteer, she said, "That shirt that I'm selling to you (which really cost me in American money about ten cents) to show you that I'm not a profiteer, that shirt will cost me just as much to put back in stock when I buy a new one. It will cost me just as much as I'm selling it to you for," and before I could ask her then why she did such a foolish thing as to sell it to me instead of putting it back in stock, she said, "but I've made a profit on that shirt, because I bought it six months ago for less."

She hadn't made a profit. She had made a loss, because when six months ago she had bought it for fewer marks, the mark was worth more. But she couldn't imagine that the mark had changed, and so her business was being run at a loss for ignorance of inflation and deflation. When your yard stick changes you make miscalculations. And we do the same thing in this country. When there's inflation nobody realizes it.

He used a briefer version of the same incident to illustrate the opening chapter of *The Money Illusion*, then continued:

Almost every one is subject to the Money Illusion in respect to his own country's currency. This seems to him to be stationary while the money of other countries seems to change. We see the rise or fall of foreign money better than we see that of our own. After

237

the War, we in America knew that the German mark had fallen, but on my way to Germany (in 1922) Lord D'Abernon, then British Ambassador to Germany, said "Professor Fisher, you will find that very few Germans think of the mark as having fallen." I said: "That seems incredible. Every schoolboy in the United States knows it." But he was right. The Germans thought of commodities as rising and thought of the American gold dollar as rising. They thought we had somehow cornered the gold of the world and were charging an outrageous price for it. But to them the mark was all the time the same mark. They lived and breathed and had their being in an atmosphere of marks, just as we in America live and breathe and have our being in an atmosphere of dollars.

An American is quite lost if he tries to think of the dollar as varying. He cannot easily think of anything by which to measure it. Even with our gold standard we have a dollar fluctuating in buying power. Yet we think of the dollar as fixed. It is not fixed in the amount of goods and benefits it can command.

I once jokingly asked my dentist—at a time when people were complaining about "the high cost of living"—whether the cost of gold for dentistry had risen. To my surprise he took me seriously and sent his clerk to look up the figures. She returned and said: "Doctor, you are paying the same price for your gold that you always have."

Turning to me the dentist said: "Isn't that surprising? Gold must be a very steady commodity."

"It's exactly as surprising," I said, "as that a quart of milk is always worth two pints of milk."

"I don't understand," he said.

"Well, what is a dollar?" I asked.

"I don't know," he replied.

"That's the trouble," I said. "The dollar is approximately one-twentieth of an ounce; there are, therefore, twenty dollars in an ounce of gold, and naturally an ounce of gold must be worth $20. The dollar is a unit of weight, just as truly as the ounce. It is a unit of weight masquerading as a *stable* unit of value, or buying power."

If we were to define a dollar as a dozen eggs, thenceforth the price of eggs would necessarily and always be a dollar a dozen. Nevertheless, the supply and demand of eggs would keep on working. For instance, if the hens failed to lay, the price of eggs would not rise but the price of almost everything else would fall. One egg would buy more than before. Yet, because of the Money Illusion, we would not even suspect the hens of causing low prices and hard times.

No one cares, or should care, what a dollar weighs. What it buys is the vital question. To confuse the fixed weight of the dollar with a fixed value is like confusing a fixed weight of a yardstick with a fixed length. If the Bureau of Standards should put out yardsticks always weighing the same, they could be used accurately for weighing sugar but not, with any great accuracy, for measuring cloth. It follows that our dollar could be used accurately for weighing sugar, but it cannot at present be used, with accuracy, for measuring value. This fact nevertheless is hidden from us by the Money Illusion.

He then showed how fluctuations in the buying power of the dollar could be gauged by means of index numbers. Specifically, he called attention to these historical instances from our past: "During the Civil War the dollar fell rapidly, so that in 1886 its buying power was only two-fifths of that of 1861. Next, the dollar's buying power rose again until it was multiplied four fold in the 31 years between 1865 and 1896. Once more the tide turned and the dollar fell until its buying power in 1920 was only one-fourth what it had been in 1896. Finally, from 1920 to June 1921 the dollar again rose rapidly in buying power, from 40 to 70 pre-war cents. Since 1921 the dollar has remained fairly stable up to the present time (1928)."

The next chapter reviewed the reasons for these fluctuations in the value of the dollar—the causes behind the periods of inflation and deflation—which he had discussed more fully in previous books. In speaking of the "direct harm" done by these variations—the harm to investors, to borrowers and lenders—he asserted: "The extent of this subtle impersonal robbing, or transfer of values from creditors to debtors through inflation or the reverse through deflation, is enormous. Professor Willford I. King estimated that, in the United States alone, there has been this sort of picking of pockets of one set of people for the advantage of another to the tune of sixty billions of dollars, and this within a period of only half a dozen years (1914-1920). All of this robbery was legal though contrary to the principles of essential right as laid down by the Constitution of the United States and the courts of the land; it was property taken without due process of law. Suppose there should be a sixty *million* dollar bank robbery; an account of it would be on the front page of every newspaper. Yet this sixty *billion* 'robbery' by inflation was so subtly accomplished that it was not generally recognized when it happened and is not recognized now. Were it not for the Money Illusion, the losses and gains of these prodigious sums would be known and the reasons for them clearly understood."

He concluded that a fixed-weight dollar is a poor substitute for a dollar of fixed buying power—witness the fourfold rise of the dollar and subsequent fall by a like amount between the years 1865 and 1920. Such "tremendous fluctuations of money produce tremendous harm, because its stretching and shrinking are unseen." This means "a constant robbery of Peter to pay Paul—a net loss to all Peters and Pauls taken together. The real solution is to be found in credit control" such as "the policy of our Federal Reserve System as to buying and selling securities and adjusting its rediscount rate."

Disclaiming advocacy of any particular plan, he put it squarely up to the reader: "Here is the problem crying for solution. What are you going to do about it? If you do not bestir yourself, and no one else does, this havoc-working, drunken dollar will remain with us always. . . . Of course stable money will not be a panacea, a cure for all business problems, any more than a stable bushel basket was a panacea. Yet besides reducing social injustice, social discontent and social inefficiency, stable money will help indirectly in solving other great problems, simply by making it easier to get at the facts, without any illusions. The fluctuating dollar keeps us all in ignorance; whereas a stabilized dollar would lay bare the facts."

In the supplementary pages of the book he discussed several stabilization proposals in detail, provided the reader with a list of additional books on the subject, and appended more than thirty expressions of opinion, ranging from Reginald McKenna and John Maynard Keynes in England to an editorial in the *Saturday Evening Post* on the unfortunate position of those who lived on fixed incomes during World War I and "were paid in dollars that had lost half their purchasing power." Also included was a quotation from an article by Carl Snyder in the June, 1923, issue of the *American Economic Review:* "Almost every strike and wage dispute grows out of a changing level of the purchasing power of money, and if this level of purchasing power can be made fairly stable, a large part of our labor troubles, so-called, will disappear."

After producing *The Money Illusion* the author next turned to more technical discussions of major business oscillations.

15. *Business Cycles*

While the discussion of the rise and fall of my father's personal fortunes is reserved for the next chapter, it was no secret at the time that the 1929 stock market crash caught him unawares. Placing his faith unreservedly in the "new economic era" he did not foresee that it was destined to collapse like a house of cards. Since economics was his chosen profession, he was widely blamed for not being more clairvoyant. He never tried to evade responsibility for his errors in judgment, though he sometimes took refuge in the realization that others had been equally misled. In reality the number of experts who foresaw the crash was so small that they could be counted on the fingers of one hand, and for the most part their predictions went unheeded until after the event.

In spite of the disastrous effect of the crash on his personal situation, Father's faith in good common stocks as the soundest long-term investment never wavered. Under most conditions he preferred stocks to bonds, because during periods of inflation the latter, while giving an assured nominal return in dollars, yielded much less in purchasing power than a corresponding investment in blue-chip stocks.

Midway in the hectic first thirty days of the crash, he expressed this philosophy in a letter to Will Eliot:

NEW HAVEN, October 28, 1929

As to advice for investment. I do not believe that in the long run investments in such securities as you mention have proved good. If we can stabilize the dollar they may prove much better in the future. But for every $100. you invested in 1896 you lost three quarters thereof by 1920, so far as the ability to buy your bread and butter is concerned. The average investor in Bonds has never been better off for any length of time than the investor in stocks, and except when prices were falling rapidly was considerably worse off.

The realization of this by large and intelligent investors is one of the leading reasons why there has been such a stampede for stocks and away from bonds. While this has led to undue speculation as witnessed by the market crash, nevertheless even with that included, if you go over any considerable period of time, you will find that what I say has scarcely any exceptions.

Two months later he delivered the seventh Josiah Willard Gibbs lecture at Des Moines, from which quotations have been given previously. At the same time he was putting the finishing touches on his book *The Stock Market Crash and After*, which was rushed onto the book stands in February, 1930.

In the preface he stated that this book was "the outgrowth of several years' study of the stock market consequent on the publication by me, in the newspapers, of weekly and daily index numbers of stock prices." He conceded that: "To publish the book now may seem audacious, but there is advantage in writing tentative conclusions while

243

impressions and memories are still fresh. Someone has said that the 'true perspective' of the historian really means he waits until everyone who could contradict him has died! It is too early to reach any absolutely sure conclusions. . . . But I trust this book will have served its purpose by contributing somewhat toward a better eventual understanding of the problem. The ordinary explanations now finding the greatest currency seem to me far too simple and naive."

In the introduction he listed some of these shallow and incomplete explanations, which blamed such divergent personalities as President Hoover, Secretary Mellon, John J. Raskob, The Federal Reserve Board, Wall Street brokers, and even Roger W. Babson for precipitating the crash simply by predicting it. Then he continued:

"Hindsight" is always clearer than foresight. Looking backward now and putting the events of the panic in perspective, we find that there were definite foreshadowings of its coming. As early as April 18, 1929, the National City Bank of New York said in a special circular: "If the rate of credit increase rises above the rate of business growth, we have a condition of inflation which manifests itself in rising prices in some departments of the business structure, over-confidence, excessive speculation, and an eventual crash."

Other observers had noted symptoms of unusual inflation of credit. On September 5th, in an address at his Annual National Business Conference, Mr. Babson said: "I still repeat what I said at this time last year and the year before; namely, that sooner or later a crash is coming which will take the leading stocks and cause a decline of from 60 to 80 points in the Dow-Jones Barometer."

On the same day, in an interview with *The Hartford Courant*, I stated that while none of us was infallible,

244

"there may be a recession of stock prices." But I did not at that time believe that there would be anything in the nature of a serious crash.

In retrospect it is easy to appreciate that preliminary symptoms of the crash were not lacking. But it is not so easy to see the underlying factors of the panic, and to judge whether it sprang from vital defects of the business structure or from more superficial causes relating to credit and finance. The avalanche came so swiftly, spreading such immediate and widespread disaster, that careful consideration of its origin is requisite.

The first symptomatic recession in the stock market in August and early September attracted comparatively little attention. In the bull market stocks had reached a level more than double that of 1926. Before the November panic, the stock price level was not only twice the level of 1926, but nearly four times the level of 1913.

The Federal Reserve Board had issued its warning of an inflated stock market back in March, 1929, with a resultant shutting off of stock market credit that at once precipitated a near-panic. This was alleviated through the action of Charles E. Mitchell, Chairman of the National City Bank of New York, who made $100,000,000 available to the market at high rates.

Here is a picture that portended and predicted the disaster that came. In the rapidly mounting aggregate of margin accounts the unsoundness of the situation stands revealed. From it many have hastily concluded that the new plateau of stock prices was wholly unwarranted and merely the result of insane speculation.

But there is another side of the picture. Since every stock price represents a discounted value of the future

245

dividends and earnings of that stock, there are four reasons that may justify a rise in the price level of stocks.

(1) Because the earnings are continually plowed-back into business instead of being declared in dividends;

(2) Because the expected earnings will increase on account of technical progress within the industry;

(3) Because less risk is believed to attach to those earnings than formerly;

(4) Because the "basis" by which the discounting is made has been lowered.

All four of these causes were at work, tending to raise the prices on the stock market during the years preceding the panic of 1929.

Under the heading "Causes of the Panic" he wrote: "Few realize today that the greatest fall of stocks in British history, comparable only with the Baring Panic of 1890, preceded and was an actuating cause of the American panic, and that a coincident fall in Paris and Berlin accompanied the British liquidation. It began with the failure of the banking house of Clarence Hatry in August, followed by his arrest in September and subsequent conviction for a gigantic forgery of stock certificates. This started the British liquidation in London and in New York." Liquidation of foreign holdings in New York resulted in a "tremendous growth of Brokers' loans" to permit New York operators to absorb the foreign holdings. "The prime cause was serious overvaluation of common stocks that had previously been undervalued." In this contention his opinion was corroborated by Carl Snyder, of the Federal Reserve Bank of New York.

Other contributory causes were: a slight recession in business, first noted in July, 1929; the Federal law imposing a tax on capital gains; the export of half a billion of gold during 1927 and 1928; overextension of loans; over-enthusiasm for the "boom"; and an unsound credit situation resulting in a vicious spiral of forced selling.

The last chapter, which was headed "The Hopeful Outlook," showed that "the factors leading to the crash were not factors of depression but of prosperity. They were factors identical with those which should bring about recovery of the long bull market that had lasted with but minor interruptions from the close of 1922. It was in the main overeagerness to profit by these factors which produced the crash. The prime fault lay in the credit structure. Just because there were golden opportunities to invest, opportunities for future dividends and profits that were not illusory but real, there had been an undue haste, an undue eagerness to invest, and people had tried more and more to do business on borrowed money."

He concluded that the panic might have been avoided if there had been no Hatry failure, less piling up of margin accounts, or if the rate of interest had been raised, instead of being lowered in accordance with the Federal Reserve easy-money policy. He was convinced: "that the threat to business due to the dislocation of purchasing power by reason of transfers of stock holdings will be temporary. Fulfillment of the pledges by the nation's business leaders that industrial programs will be adhered to, that wages will not be reduced, and that the 'tempo' of production on which all our prosperity has been built will be maintained, should suffice to bridge across the business recession that slightly antedated and accompanied the crash.... The only 'fly in the ointment' is the danger in a few years of gold shortage and long gradual deflation like the deflations after the Civil War and after the Napoleonic Wars. And even this danger may be averted if wise banking policies and gold control are adopted in time. For the immediate future, at least, the outlook is bright."

The ink was scarcely dry on this opus, when the disastrous decline was resumed. What had seemed to be the "bottom" of mid-November, 1929, was only the lull before the real storm, which by the end of 1932 was to carry stock prices down to the previous low of mid-1921. Perhaps it was wishful thinking which blinded him to the real potentialities of the situation. Perhaps he prepared the book too hastily, in an understandable attempt to strike while the iron was hot. His preface indicated that he recognized the danger of drawing premature conclusions, but having set himself the task he carried it through to the best of his ability with the facts and figures available to him.

Nor was it all wasted effort. It prepared the way for a more important book, *Booms and Depressions*, which was published late in 1932. He had touched briefly on the subject of business cycles in *The Rate of Interest* and *The Purchasing Power of Money;* and he had written two papers along this line for the *Journal of the American Statistical Association:* "The Business Cycle Largely a Dance of the Dollar," in December, 1923, and "Our Unstable Dollar and the So-Called Business Cycle," in June, 1925. And on the first day of 1932 he addressed the American Association for the Advancement of Science at New Orleans on "The Debt-Deflation Theory of Depressions." His book *Booms and Depressions* went to press in July and was dedicated "To Wesley Clair Mitchell, the world's acknowledged leader in the study of the subject of this book."

In the preface he limited "the scope of the present work, for the most part, to the role of nine main factors, not because they cover the whole subject, but because they include what seems to me to be outstanding influences in

the present, as well as in most other major depressions. . . .
Being so unfamiliar with the immense literature, I decided
to submit the first draft of this book in mimeographed form
to a number of authorities, several of whom have given
much of their lives to the study of the so-called business
cycle. With few exceptions these have found in the theory
much that they regard as both new and true. . . . The main
conclusion of this book is that depressions are, for the most
part, preventable and that their prevention requires a
definite policy in which the Federal Reserve System must
play an important part. No time should be lost in grap-
pling with the practical measures necessary to free the
world from such needless suffering as it has endured since
1929. . . . Ignorance cannot much longer serve as an excuse
for neglecting this greatest of all practical economic
problems."

These passages are from the introductory chapter:

> A Depression is a condition in which business be-
> comes unprofitable. It might well be called the Private
> Profits disease. Its worst consequences are business
> failures and wide-spread unemployment. But almost
> no one escapes a degree of impoverishment. Some of
> the mightiest and best managed enterprises are among
> the worst sufferers. If they do not break, it is often
> only because they are saved by their reserves. Many
> rich stockholders, too, are compelled to live on re-
> serves; while many persons who had lived modestly are
> compelled to live from hand to mouth; and many who
> already lived from hand to mouth become jobless and
> live on charity.
>
> A depression seems to fall upon mankind out of a
> clear sky. It scorns to choose a moment when the
> earth is impoverished. Is the soil less fertile? Not at
> all. Does it lack rain? Not at all. Are the mines

exhausted? No. Are the factories then lamed in some way—down at the heel? No; machinery and invention may be at the very peak. But perhaps the men have suddenly become unable or unwilling to work. The idea is belied by the spectacle of hordes of workmen, besieging every available employment office.

Perhaps, then, the world has become over-populated. But how could that happen in so short a time? When the calamity starts there seems to be (at least in America) enough of every good thing to go around; everybody wants it, and nearly everybody wants it enough to work for it; yet some cannot get it, and many who can get some of it must be content with less.

Those who, at the beginning of a depression, cry "over-production" and expect recovery as soon as over-production ceases usually become disillusioned when later almost universal poverty appears. . . . Perhaps the secret, then is to be found in the machinery of distribution. Between the producer and the consumer there must be a chasm in need of a bridge. But no; there are plenty of *physical* bridges, ships and canals—only the shippers are few.

There is, however, another distributive mechanism whose name is money. There is no more reason why this money-mechanism should be proof against getting out of order than a railroad or a ship-canal. Moreover, profits are measured in money. If money, by any chance, should become deranged, is it not at least possible that it would *affect all profits, in one way, at one time?*

In the October, 1933, issue of *Econometrica* he wrote a paper on "The Debt-Deflation Theory of Great Depressions." In it he aimed partly to summarize the conclusions reached in *Booms and Depressions*, "and partly to fit them into the conclusions of other students in this field." Here in briefest form was the meat of his book "purposely expressed dogmatically and without proof. But it is not a creed in the sense that my faith does not rest on evidence and that I am not ready to modify it on presentation of new evidence. On the contrary, it is quite tentative."

The following paragraphs have been condensed from this paper, and occasionally paraphrased for the sake of further brevity:

The old and still persistent notion of "the" business cycle, as a single self-generating cycle, is a myth. There are many forces, many co-existing cycles. The tendencies making mostly for economic dis-equilibrium fall under three headings: (a) growth or trend tendencies, (b) haphazard disturbances, (c) cyclical tendencies.

There are two sorts of cyclical tendencies. One is "forced" or imposed on the economic mechanism from outside, either by astronomical forces or custom or religion. The "free" cycle, not "forced" but self-generating, operates analogously to a pendulum or wave motion. It is the "free" type which is apparently uppermost in the minds of most people when they talk of "the" business cycle.

There may be equilibrium which, though stable, is so delicately poised that, after departure from it beyond certain limits, instability ensues. Such a disaster is somewhat like the "capsizing" of a ship which, under ordinary conditions, is always near stable equilibrium but which, after being tipped beyond a certain angle, has no longer this tendency to return to equilibrium, but, instead, a tendency to depart further from it.

Ordinarily and within wide limits, all economic variables tend toward a stable equilibrium. Unless some outside force intervenes, any "free" oscillations about equilibrium must tend progressively to grow smaller, just as a rocking chair set in motion tends to stop. But the exact equilibrium thus sought is seldom reached and never long maintained. Theoretically there may be over- or under-production, over- or under-consumption, and over or under everything else. It is as absurd to assume that the variables in the economic organization will "stay put," in perfect equilibrium, as to assume that the Atlantic Ocean can ever be without a wave.

In practice, general over-production has never been a chief cause of great dis-equilibrium. The reason for the common notion of over-production is mistaking too little money for too much goods. While any deviation from equilibrium of any economic variable theoretically may, and doubtless in practice does, set up some sort of oscillations, the important question is: Which of them have been sufficiently great disturbers to afford any substantial explanation of the great booms and depressions of history?

There is some grain of truth in most of the alleged explanations commonly offered but this grain is often small. Any of them may suffice to explain *small* disturbances, but all of them put together have probably been inadequate to explain *big* disturbances. In particular, I doubt the adequacy of over-production, under-consumption, over-capacity, price-dislocation, maladjustment between agricultural and industrial prices, over-confidence, over-investment, over-saving, and the discrepancy between savings and investment.

In the great booms and depressions, each of these factors has played a subordinate role as compared with two dominant factors, *over-indebtedness* and *deflation*. These two economic maladies are more important causes than all others put together. Some of the minor factors often derive some importance when

252

combined with one or both of the two dominant factors. Thus over-investment and over-speculation are often important; but they would have far less serious results were they not conducted with borrowed money.

In addition to the two primary factors, debt and deflation, there are seven secondary factors, making in all nine variables, as follows: debts, circulating media, their velocity of circulation, price levels, net worths, profits, trade, business confidence, interest rates. The chief interrelations between these nine factors may be derived deductively, assuming that, at some point of time, a state of over-indebtedness exists.

Then we may deduce the following chain of consequences: (1) Debt liquidation leads to distress selling and to (2) Contraction of deposit currency, as bank loans are paid off, and to a slowing down of velocity of circulation. This causes (3) A fall in the level of prices, (4) A still greater fall in the net worths of business, precipitating bankruptcies and (5) A like fall in profits, which in a private-profit society, leads the concerns which are running at a loss to make (6) A reduction in output, in trade and in employment. These losses lead to (7) Pessimism and loss of confidence, which in turn lead to (8) Hoarding and slowing down still more the velocity of circulation. These eight changes cause (9) Complicated disturbances in the rates of interest, in particular, a fall in the nominal, or money, rates and a rise in the real, or commodity, rates of interest.

In actual chronology, the order of the nine events is somewhat different from the above "logical" order, and there are reactions and repeated effects. But it should be noted that, except for the first and last in the "logical" list, all the fluctuations listed come about through a fall in prices.

When over-indebtedness stands alone, that is, does *not* lead to a fall of prices, the resulting "cycle" will be far milder. Likewise, when a deflation occurs from other than debt causes and without any great volume of debt, the resulting evils are much less. It is the combination of both—the debt disease coming first, then precipitating the dollar disease—which works the greatest havoc.

If the over-indebtedness with which we started was great enough, the liquidations of debts cannot keep up with the fall of prices which it causes. In that case, the liquidation defeats itself. While it diminishes the number of dollars owed, it may not do so as fast as it increases the value of each dollar owed. Then, the very effort of individuals to lessen their burden of debts increases it, because of the mass effect of the stampede to liquidate in swelling each dollar owed. Then we have the great paradox: *The more the debtors pay, the more they owe.* The more the economic boat tips, the more it tends to tip.

The debts of 1929 were the greatest known, both nominally and really, up to that time. They were great enough not only to "rock the boat" but to start it capsizing. By March, 1933, liquidation had reduced the debts about 20 per cent, but had increased the dollar about 75 per cent, so that the *real* debt, as measured in terms of commodities, was increased about 40 per cent.

Unless some counteracting cause comes along to prevent the fall in the price level, such a depression as that of 1929-33 tends to continue, going deeper, in a vicious spiral, for many years. On the other hand, it is always economically possible to stop or prevent such a depression simply by reflating the price level up to the average level at which outstanding debts were contracted, and then maintaining that level unchanged.

254

That the price level is controllable is not only claimed by monetary theorists but has recently been evidenced by two great events: (1) Sweden has now for nearly two years maintained a stable price level, practically always within 2 per cent of the chosen par and usually within 1 per cent. (2) The fact that immediate reversal of deflation is easily achieved by the use of appropriate instrumentalities has just been demonstrated by President [Franklin] Roosevelt.

Those who imagine that Roosevelt's avowed reflation is not the cause of our recovery but that we had "reached the bottom anyway" are very much mistaken. Had not "artificial respiration" been applied, we would have seen general bankruptcies, insolvency of our government, and some form of political revolution.

If reflation can now so easily and quickly reverse the deadly down-swing of deflation after nearly four years, it would have been easier to have stopped it earlier. It would have been still easier to have prevented the depression almost altogether. In fact, in my opinion, this would have been done had Governor Strong of the Federal Reserve Bank of New York lived, or had his policies been pursued after his death. In that case, there would have been nothing worse than the first crash. We would have had the debt disease, but not the dollar disease—the bad cold but not the pneumonia.

In summary, we find that (1) economic changes include steady trends and unsteady occasional disturbances which act as starters for cyclical oscillations of innumerable kinds; (2) among the many occasional disturbances, are new opportunities to invest; (3) these, with other causes, sometimes conspire to lead to a great volume of over-indebtedness; (4) this, in turn, leads to attempts to liquidate; (5) these, in turn, lead (unless counteracted by reflation) to falling prices or a swelling dollar; (6) the dollar may swell faster than the number of dollars owed shrinks; (7) in that case, liquidation does not really liquidate but actually aggravates the debts, and the depression grows worse instead of better; (8) the ways out are either via laissez faire (bankruptcy) or scientific medication (reflation).

The concluding chapters of *Booms and Depressions* discussed palliatives, remedies and the world movement for stable money, with more than a glance in the direction of the compensated-dollar plan and other proposed solutions. Here are his final paragraphs, in considerably condensed form:

What we call the Capitalistic System might better be called the System of Private Profits; and a depression, being a profit disease, is one to which Capitalism is peculiarly liable. Nicholas Murray Butler has recently affirmed that the system is on trial today. Unless Capitalism shall clean house by taking the dirt of depression out of profits, some form of Socialism may tear the house completely down.

Socialistic thinkers of all degrees make common cause against private profits, and add that, without such profits, crises would disappear. Accordingly, in 1929-32, the plight of the capitalistic world drew a good deal of derision from the Russians, who, though not prosperous, were apparently going up while we were going down.

I shall not here debate the comparative merits of the two systems. Each system has been compelled to borrow from the other. The Capitalistic system, for instance, is not wholly capitalistic: witness government itself, public schools, the post office, and the

Panama Canal. On the other hand, Russia, which furnishes the only large-scale example of a socialistic experiment, has, in ten years, drifted perhaps as far toward Capitalism as we, in a thousand years, have drifted toward Socialism.

Writing in the July, 1948, issue of *Econometrica*, from which several passages have already been quoted, Professor Schumpeter made these concluding comments:

> The monetary reformer also stepped in to impair both the scientific and the practical value of Fisher's contributions to business-cycle research. But in themselves they are much more important than most of us seem to realize. They are models of econometric research and have perhaps influenced the development of its standard procedure. With admirable intuition, he listed all the more important "starters" of the cyclical movement.
>
> But in order to realize this, we must again perform an operation of "scrapping the facade." The "starters" are not where they belong, viz., in the place of honor at the beginning. They are shoved into Chapter IV. On the surface, we have overindebtedness and the process of its deflation, "the root of almost all the evils." And expansion and contraction of debt, associated as they are with rising and falling price levels, land us again in monetary reform, the subject Fisher was really interested in when he wrote the book.
>
> This time the Compensated Dollar, while still recommended, received but modest emphasis. Instead of the vigorous advocacy of this particular plan that we found in *The Purchasing Power of Money*, we find in Part III of *Booms and Depressions* (entitled Factual) a simple and popularly worded survey of means of monetary control in which hardly any economist will

find matter for disagreement and which includes practically all the policies of "reflation" that were either adopted or proposed in the subsequent years. I do not want to belittle the merit or to question the wisdom, of almost everything Fisher wrote there. On the contrary, considering the date of publication, I believe him to be entitled to more credit than he received. But I do wish to emphasize that this was not the only merit of the book and that, though but imperfectly sketched, something much larger and deeper looms behind the facade.

The *Investigations, Appreciation and Interest, The Nature of Capital and Income, The Theory of Interest, The Purchasing Power of Money, Booms and Depressions,* are the pillars and arches of a temple that was never built. From Cantillon through A. Smith, J. S. Mill, and Marshall, leaders of economic thought made their impression, on their epoch and on posterity, by systematic treatises. Fisher never expounded his thought in this way. The busy crusader had no time for it. He formed no school. He had many pupils but no disciples. In his crusades, he joined forces with many groups and individuals. In his scientific work, he stood almost alone.

Strange as it may seem in the case of a man of such monolithic purity of purpose, of such width of social sympathies, of such unqualified adherence to one of the ruling slogans of his day—stabilization—he always remained outside of the current and always failed to convince either his contemporaries or the rising generations. But those pillars and arches will stand by themselves. They will be visible long after the sands will have smothered much that commands the scene today.

Three small books followed close on the heels of *Booms and Depressions.* They were tracts, not treatises. Each aimed to widen the base of informed public opinion on the subject of monetary reform, so that pressure might be brought on "the powers that be" for effective remedial action to end the depression. One book was scarcely released when changed conditions influenced the author to undertake another, in an effort to attack the problem from a slightly different angle.

In May, 1933, he published a slim book which he simply called *Inflation?* In addition to being a further popularization of the commodity dollar plan, this book tried to interpret current events in Washington for the benefit of the bewildered layman, who, even though he may have vaguely approved President Roosevelt's "reflation" policy, did not pretend to understand it. Like the stock market book, this one was so timely that it was outdated thirty days after publication.

Five months later he revised it and brought it up to date under the title: *After Reflation, What?* At that time he hoped that President Roosevelt would follow up his reflation policy with permanent stabilization. In lieu of a dedication, the book opened with two quotations, each dated July 3, 1933. The first was an excerpt from the President's radiogram to the London Economic Conference: "The United States of America seeks the kind of a dollar which a generation hence will have the same purchasing power and debt-paying power as the dollar we hope to attain in the near future." The other was a contemporary comment on this radiogram by the British economist, John Maynard Keynes: "Mr. Roosevelt ... is magnificently right."

Sandwiched in between these two topical books was an equally brief but somewhat more specialized volume called *Stamp Scrip.* It recorded the history of a phenomenon which sprang up spontaneously in many communities throughout the country. The author of the book did not originate the plan, but officials of more than five hundred municipalities in every state of the union sought his advice on the best methods of instituting such a program as the book described. This voluminous correspondence now reposes in the archives of the New York Public Library. The book was written largely to simplify this correspondence and to offer a concise answer to the many problems arising from such an undertaking.

Admittedly a temporary pump-priming expedient, the scheme was to place certificates in circulation locally, which would be self-redeeming, by virtue of the fact that the holder was required to affix a special two-cent stamp on the back each week. The dollar required for redeeming the certificate at the end of its year of circulation was thus collected by the municipality through the sale of stamps. In the meantime, it served the community like ordinary money, except that its velocity of circulation took a noticeable upturn just before the weekly date when a new stamp had to be affixed. Although the plan attacked the problem at "a minor point" the author of *Stamp Scrip* felt it might well become "a key point" in stimulating recovery by temporarily expanding the circulating media of the community and thus counteracting the ill effects of a prolonged period when money was abnormally scarce.

After adding these three items to the growing shelf-full of books on stabilization, he undertook to write, at a somewhat more leisurely pace, *Stable Money, a History of the Movement*, with the assistance of Hans R. L. Cohrssen. This volume contained 425 pages, the last fifty of which were devoted to appendices. A sizable portion of the autobiographical section of this book was included in the chapter on the commodity dollar. It went to press in August, 1934, and was dedicated to President Roosevelt.

The introduction again quoted President Roosevelt's radio message to the London Economic Conference, then continued: "Although the President has expressed the same thought many times, so that millions on millions of people must have heard it, and although his influence on the average man's ideas is far greater than that of any one else in America and probably in the world, nevertheless the ordinary ear is still deaf even to the mere idea of stable money —all because, behind that ear is a brain in which, as a fixed part of its 'mental furniture,' is the almost ineradicable 'money illusion.'

"But fortunately, besides such naive and unreasoning popular psychology, there are always a saving few who learn the lessons of history. Just as New York City got its health department seventy years ago from an epidemic, just as many cities get a good fire department after a bad fire, and just as safety at sea became a new object of solicitude after the Titanic disaster; so a stable dollar can come only after instability has worked enough havoc to cause some pivotal men to be emancipated from the money illusion."

The book was "intended to be not so much a history of these catastrophes, due to unstable money and endured by unsuspecting millions subject to the money illusion, but rather a history of the efforts of a few to remedy or prevent such catastrophes. . . . Only a few even now realize that the waning of Hoover and the waxing of Roosevelt were little more than the political reaction to an enlargement of the dollar. . . . Some historians do realize that deflation 'made' Bryan politically and that subsequent inflation 'unmade' him. . . . Lord D'Abernon, one of the keenest British students of money, went so far as to say that, in his opinion, 80% of the labor discontent in Europe after the War was due to this cause." Unstable money is not "the

261

sole economic determiner of history," but "its role is a big one."

In spite of the special efforts by the Stable Money Association and the Committee for the Nation to see that the book achieved a wide distribution, "the ordinary ear" remained deaf to the propaganda. The Committee for the Nation was made up of public-spirited men who hoped to prime the pumps of industry so as to put the economic machinery in working order again. The next chapter deals with Father's round-the-clock efforts to effect national as well as personal recovery.

16. Fighting the Depression

A chart might be made to plot the course of Father's personal fortunes, simply by listing the succession of cars which he owned. The 1916 Dodge lasted four years. It was followed by two Buicks in fairly rapid succession; and when Index Visible began to pay off in 1925 he splurged with a chauffeur-driven Lincoln. Then late in the summer of 1929, while he was spending $30,000 to enlarge his offices, he acquired a La Salle convertible for his personal use and invested in a Stearns-Knight, one of the few American cars which could justly be classed with the Rolls-Royce. The Stearns survived seven years, largely because there were so few potential buyers during the depression. But in 1936 it was supplanted by a Tudor Ford, which in turn gave way to a slightly used Buick two years later.

The stock market crash found Father heavily in debt, not because of car purchases or office expansions, but because he had borrowed from the banks, in order to take advantage of his mouth-watering "rights" to buy additional Remington Rand stock, which accrued to him as an outgrowth of the original merger agreement. He also subscribed heavily to several younger enterprises, hoping that by getting in on the ground floor they might pay off as spectacularly as Index Visible. Some of these ventures, seen with the advantage of hindsight, make him appear rather gullible. Others might well have turned out profitably except for their unfortunate timing with respect to the crash. But the promoter of what was perhaps the most promising of them was so carried away by enthusiasm in his stock-selling operations that he was eventually indicted for misrepresentation; and while Father's trial testimony was filling the front pages of the New York papers, I overheard two strangers discussing the lurid details at the table next to mine in a restaurant. One of them summed it all up thus: "Gosh, he's supposed to know all the answers, and look how he got burned!"

Even when things looked blackest, Father never gave way to defeatism, but remained amazingly optimistic. The bare facts of his financial history, stated bluntly, sound rather lurid. An impecunious scholar marries a well-to-do girl, pyramids his own fortune on top of hers, then fritters everything away in foolish speculation. But his case was by no means that simple. His 1925 letter to me, given at the end of Chapter 13, reveals the fundamental unselfishness of his motives in seeking more worldly goods—in order to promote his favorite causes. Being human, however, he was not content with scoring a single ten-strike but succumbed to the temptation of reaching for half a dozen more.

He hoped to build his fortune into something so substantial that he would be able to establish a foundation to carry on his good works after his own death. With this eventual purpose in mind, in 1928 he gave Carol and myself a small proportion of his Remington Rand stock for us to have as nest-eggs, so that in his will he could leave the bulk of his estate to the foundation. His wire to me in California, replying to my inquiry about the advisability of selling some of my Remington Rand in order to diversify, reflects his current state of mind:

November 17, 1928

SUGGEST YOU MIGHT RISK HALF YOUR PRESENT HOLD-INGS BY BORROWING ON IT AS COLLATERAL AND USING PROCEEDS OF LOAN FOR BUYING MORE. SIX MONTHS OR A YEAR LATER YOU COULD PROBABLY SELL AT SUBSTAN-TIAL ADVANCE AND THEN DIVERSIFY.

I disregarded this advice, but we would each have fared much better if we had followed it to the letter. At the peak of the boom Father could have liquidated enough of his Remington Rand stock to pay off all his heavy bank loans, and still have retained a net of between eight and ten million dollars. Instead, he waited for that elusive additional rise which never came, and lost his proverbial shirt. Just before the crash Remington Rand was selling for $58 per share. A year later it was still worth $28 per share. This seemed like a dizzy figure in comparison with its ultimate nadir, when it sank to one dollar.

Though I never heard him use it as an alibi, the crucial period of the 1929 decline coincided with his Mother's final illness. (She was eighty-three when she died and had been a widow for forty-five years.) Even if this personal anxiety had not conspired to distract his attention at such a critical moment, the end result would probably have been the same, because his unquenchable optimism was such a two-edged weapon. Without it he could hardly have carried on, but it also blinded him to the possibility of accepting his comparatively moderate 1929 losses and goaded him on to full disaster. His J. Willard Gibbs address at Des Moines on the last day of 1929 contained no hint of his personal worries; nor did the books which he was writing at that time. As his position worsened, when all his collateral was pledged with the banks, including Mother's blue-chip Allied Chemical and Dye stock, and when the banks were clamoring for more collateral or a reduction of loans, he found himself in the unenviable position of asking Aunt Caroline to lend him a sizable block of her Allied Chemical stock, to bolster his position at the banks. At one midway plateau in 1932, when he was sure that the tide had finally turned, he proudly restored part of this collateral to her intact, not foreseeing that the continuing deflationary spiral would virtually wipe him out and necessitate his liquidating the remainder of her collateral, leaving him with an ultimate debt to her of roughly three quarters of a million dollars.

Perhaps as an indirect result of all these financial worries, he was laid low with an attack of pneumonia in January, 1931, which might easily have ended the career of someone less resilient. At the same time he and Mother were undergoing the additional strain of Carol's divorce proceedings, which had been pending for several years. Viewed against the background of their own "ideal" marriage, Carol's divorce—ten years after her Four-sixty wedding and Whimsy Cot honeymoon—was in some respects more difficult to accept than Margaret's death. Not the least difficult feature was the separation of their two grandchildren, because the girl accompanied her mother to Switzerland, while the boy remained in Ohio with his father. Once the divorce was accomplished my parents took it more philosophically, and Father quickly rebounded from his pneumonia, to attack the problems of the depression with renewed vigor.

That April he journeyed to Santa Barbara, to seek further assistance from Aunt Caroline. On the westward journey he carefully reviewed all the detailed figures, and wrote Mother that their combined net worth was still more than a million, "but some of the assets need nursing, or they will crumble to dust. Our predicament is not any nearness to a zero valuation, but lack of cash." From Santa Barbara he wired her of the successful completion of his mission, and on the return journey he wrote from the train:

> April 20, 1931
>
> The relief and satisfaction from Sister's help are very great. She is helping purely on the basis of love and affection—for you particularly. She was severe at times, but not unjustly so and she was throughout most sympathetic.
>
> I'm sorry to have made mistakes causing me to be such a nuisance, but I think Sister is quite reconciled to whatever may happen, if my optimism misfires; and rather enjoys being a *Dea ex Machina*, the great power to solve the problem.

As his position deteriorated still further and Aunt Caroline finally appreciated its magnitude and complexity, she felt obliged to turn over the handling of all the intricate details of their financial relationship to a committee consisting of her lawyer and two nephews. Though Father realized how distasteful discussion of every minute ramification was to her, he found the new arrangement very constricting. He had always been superconscious of the sharp line of demarcation between generations, and disliked having to render an accounting to such "youngsters," despite their admitted maturity of judgment. At best it was a cumbersome arrangement, but everyone concerned managed to steer an amazingly even course through the treacherous waters. Afterwards Father felt, however, that the final reckoning need not have been quite so disastrous for him or for Aunt Caroline, if he could have been freer to make quick decisions at the most critical stages.

Intermingled with these personal tribulations were the professional activities mentioned in the preceding chapter and his continuing efforts to solve the problem of the Depression on the national level. With regard to the latter, he was especially energetic during the final year of the Hoover administration and in the first months of the New Deal. Early in the crisis he sought and was granted an interview with under-Secretary of the Treasury Ogden Mills, to suggest five alternative ways by which the price level might be raised, in order to end the vicious downward spiral. In a letter to Mother written after this meeting with Mills, he wrote: "I told him he and Hoover should choose *some* way and go right after it."

In accordance with his usual practice he attended the year-end sessions of the American Economic Association, of which he was a former president, the American Statistical Association and the newly formed Econometric Society, for both of which he served as president in 1932. As noted in the previous chapter, he also addressed the American Association for the Advancement of Science at New Orleans on the first day of January, 1932, on "The Debt-Deflation Theory of Depressions." His letter to Mother written en route from New Orleans to Washington enumerated various compliments friends had paid him at these gatherings and continued:

January 3, 1932

... But the most pleasing thing is that this new generation of rising economists is following in the path which I tried to block out. I hope they may make Economics a truer science and more like the older sciences. I switched from Gibbs' sort of work to Economics in the hope of helping lay the foundations.

For years I was greatly disappointed because there seemed so little market for my wares and so much resistance to their novelty. But now of a sudden I'm realizing that the seed planted really took root.

The sixty-five-year milestone found him in Florida, where he visited Dr. Kellogg at Miami Battle Creek and participated in the Rollins College animated magazine at Winter Park. On this occasion he and Jane Addams and Edward A. Filene were among those who were awarded honorary degrees. After the impressive ceremonies he wrote Mother: "Bouquets are grateful after years of bricks thrown at me, though I haven't minded them and have had all the recognition I deserve anyway." A few days later he lectured on the depression to an overflowing audience in one of the college auditoriums, and wrote Mother: "President Holt said he did not see how I could make so technical a subject so clear."

A month later he testified for a day and a half before a Congressional hearing on the Goldsborough bill for stabilization, which was largely an embodiment of his own suggestions on the subject. At Goldsborough's request he stayed in Washington an extra day to correct the stenographer's transcript of his testimony. "This took me from noon yesterday till eleven last night. 'Long-winded' did I hear you say? 'Not a superfluous word in the book,' say I!" He talked again with Mills and also with Eugene Meyer, head of the Federal Reserve system, but he had no success in convincing them of the necessity for reflation and stabilization. These excerpts from his letters to Mother convey his impressions of the Washington kaleidoscope:

WASHINGTON, May 18, 1932

Jim Rand (President of Remington Rand) and I saw Goldsborough before the hearing, then listened to Meyer and Adolph Miller. After lunch, I was called again and made my second talk, answering Meyer and Miller.

A dispatch from London arrived too late for me to use in my testimony, showing that two former Chancellors of the Exchequer, Horne and Churchill, and the present Chancellor Chamberlain have come out for reflation and stabilization—my program and Goldsborough's. Everything seems to be coming my way now on this subject. After dinner Jim and I called on Carter Glass but got nowhere.

NEW HAVEN, June 1, 1932

I called Mr. Rand in Buffalo from New York yesterday (on his own wire) but he had not tabulated any returns from his questionnaire to Bankers (gotten up for Hoover, very confidential). An hour ago Jim called me here and read me the returns to date. They looked good.

He sent out the questionnaire to 15,556 Bank Presidents. 2,245 returns had so far been tabulated. 1524 to 393 favored balancing the budget immediately. Large appropriations for public works were frowned on, 310 being for and 1804 against. 1218 favored Rand's gold-silver dollar idea. 1758 to 309 favored cutting the tariff in two, if other countries will do the same. The grand scheme of U. S. selling Bonds for time deposits, which I believe would "do the trick" brought 1086 replies for and 895 against.

Did you notice this morning that U. S. is favorable to England's suggestion of a conference on stabilizing the price level? This was also in the questionnaire and the Banks favored it 1497 to 536. I tried to get such a conference in the Taft administration, but it did not reach a vote in the House. In Wilson's administration, they never got to it before the War. In 1927 I planned to get Mussolini to do it. Now at last it is in sight.

NEW HAVEN, June 2, 1932

Last night, after I had gotten to bed, Rand called from Buffalo to say that Hoover had called him to ask for the figures. Rand said he had mailed them. Hoover said he couldn't wait and wanted them for an all-night conference.

Rand couldn't get them in Buffalo, as they were locked in his safe down town, and he couldn't think of any faster way of getting them than phoning me. So I trotted down stairs and phoned him back the figures.

WASHINGTON, June 29, 1932

Much to my surprise when I phoned the White House, Sec'y Ritchie said I could see the President at six. I have just come from there.

I was taken upstairs where the President has a desk. He did not look as tired as I expected but he seemed disgusted and discouraged. I told him I had come to think that the "Rand plan" was our best bet now. He said the trouble was that the Banks would not function voluntarily. They were selfishly seeking their own liquidity and though they had been handed several billions already they were not passing it on to the public. I said we could not blame the individual bank, as it had to save itself and devil take the hindmost.

270 ·

He said it might be better for the Government to lend direct. I said there was not time. A servant brought in two orangeades. He asked me to go over the plan step by step.

As I was going he asked if I had seen the Democratic wet plank and showed me a typed copy. I said that would put prohibition into the campaign and I was sorry. He said he was.

I must have been with him a half hour, the longest I ever had with a President.

WASHINGTON, June 30, 1932

I've tried to see Mills and Meyer today but could not get appointments. I think I've done all I can by seeing Hoover, though I'm not very optimistic now.

I'm rather glad the Democrats have made Prohibition the issue. It will, to some extent, prevent the campaign frightening the public over the economic problems, which they don't and can't understand.

In July a group of Connecticut Republicans urged Father to run for the Senate, either in place of the current incumbent Hiram Bingham, in the unlikely event that the state organization would consent to switch horses, or on an Independent ticket, which they hoped might split the Republican vote sufficiently to defeat Bingham. Father replied that he would "rather run in the triangular race and get defeated than run instead of Bingham and get sentenced to six years in the Senate." A few days later he wrote Mother: "I'm inclined to think I'd better try for the Senate after all. It fits in after my work at Yale is finished and the book (*Booms and Depressions*) is off. The Senators are just the ones who need to be educated." He finally decided against running, however, feeling that he could contribute more by remaining on the side lines.

Toward the end of July he went to Albany to interview the Democratic nominee, Franklin Roosevelt, whom he had first met during the Cox campaign twelve years before. En route to Albany he wrote to Mother: "Now is the time to educate him." After the election he expressed his disappointment that Roosevelt and Hoover would not cooperate in combating the crisis on a bi-partisan basis during the interval before inauguration, in this letter to Henry L. Stimson:

New Haven, November 11, 1932

Dear Harry:

Although I voted for Hoover, I confess that I was greatly disappointed that no one took the opportunity to educate the public on what the campaign was really all about, namely the depression and the uncorrected deflation which caused it. I suppose this represents the yearnings of an educator as against the requirement of "good politics," but it was a wonderful opportunity missed.

Some months ago in a directors meeting consisting mostly of business men, I suggested and the others agreed that it would be a wonderful reassurance to business especially after the unfortunate "campaign of fear," if Hoover and Roosevelt could bury the hatchet, forget the bruises and blows below the belt, real or fancied, and in the interest of the country get together and keep together between now and March 4. This could, perhaps, be accomplished if Roosevelt were invited to attend Cabinet meetings and if Hoover or Roosevelt or both would make a public statement to the effect that so far as the depression is concerned they were working harmoniously and there would be no great discontinuity in policy. You are the only one in Washington, to whom I could write this without feeling that it would be resented as butting in.

I believe that nothing would be more conducive to Hoover's vindicating himself than his showing a disposition to share the credit with Roosevelt and give him a good start by having him splice the beginning of his policy with the end of Hoover's. It would show that Hoover was not only a "good fighter," as you pointed out and which the public applauded, but also a "good sport," which the public likes particularly.

I shall never forget, after Wilson won over Taft, how Wilcox, Taft's manager and McCormick, Wilson's manager were dramatically brought together at the Gridiron Club dinner in one of its "stunts" and shook hands after a campaign with far more mudslinging than the present one and in which these two men in particular had practically called each other insulting names.

Alvin T. Simonds, a backer of the Harvard Business School and a Vice President of the Stable Money Association, had a private conference all one Sunday in August, 1931, consisting of himself, the Governor of the Federal Reserve Bank of Boston, the Federal Reserve Agent at Boston, the head of the Harvard Business School and myself. We practically all agreed on the importance of bond-buying, such as was adopted a year and a half later and which I had mentioned to you at Woodley a month or two before that conference. But the two Federal Reserve men thought it would be "safer" if they waited! That waiting, in my opinion, cost the country the major part of the depression.

A week before Roosevelt's inauguration he sent the President-elect a nine-page letter outlining his current suggestions for getting the country out of the depression. When the New Deal was scarcely a month old, he returned to Washington to help draft remedial legislation. His letters to Mother describe these hectic days, with particular reference to activities of The Committee for the Nation, consisting of such business leaders as James H. Rand:

WASHINGTON, April 8, 1933

I'm at a public stenographer's waiting for her to copy the manuscript of a bill for stabilizing the dollar after reflation of the price level. The President and most members of both houses of Congress now realize that we *must* do it. The only question is *how*.

I had had a long conference with Goldsborough, Senator Bulkley of Ohio and others. Prof. [George F.] Warren of Cornell came and Rand and several of the Committee for the Nation. The people working out the details now are ex-Senator Owen, Warren, myself and Goldsborough.

WASHINGTON, April 9, 1933

Owen, Warren, Rumely, Goldsborough and I have conferred all day and will meet tomorrow, which will be the third day. Rand, Vanderlip, etc. had one program and Goldsborough and Owen another. They are now combined and after the details are all worked out the result will be taken to the President, as the united suggestion of us all.

WASHINGTON, April 12, 1933

The Committee for the Nation have been having their sessions all day both before and after seeing the President. He did not commit himself, but I am confident that he is for reflation in some way and soon.

I had a talk with Att'y Gen'l Homer Cummings, who spoke quite frankly. I assume Sec'y Woodin is the stumbling block. It is interesting to see how people's moods here go up and down just as mine have done.

I think it is true that F. D. R. is ready to change his mind easily. I believe in this for myself, but it is very worrisome to have a President do it. He seems now to be wobbly about Bank Deposit Guarantee, because New York bankers via Woodin have questioned it again. But Senator Glass, now that he has been won over to it, is as determined for it as he was against it and resents Woodin's defection.

When the President's program was fully crystallized a week later and the gold standard definitely abandoned, Father expressed his elation in this letter to Mother:

WASHINGTON, April 19, 1933

Now I *am* sure—so far as we ever can be sure of anything—that we are going to snap out of this depression fast. I am now one of the happiest men in the world. Happy that we are to get back prosperity, happy to have had a share in the work which turned the scales and in the laying of the foundations years ago. I feel that this week marks the culmination of my life work. Even if I had no more of life, I would feel that what I have had has been as worth while as any man has a right to expect.

Even you haven't really known what I've been through this last month, between the mountain and the precipice. I felt that the only hope lay, not only for the country which is the important thing but for our own little selves, in Washington here; and the balance trembled back and forth. It is evident that F. D. R. has not until recently been sure which turn to take. Now that the right turn has been taken my work is over, except for details.

My next big job is to raise money for ourselves. Probably we'll have to go to Sister again, but I hope

275

this can be avoided. I have defaulted payments the last few weeks, because I did not think it was fair to ask Sister for money when there was a real chance that I could never pay it back.

I mean that if F. D. R. had followed Glass we would have been pretty surely ruined. So would Allied Chemical, Sister, and the U. S. Gov't. The great prairie fire was ready to destroy everything before it. *Now* I can go to Sister with a clean conscience and a restored faith that she will not lose anything.

Today the peg which kept our dollar up in foreign exchange has been pulled out. And lo! The stocks and commodities soar at once! It seems miraculous to those not versed in these mysteries. And there will be grumbling and misunderstanding without end.

WASHINGTON, May 4, 1933

I'm just back from the U. S. Chamber of Commerce dinner at which President Roosevelt spoke. It is wonderful to have things coming my way so fast. He spoke of raising the price level and getting international cooperation.

The greatest news is that last night to a group of friends he definitely committed himself to reflation to the 1926 level and *stabilizing* at that level. We may thank God that we have a President who has the knowledge, understanding and courage to see and do what must be done.

Three months later he visited Hyde Park for the first of two interviews with President Roosevelt, which he described in this detailed letter to Mother:

POUGHKEEPSIE, August 9, 1933

This is a letter "for the record" which please keep for future reference. I'm writing it in the Poughkeep-

276

sie R. R. station waiting for the train to New York after a half hour with the President—while our talk is still fresh in my memory.

The house is a very livable appearing one. The day was perfect and I really enjoyed every minute of the long wait, spending part of it on the big flag-paved roof-less entrance porch in the sun with a view of the blue sky above the big green trees surrounding the house and a vista of a cornfield. But most of the time I waited in the big hall and used some of the time writing out headings to cover what I wanted to say and to leave with the President.

One other person (a Mr. McEmery I think) was waiting and before I was called, Att'y Gen'l Cummings and Mrs. Cummings came with an assistant. Secretary McIntyre also came and went using the phone several times.

A limousine drove up and a fine looking lady came in. I had already realized who it was before she came up to me and said, "I'm the President's mother. Does the President know you are waiting?" She phoned, then went upstairs. Shortly after, two small children and a colored nurse came in and went upstairs, the children laughing happily. But at the top of the stairs one of them tripped, fell and cried and then I heard Madame R. say, "Don't cry" and when that did not avail "Granny doesn't like crying babies. We'll have to put you to bed and give you a long rest just like a baby" which seemed slowly to bring results.

Later Madame R. came downstairs and said "I'm sorry to see you are still waiting; come into the library." So we went there joining Mr. & Mrs. Cummings and then out into her "mosquito room" when, at last Sec'y McIntyre came and said the President was ready to see me.

I was led through a tortuous back hallway to a tiny room where the President was sitting and signing some documents. He said cordially "Well, how are *you?*"—was sorry for keeping me waiting but had had imperative demands on his time because of the Cuban situation which was serious.

I said, "Then you are pressed for time?"

"Very."

"Would you rather I'd come some other time?"

"Oh, no."

"Shall I take five minutes? Or what?"

"Fifteen or twenty will be all right."

He used most of the time himself asking what I thought of how to solve various problems and evidently being really anxious to get my opinions. He seemed also to be convinced or impressed by my answers which evidently gave him some new ideas. I don't think he was merely trying to be polite. He referred to his talk yesterday with Warren and [James Harvey] Rogers and "Jimmie Warburg."

He said "J. W. wants me to fix a definite price of gold etc. as people now can't make future contracts. I said 'that's poppy-cock. The bankers want to know everything beforehand and I've told them to go to he——.' "

As he apparently didn't hesitate to tell Warburg he was wrong, I think he would have told me. In fact he did raise objections and in one case said "That's a splendid idea but it would require legislation" to which I replied, "Yes, that precludes it for the present. I keep forgetting that you're not the whole government!" which made him smile.

It was the most satisfactory talk I ever had with a President and the most important. I have had talks with Theodore Roosevelt, Taft, Wilson, Harding and Hoover. They were all very nice to me but I never

278

felt I got as good a reception of my message before.

He began by asking if I agreed with Warren and Rogers that if he (Roosevelt) got the Federal Reserve to buy newly mined gold at say $29 an ounce it would help raise commodity prices. I said I did and read him No. 2 of the headings which I had prepared:

2. Open a free market for gold in New York— U. S. to buy gold at market price and offer to sell gold at not less than say $30 an ounce for the present.

When he asked me what I thought about announcing his proposed price level, I read him my No. 1:

1. Declare your objective to be a price level up at least to within 10% of the level of 1926 and not to be above 1926, dependent on the absorption of unemployment.

He seemed to like that, especially the last re the unemployment, and said "That's a good way to put it." He repeated what he has publicly said re raising the price level to the average level at which debts were contracted.

He asked if I'd advise the Federal Reserve soon to both buy and sell gold at say $30 an ounce. I explained that it would be well to have two prices, one for buying and a higher one for selling (by the Government). He had apparently not thought of that. I told him otherwise whenever the Government announced a rise in price, speculators would buy of U. S. today and resell to U. S. tomorrow. He saw the point at once. I showed how this speculation, injurious to U. S., would be avoided by two prices. He said "How far apart would you have them?" I said "Not over 2% and perhaps only 1% but now I'd have more."

He asked how often I'd have the Federal Reserve go into the gold market. He said Rogers thought once a week but he thought that would be too often. I told him I thought once a week or oftener.

He asked what I thought of his trying to get England to cut loose from the franc and tie the pound to the dollar. I said I thought that would be *great* and that if U. S. and England both adopted a commodity standard in place of the gold standard the whole world would, and that in England there was more understanding of all this than in U. S., mentioning McKenna, d'Abernon, Vernon, Stamp, etc.

He agreed and said "Even Neville Chamberlain seems to be coming round but not Montagu Norman." He said "If we do this, what ratio should we adopt between the dollar and the pound?"

I said I would ask England to select its *price level* first and U. S. to select its own and then fix the ratio of money to match. That seemed to appeal to him and I pointed out that just as he had said in his message to the London Economic Conference that U. S. wanted to select its own price level, England would want to too.

I read him my other three suggestions:

3. Open closed banks, or at any rate give the depositors their money by buying preferred stock or buying the banks' frozen assets.

4. U. S. to lend to each employer $2 per day for 100 days for each additional employee added to the payroll—without interest for the 100 days and thereafter with interest for one year. For this job commandeer the Commercial Investment Trust and have the banks act as its agents, using as security (if needed) accounts receivable.

5. Recall gold certificates in exchange for old ones and for any presented after Sept. 1 tax them at very high rate. The gov't could then

take the gold now held against any not presented before Sept. 1 and probably realize a profit of $200,000,000 because of certificates lost during the last 50 years.

He asked re "4" how U. S. would get the money to lend to employers and we had a long discussion. He seemed not to realise that the Federal Reserve could be forced to disgorge to U. S. gold because its profits are limited to 6% and to have thought that the gold belonged to the banks. I had a talk re using George Le Blanc and he made a note about it. I said G. Le B. was the only banker, except McKenna and Strong, with whom I'd talked who seemed to realise the relation of banking to the price level.

Our talk was alone and undisturbed until McIntyre (who, at the start, had been told "now leave us alone, McIntyre") returned to say that Att'y Gen'l Cummings was very anxious to see him *before* lunch. Pres. R. said "Tell him to wait. We're not quite through." As I went, he said; "I'll hope to see you soon."

He looked well and cheerful, showed no self-consciousness or big-headedness, talked to the point without waste of words and yet without haste. It was wonderful to have so full and satisfying a talk with this, the most powerful man in the world today. But the greatest satisfaction is to realize that at last there is a statesman who has the audacity as well as the understanding to do the things which for twenty years, I've been trying to get done.

I had hoped, you remember, that Mussolini would be the one, but all he did was to stop Italian deflation. Roosevelt is reversing deflation ("reflating") and proposes to tie the dollar to the commodity price level and to get first England and then the whole world to follow.

281

But the realization of Father's dream was not as simple or easy as he anticipated, and two letters which he wrote to me in Europe make it plain that there were several facets of the New Deal with which he was not in complete sympathy:

August 15, 1933

I have meant to write oftener to tell you more of the goings on here. It's all a strange mixture. I'm against the restriction of acreage and production, but much in favor of reflation. Apparently F. D. R. thinks of them as similar—merely two ways of raising prices! But one changes the monetary unit to restore it to normal, while the other spells scarce food and clothing when many are starving and half naked.

I saw F. D. R. a week ago, and found him a *very* satisfactory man to talk to and very much set on carrying out his program. Despite my disagreements on certain things, I think he is a *great* President. A friend of mine, Tom Bayard (formerly Democratic Senator from Delaware) said on inauguration day— *before* F. D. R.'s inaugural address; "Theodore Roosevelt will ultimately be known as 'President of the U. S.—a sixth cousin of the famous President Franklin Roosevelt!'"

March 8, 1934

Yes, the gold act was a fine birthday present (for me); but I can't help feeling that the president could have gone much faster if he hadn't mixed in so many things which were holding us back instead of getting us out of the depression.

The N. R. A. was a National Retardation Affair, as Professor [Willford I.] King says, though I do think in the long run it will be a good thing to get labor, capital and the public to play ball together.

That fall he was summoned to Hyde Park for another talk with the President, the details of which he set down in this brief memorandum:

September 6, 1934

The President said that he had been talking with his uncle, Frederick A. Delano (President of the Stable Money Association) in regard to me and wanted to ask my help in solving what is now his main problem. He wishes to get all the unemployed at work as soon as possible and estimates that it would cost about five billion dollars to provide for the five million men for one year.

He wanted to know how this money could be obtained. He was thinking in terms of employment by the Government rather than re-employment in private industry. I told him I thought the best way was to stimulate re-employment in the old industries as fast as possible, that public works were slow, clumsy, inefficient and costly. I reminded him of the plan that I had offered a year before.

We were interrupted by Mrs. Roosevelt coming to remind the President that he was expected at once to go off to a picnic. He said "Dr. Fisher and I have not finished" and asked if I would come again in the afternoon, which I did. Splitting our engagement in two was really very fortunate, for it gave me an opportunity meanwhile to work out a preliminary answer to his question. When I returned I had a typewritten preliminary answer embodying eleven points, and the President read it out loud, with running comments. When he finished, he said: "Grand! Perfectly grand!"

Father disapproved of the "packing" of the Supreme Court and he looked on the third and fourth terms with disfavor, but he continued writing long letters of advice to the White House. In a four-page document written a few weeks after the 1944 election he suggested positive action under three headings: (1) How to stop inflation and deflation, (2) How to reform "our terrible Federal Income Taxation" in order to encourage savings, and (3) How to convince the business world of the President's loyalty to American free enterprise in contrast to any form of statism.

Improved national conditions did not benefit Father's personal situation as much as he had hoped. The depression had lasted too long. His dark horses died on their feet. That Mother's loyalty to him never wavered throughout his financial tribulations is shown by the expression on her face in the photograph taken on the fortieth anniversary of their wedding in 1933. I can recall hearing only one conversation in which there was even the slightest suggestion of criticism or resentment. Once at Whimsy Cot, Mother asked a little plaintively what Father expected to live on, if his investments remained on a non-dividend-paying basis. He replied with a touch of impatience: "I don't care if they *never* pay dividends, as long as their earnings reveal substantial underlying value." But when earnings sank out of sight, he recognized that these long shots would probably never amount to anything in his lifetime.

To climax his personal difficulties the Internal Revenue Bureau, in a routine examination of his books, discovered a deficiency of nearly $75,000 in the taxes paid for the boom years of 1927 and 1928. The dispute arose because of differing interpretations with respect to certain transactions between Father and half a dozen of his friends, to whom he had "sold" blocks of Remington Rand stock with the privilege of subsequent repurchase at a higher price. By this device he bettered his own cash position without parting permanently with the stock, which he felt sure would continue soaring to a figure even higher than at which he was entitled to repurchase it. He argued that these transactions should really have been considered "loans" rather than "sales" (on which the tax authorities ruled that he should pay a fat Capital Gains tax), but, as his lawyer's brief stated, he had "signed without much examination" the Tax Returns for the years in question. This was an unfortunate instance of delegating too much authority, and the resultant drawn-out and costly litigation came when he could least afford it.

In addition to his main debt to Aunt Caroline, therefore, the continued decline in the stock market made it impossible for him to fulfill these Remington Rand stock repurchase agreements; and when the Internal Revenue men landed on his neck he secured releases from the six or seven individuals concerned, in order to simplify his complicated financial picture, although he continued to consider himself morally obligated to them. In due course the Internal Revenue matter was settled by compromise. To help raise cash Four-sixty was sold to Yale, my parents retaining the privilege of life use. Periodically they discussed the advisability of moving into smaller quarters, which would require a lower rent than the figure stipulated in the contract with Yale, but the Herculean task of moving out of the only home they had known prevented their doing so until after the start of the Second World War.

Partly to enable them to stay at Four-sixty, Aunt Caroline set aside some of her remaining shares of Allied Chemical stock to be held in trust for Mother's benefit. The income from this trust fund together with Father's substantial director's fees from Remington Rand, Sonotone and a few other corporations, enabled them to keep Four-sixty going on a more frugal basis than during the boom years. By cutting out the frills Mother managed to run the large house with one general helper, and Father's drastically reduced office staff rattled around in its cavernous quarters below decks. Even so he had to pay some of the rent to Yale in notes, and in the end he was obliged to ask Yale to cancel the legal obligation of these unpaid notes, although in this case he also considered himself morally obligated. All his remaining assets which had any market value, including Whimsy Cot, were finally turned over to Aunt Caroline in partial settlement of his large debt to her, and in her will she forgave him the balance.

In 1935 Father reached sixty-eight, the prescribed age for retiring from Yale. Since his teaching activity had been limited for some time to a single half-year course, formal retirement meant little change in his routine, other than a slight shifting of emphasis. His declining years were to be anything but inactive.

PART THREE

1935-1947

17. *Active Retirement*

Before his actual retirement from Yale, when the pressure of the first hectic months of the New Deal had lessened, he felt sufficiently relieved to go to Mexico as a delegate to the International Statistical Institute. From there he wrote to Will Eliot:

> PUEBLA, MEXICO, October 17, 1933
>
> Today I had a three-hour interview with General Calles, the "Strong Man of Mexico." He could have remained President all his life I suppose, as Diaz did, but he had the good sense to let others have that office while he, by virtue of his abilities, still remains the center of power.
>
> He has been studying my books, he says, for a long time and recently has had three of them translated into Spanish for his personal use. He told me he had become convinced of the importance of reflation and stabilization, the two parts of my own program now publicly adopted as the program of Mr. Roosevelt.

In the same year that he retired from Yale (1935) he tackled the problem of stable money from a slightly different angle. In a book called *100% Money* he urged the adoption of a plan which was first proposed by a group of University of Chicago economists led by Henry C. Simons and including Paul H. Douglas. Under this plan

289

the banks would be required to keep a 100% reserve behind their checking accounts, rather than the customary 10%. It was "designed to keep checking banks 100% liquid; to prevent inflation and deflation; largely to cure or prevent depressions; and to wipe out much of the National Debt."

Despite the opposition of conservative bankers to the plan the author contended that "the only obstacle standing in the way of adopting *100% Money* is the momentum of the past, which includes (1) a widespread blind and fanatical adherence to the old fashioned gold standard, and (2) the mistaken belief of unenlightened bankers that they can make more money under a partial reserve system."

Prepublication copies of the book were sent to one hundred and fifty laymen, economists and bankers "in order to get criticism from every angle and to test every feature of the plan." The list of those who contributed helpful suggestions included for the first time the name of Professor Schumpeter, the group of University of Chicago economists who had initiated the proposal, Laughlin Currie of the Federal Reserve Board, Spruille Braden, Owen D. Young, Frank A. Vanderlip, George Le Blanc, and two St. Louis bankers, W. L. Gregory and F. R. von Windegger, who had "read two successive drafts of the manuscript. Though, at first, they were doubtful about the merits of the plan, they have, after further study, endorsed it fully."

Robert H. Hemphill, former credit manager of the Atlanta Federal Reserve Bank, contributed a foreword, which said in part:

> To the "man in the street," or to one whose wages, salary or income is paid in currency or coin, banking appears to be a remote subject, in which he can have little direct interest. To such a man it may be a great

surprise to read that the amount of his wages, salary or income depends on the total of loans outstanding by the commercial banks of the nation. And yet such is the case.

The scarcity of money is our paramount national problem. We have ample producing and distributing facilities to supply everyone with an abundance of the essentials for a high standard of living, and we are desperately anxious to produce, but we haven't sufficient money to effect the exchange of our goods and services.

It is only in very recent years that we have collected sufficiently accurate data to calculate the amount of money which must be in circulation to make possible a given national income. We find that this ratio is about one to three.

According to my estimates we had in circulation in 1929 twenty-seven billions of dollars in cash and demand bank deposits. Our national income for 1929 was eighty-one billions of dollars. In 1932 the volume of currency, coin and bank deposits in circulation had shrunk to approximately sixteen billions of dollars, and our national income had shrunk in precisely the same proportion, to approximately forty-eight billions of dollars.

The vast majority of our transactions are paid by checks drawn against the demand deposits in commercial banks. These deposits are created by the commercial banks and the people who borrow from them. . . . Neither the banker nor the borrower ordinarily realizes that a loan just completed is putting into circulation that much new money. Neither realizes that he is starting an endless chain of successive transactions which will continue as long as this credit substitute for money remains in circulation.

If all bank loans were paid, no one would have a bank deposit, and there would not be a dollar of currency or coin in circulation. This is a staggering thought. If the banks create ample synthetic money we are prosperous; if not, we starve.

If all the 14,500 banks of the nation begin calling their loans simultaneously, the aggregate destruction of this synthetic money is enormous. Almost immediately, practically no one seems to have the normal amount of money to spend. This is a "depression." As the depression deepens, prices and values decline and the banks are forced into further and more drastic efforts to preserve their solvency. The principal reason this depression continues is that the banks are not lending, and the money with which to expand business does not exist. That is the essence of the story.

In Professor Fisher's book, he presents in lucid detail the operation of this erratic banking-monetary system, and the obvious remedy. . . . It is so important that our present civilization may collapse unless it is widely understood and the defects remedied very soon.

Here is a brief outline of the proposal and its alleged advantages, as set forth in Chapter 1 of *100% Money:*

Under our present system, the banks create and destroy check-book money by granting, or calling, loans. . . . Thus our national circulating medium is now at the mercy of loan transactions of banks; and our thousands of checking banks are, in effect, so many irresponsible private mints. It is obvious that such a top-heavy system is dangerous—to depositors, to the banks, and above all to the millions of "innocent bystanders," the general public.

Only a few sentences are needed to outline the proposed remedy, which is this:

292

Let the Government, through an especially created "Currency Commission," *turn into cash* enough of the assets of every commercial bank to increase the cash reserve of each bank up to 100% of its checking deposits. Then all check-book money would have actual money—pocket-book money—behind it. (In practice, this could be mostly "credit" on the books of the Commission, as very little tangible money would be called for—less even than at present, so long as the Currency Commission stood ready to supply it on request.)

This new money would merely give an all-cash backing for the checking deposits and would, of itself, neither increase nor decrease the total circulating medium of the country. A bank which previously had $100,000,000 of deposits subject to check with only $10,000,000 of cash behind them (along with $90,000,000 in securities) would send these $90,000,000 of securities to the Currency Commission in return for $90,000,000 more cash, thus bringing its total cash reserve up to $100,000,000, or 100% of the deposits.

After this substitution of actual money for securities had been completed, the bank would be required to maintain *permanently* a cash reserve of 100% against its demand deposits. Thus, the new money would, in effect, be *tied up* by the 100% reserve requirement.

The checking deposit department of the bank would become a mere storage warehouse for bearer money belonging to its depositors. There would then be no practical distinction between the checking deposits and the reserve. The bank's deposits could rise to $125,000,000 only if its cash also rose to $125,000,000. And if deposits shrank (below $100,000,000) it would mean that depositors withdrew some of their stored-up money, taking it out of the bank and put-

293

ting it into their pockets. In neither case would there be any change in the total.

So far as this change to the 100% system would deprive the bank of earning assets and require it to substitute an increased amount of non-earning cash, the bank would be reimbursed through a service charge made to its depositors. . . . In conclusion, if our bankers wish to retain the strictly banking function—loaning—which they can perform better than the Government, they should be ready to give back the strictly monetary function which they cannot perform as well as the Government.

Nearly four hundred "influential" persons in many walks of life put themselves on record as favoring the plan, with occasional minor reservations, but the number of bankers on the list was disappointingly small. Likewise, passage of the bills which Congressmen C. G. Binderup of Nebraska and Jerry Voorhis of California introduced to implement the plan, were blocked by that old devil—the money illusion. Academic interest was so widespread, however, that two more editions were required within a decade, and it was translated into several foreign languages.

Altogether there were close to one hundred and fifty separate domestic and foreign editions of his twenty-nine titles—two of which remain to be considered in the next chapter. One title—*After Reflation, What?*—was even translated into Latvian. *The Money Illusion* chalked up the record for foreign distribution, with translations into fifteen languages; and *How to Live* held the domestic record, with nearly half a million copies sold of twenty-one editions. But the royalties received were never commensurate with the effort which went into these books. Since the author was primarily a propagandist, his main consideration was not the amount of royalties earned, but the number of converts won.

One item from his pen was unique because it was so far removed from being propaganda. It was a short article published in the February 22, 1936, issue of *Liberty*, under the title: "I Walked and Talked with Lincoln." Except for some superfluous introductory sentences, it is given here almost in its entirety:

On a midsummer night in 1935, I had a profound personal experience. I remember each detail. I was chatting with friends on the roof of a Union League clubhouse in Philadelphia. Among them was my brother-in-law, Nathaniel T. Bacon. Downstairs there was to be a lecture, which we were to attend. But we delayed so long that when we looked down, we saw the street crowded—blocking the front door.

There was a narrow back stairway leading from the roof to the lecture hall. After descending to the passage, we found the door blocked. Temporarily a statue of Lincoln had been placed in the entrance. It represented him in a half-reclining posture.

Some one shouted "Move Lincoln," which we did. Then we slipped by and took our seats. Lincoln filled all my thoughts. What the lecture was about I cannot remember. After it was over, the audience broke up into groups, for friendly talk.

Nat Bacon and myself were standing near "Lincoln." On looking down at the homely, wonderful face, my attention was attracted by a slight movement in one of his legs.

I said, "Nat, did you see that?"

He replied, "I most certainly did."

We both watched intently. Lincoln's head moved and his eyes opened. Then very slowly and quietly, he rose and began to walk.

Nat Bacon stepped forward promptly and seized one arm of the now erect figure, and on the other side I offered mine. Lincoln took both, as if this were a daily practice. We walked back and forth.

The room was silent. Everybody stared, petrified. Then Lincoln spoke. He looked at neither of us, but spoke as if resuming some old conversation: "You see, I tried, in that speech, to make them understand that we were not really enemies. I wanted them to share with all of us the feeling that, on both sides, there should be malice toward none and charity toward all. Both sides had striven to do right as God had given them to see the right. I voiced the hope, which I myself felt, that now at last there would be peace— a peace so deeply rooted that the scourge of war would vanish from the earth."

I do not remember all that Lincoln said, but I do remember the deeply satisfying sense of comradeship with him. He had not looked at either of us. Yet we both felt the warmth of his presence and of his affection—for us and for the world of men. The sense of reality was unqualified. I cannot remember any end to that walk. I had a feeling that I would walk with him on and on forever.

The next morning, as I was waking, my first remembrance was of that wonderful experience. My eyes moistened with the memory. I longed to tell the world. Of course the world would be skeptical. "There were scores of witnesses," I said to myself, but unfortunately, I had neglected to take their names.

"Anyhow," I thought, "Nat Bacon was there—he will confirm my story." Suddenly I remembered that Nat had been dead for several years.

I opened my sleepy eyes. Where was I? This was New Hampshire — Nashua — a surgical ward — the morning after I had undergone a slight bit of surgery. The anaesthetic had been local, but the night's sleep had perhaps been colored by it.

Had it all been a dream? Many of my ordinary dreams I recognize as dreams before I even wake up. And nearly all of them I forget a few minutes after waking. But this one I shall never forget. It was not so much a dream as the fulfillment of a dream, dreamed subconsciously through the years. And there was an abiding sense of an intimate association with the most ideal character in our history.

On the Lincoln's birthday which immediately preceded the publication of this article, he wrote to Mother:

WASHINGTON, February 12, 1936

This afternoon about 5:30 I walked to the Lincoln Memorial and back. The pool in front of it was partly cleared and filled with skaters. As I approached I thought I saw a lot of people lining the top of the steps, but I found they were not people but floral tributes.

As I entered, a "rough diamond" of a man entered too and instinctively removed his hat. Lincoln was in a glory of light directed on him from above. I felt as if he might step down and walk with me arm in arm, as he had in the dream.

I read every scrap of the inscriptions, gazed again at the noble statue, and came away with my eyes streaming and my heart newly inspired with his noble personality.

That fall he went to Greece to attend another International Statistical Institute gathering. Mother accompanied him this time as far as Switzerland, where my sister Carol had settled permanently as one of Jung's disciples in

Zurich. Father's letter to me from Athens gives the high points of his Busman's holiday:

ON TRAIN FROM ATHENS, October 4, 1936

Scheibler travelled with me, just as he did nine years ago when I went to see Mussolini. At one place in Yugoslavia we had to change cars. In the two-hour wait we climbed a foothill. At the top there was a quaint church and an Inn where the Innkeeper tried to palm off on us as apple juice, some hard cider.

We arrived in Athens a week ago today, and Mr. Loverdos met us. He had translated my "Money Illusion" and some articles into Greek. He is an Economist for the National Bank of Greece and wanted to spend a week of his vacation showing me around. He insisted on spending money on me, even paying taxi fares, etc. Upon our arrival he escorted us to the Acropolis, which was the first item on the program of the Institute. It gave me a great thrill, and I saw it a second time by moonlight night before last.

There were not so many excursions and social functions as at Mexico three years ago, but there were three great dinners and there was an all-day excursion to Marathon to see the water-works built by American engineers, including a huge dam of *marble*, because it was "cheapest"!

One day I got a notice of a registered package at the Post Office, and Loverdos went with me. I imagined it was from Mother and might be important. After waiting an hour for the proper official to open the safe, I found the package was from London. I could not tell them what was in it. So it was opened. It was "Colojel" (a new laxative) ordered by mail from New Haven. They had never heard of it, of course, and it took another hour of palaver before I could go. Loverdos saved the day by pointing out

298

that Greece would be cutting a ludicrous figure in the eyes of a "distinguished" foreigner.

They were first for making me pay a big duty, then for letting me have it free of duty—provided a statement could be obtained from the medical authorities of Greece and provided that the ministry of Hygiene consented and also the Post Office ministry, because the package should not have been sent by registered mail but by a special parcel post.

In the end we were sent to a tax authority, who finally took the responsibility on condition of my signing something—very likely an oath that it was not a bomb—of letting me take the package. The ludicrousness of it all made me enjoy the whole experience, though I managed to keep my face straight.

Loverdos took me to the native out-door restaurants for two late night dinners. We had proposed having him to dinner at the Hotel the first time. We said "O. K." to his counter-proposal provided we should pay the bill. We went and enjoyed it hugely—the balmy outdoor air, dirt floor with tiled dancing space and small orchestra.

The food was delicious and while Loverdos was absent I told Scheibler we must rebel against Loverdos. So he promised to hold him when the proper time came. As soon as Loverdos returned I told him there was to be a "revolution." He said he didn't understand. I told him to wait.

Later he started up evidently intending to pay the bill. Scheibler grabbed him and I shouted "La Revolution" and handed Mr. Balfour, another American, the money to pay, as he knew the ropes. Loverdos surrendered and the "revolution" was quickly over. But he was incorrigible. The next night he took us to another restaurant, and when he found we liked Greek melons, he ordered three more, though we were all "full up."

We didn't see the King, as we had expected. He decided to receive the officers only, so I brought my cut-away for nothing. But I was more disappointed not to see Metaxas, the dictator. Loverdos took me to see his friend a former premier (Themistocles Sophoulis) who speaks English well, at his villa in a suburb.

Afterwards Loverdos said he could understand the ex-premier's English better than my American English! The premier knew of my writings on money and when I explained to him the 100% Plan he caught on quicker than any one else I ever met and saw its value at once. He said he often wished he could write a book on "human stupidity."

As in Mexico, I was astonished to find so many who knew of my work. At one of the sessions the Minister of Finance read a paper on Income Tax. I ventured to offer some comments and he sought me out and asked me to send him more suggestions, adding: "You don't know it, but I'm a pupil of yours."

But the pleasantest thing of that sort was via Sir Josiah Stamp. Snyder (of the Federal Reserve Bank) brought him to me in the Hotel lobby saying, "Sir Josiah has a scheme for disposing of the vast stock of American gold now that the gold standard is doomed to go."

Sir Josiah then asked me, with a twinkle in his eye, "But first what would you propose?"

Knowing he wasn't serious, I replied, "Dump it in the middle of the Atlantic!"

He said, "My plan is better. Erect a monument out of it to Irving Fisher—Why not?—You've done more than anyone else to bring about this monetary reform."

300

I replied, "I didn't know you had kissed the Blarney stone."

He said, "Oh, yes," and told me all about being held by the heels and hanging down over the precipice, with a drop of some hundreds of feet before your eyes. He said the stone is well polished from the kissing.

Next day I inquired if he had started work on my monument. He said, "No, but I'm talking it up."

I said I'd be interested to know the site. "Oh," he said, "right next to the Statue of Liberty."

The last thing I did in Athens was to lecture in the University, this being one of the many engagements brought about by Loverdos. I lectured on the World Monetary Problem. I got great applause. The deputy Governor of the Bank of Greece was effusive and said he agreed with a friend who called my lecture "of crystallic clearness." Another functionary of the Bank of Greece provided me with the names of the three men in London who are now (presumably) stabilizing the money for most of the world. Sir Leith Ross of the Treasury is one and his chief advisor is R. H. Hawtrey, whose sentiments are like mine and who has kept out of sight even more than I and done much more. I told Sir Josiah the monument should be to Hawtrey.

My biggest thrill is to have lived to see my dreams coming true and to be, with Hawtrey and others among the unknown soldiers who have fought a winning fight in a great cause.

P. S. at Zurich, October 7, 1936:

I got "home" late last night and went to bed without reading the accumulated mail. This morning Mother read hers from you and then waited breathlessly for the one addressed "Prof. and Mrs." as her letter left her guessing.

301

Of course she guessed right but the joint letter was all the more thrilling and Mother read it with a trembling voice. No marriage is complete until it has borne fruit and we both love to think now of your happy anticipation. May he or she, like you and we, be in turn a torchbearer in the unending procession of life.

During the following winter, as he approached an important milestone, he wrote these letters to Mother, who was spending some time with Aunt Caroline in Santa Barbara:

NEW HAVEN, February 23, 1937

I wish we could have read Carrel's book [*Man the Unknown*] together, because it states my own fundamental standpoint. I never found a book which did this so well. He has, incidentally, saved me having to write one book!

There are lots of things in it I'd like you to see. I've read it once, reread the passages I marked, reread those I doubly marked and reread those I triple-marked. Nowadays I almost never do that with any book.

One thing you unconsciously dinned into me, which he expresses: "The pure intellectual is an incomplete human being." The way you did it was by being something else which Carrel also expresses: "Moral beauty is an exceptional and very striking Phenomenon. He who has contemplated it but once never forgets its aspect. This form of beauty is far more impressive than the beauty of nature and of science. It gives to those who possess its divine gifts, a strange, and inexplicable power."

Well! I first contemplated that sort of beauty incarnate, through the crack of a door and have been contemplating it ever since.

It used to irk me a little that you didn't seem to set more store by my brains. One reason I switched from Mathematics to Economics was because Economics, being more human, would appeal to you more. But I gradually came to see that instead of being so proud of my brains, I ought to be ashamed of my imperfections and that what was needed was not so much for you to get what I had to offer as for me to get what you had to offer; and I've tried a little but—like Peter—"afar off."

Carrel speaks my language, says nothing to jar me re creeds, is fully as heterodox as I; yet his book is largely to insist on the value of the sort of thing you have in such full measure and which is in danger of passing out of this mechanized world. Your dear wise Mother, when we came to Four-sixty had a poem about the marriage of my sort of knowledge and your sort of wisdom. I appreciate what she meant more now than I did then. And Carrel's book is almost about the marriage of those two parts of human life.

NEW YORK, February 25, 1937

I lunched with Alexis Carrel, at the Rockefeller Institute for Medical Research. We each admire the other's work and agree on everything except free will, in which he agrees with you! He thinks my 100% Money plan ought obviously to be adopted.

He has not seen me since ten or fifteen years ago at Battle Creek and says I look younger. So many people say this spontaneously that I'm beginning to believe it.

NEW HAVEN, February 27, 1937

Many people feel trepidation on reaching three score and ten. I feel really exultant. "I've been and gone and done it!" Of course, I know it means getting nearer the jumping off place (as Sumner used to call it) but I seem to smile inside at that, perhaps because I went through the trepidation stage in Saranac. The real reason is I'm in good health and Emerson said: "Give me health and a day and I will make the pomp of emperors ridiculous."

A few weeks later he was in Washington again working with Congressman Binderup and ex-Senator Owen, in another effort to frame a workable stabilization measure. This time he was not very sanguine that it would pass Congress, or if it did pass that F. D. R. would sign it. However, he commented philosophically to Mother: "It takes a lifetime to move Washington. Yet there is a building from year to year and *some* day I feel confident something will be done to crown the efforts of the many people who have worked so hard."

1937 was the year he was awarded two honorary LL.D. degrees—one by the University of Athens and the other by the University of Lausanne—although he could not be present to accept either of these bouquets in person. Perhaps even more pleasing was the publication of a volume entitled *The Lessons of Monetary Experience*, to honor him on reaching seventy. Edited by Arthur D. Gayer, this volume contained essays by twenty-two economists, representing fourteen different countries. The list of contributors ranged from James W. Angell of Columbia University and Marriner Eccles in this country to T. V. Soong in China and J. M. Keynes in Britain.

In the meantime, Father continued his usual activities without any noticeable slackening of pace. He spent Monday and Tuesday of nearly every week in New York attending directors' meetings, and there were numerous Washington conferences, as well as speaking engagements all over the map. He was alone in the library at Four-sixty when the hurricane of September 21, 1938, surprised the whole of New England. His concentration on his work was so complete that he was entirely unaware that anything unusual was in progress until he went outside to mail some letters and found trees down everywhere. Even then he thought it must be a local freak of nature and didn't appreciate what the big blow had meant to Mother, who was still at Whimsy Cot on the exposed Rhode Island shorefront. Telephone service was not restored for several days, so that his first direct word from her came via the chauffeur, who drove the housekeeper to New Haven after transferring Mother safely to Aunt Caroline's in Peace Dale.

Several of the Whimsy Cot windows were broken by flying debris, and the rest all leaked like sieves, so that Mother sloshed around in her bedroom with overshoes on. She and the chauffeur had to scrounge for nails to fasten improvised braces against the living-room doors toward the ocean, to prevent their being blown from their hinges. All the windows were so obscured by scum that she was not aware until the following morning that the giant waves had inundated the wide lawn to within a few feet of the porch. In describing her experiences she expressed the hope that Hitler might some day have a little sense knocked into him by being forced to live through such an ordeal. She summarized her impressions in this vivid quatrain:

Fierce shrieking whistle of the wind, with flooding rain,
Black waves mountains high, with thunderous jar;
A sense of littleness, all striving vain,
At last the stead'ing comfort and far nearness of
    a star.

305

Though she never admitted it, the hurricane was certainly a factor in her decision to rent Whimsy Cot—to the Stephen Vincent Benéts—for the next season, and she never occupied it again.

To celebrate Christmas that year the family gathered around the small collapsible tree, which had first been used at Cannes in 1893. A few of the original marzipan ornaments still survived, though they had long since become inedibly petrified. For this occasion the tree was placed on a tip-table in the center of the music room. While we were all engrossed in our packages, an involuntary gasp from Mother made us turn in time to see the tree burst into a mass of flames. A candle had burned to the socket and ignited the artificial foliage. I stepped quickly into the back hall, unhooked the fire extinguisher from its rack on the wall and carried it into the room. Then I stood uselessly at one side, while my wife and the others stamped out the burning tissue wrappings which had fallen onto the floor under the table. I looked at the ceiling and saw that it was not even darkening over the tree, and I realized that the chemical extinguisher might do more harm than good, if I sprayed it on the furniture needlessly. So, in a few minutes the fire was out, and the only real damages were some scorch marks on the Oriental rug under the table, and a hole in one of my wife's nylons, which were all covered by insurance.

When the excitement was over my wife spied the extinguisher and commented on my presence of mind for fetching it. Whereupon Father turned towards me and asked in astonishment: "Did you bring that in?" as if it had somehow walked into the room all by itself. While we ruefully contemplated the blackened wire framework of the tree, which had symbolized the Four-sixty Christmas for forty-five years, my wife and I involuntarily exchanged

306

glances. Our unexpressed premonition proved to be correct. That was the last Christmas which my parents celebrated together.

Prior to turning the house over to Yale in the fall of 1939, they sold the major portion of its contents at private sale, keeping only the minimum which might be required for furnishing a small apartment. My childhood playmate, Jim Toumey, who had crouched with me under the piano while the Giant's mumbo-jumbo crept relentlessly nearer, said that the dismantling of Four-sixty typified for him the end of an era. Mother's feelings at leaving the home her father had built for her as a wedding gift may be read between the lines of her final entry in the guest book:

October 28, 1939

Sister drove from Peace Dale and took tea with us, bringing lovely chrysanthemums from Oakwoods. She started back about 4:15 and left Jennie to help with the last packings, and is going to send for me and Jennie on Thursday November 2nd for the last move. I. F. will stay on a little longer and expects to join us in Santa Barbara about the middle of January, 1940.

The plan was for Mother to spend a few days in Peace Dale before going to Santa Barbara with Aunt Caroline for the winter, and then return to Whimsy Cot in the spring. In spite of its long span, the relationship between the two sisters had always remained in the little-sister, big-sister category. Neither of them seemed to be capable of forgetting that there was a difference of eleven years in their ages. And, despite the sensitive consideration of each for the other, it was as if Mother was returning to the protecting wing of her older sister, virtually in the capacity of a dependent.

307

When the train which carried them to California passed through New York, Father went aboard to wish them bon voyage, without having the slightest premonition that he was seeing Mother for the last time. After their arrival in Santa Barbara, the two sisters celebrated a quiet Christmas together and entertained a dozen friends for lunch on New Year's Day. A week later, as if not wishing to sadden the holidays for anyone, Mother died following an illness of less than thirty-six hours. Coronary thrombosis was the official diagnosis. Father, my wife and I and the Leonard Bacons flew to California for the funeral service, and three weeks later George Stewart officiated at a memorial service in New Haven.

Out of the many expressions of sympathy which we received, here is a single sentence from one written to me:

> Your mother had an "aura" about her of understanding life, its difficulties, its joys and its rewards; and a graciousness of sympathy and unselfish interest in others that actually left a little bit of herself with those whose lives she touched.

On the very day of Mother's funeral Father started a diary, in order to set down the important events of his remaining years, which would have been recorded in his letters to her if she had lived. Here is part of his first and longest entry:

> SANTA BARBARA, January 12, 1940
> Today was the funeral of my darling wife who has been the center around which my whole life has been turning, ever since we were married—in fact ever since we were engaged.

Since I had been told fourteen years ago that her heart might stop at any time, I have been wondering what life would be when this parting came. I feared I might be crushed so that life would not seem worth living. I never felt sure until the end came.

When she died I must have been answering a question on the preventability of heart disease, just after a lecture on "Health as a Money Investment" at Boston University. But the telegram saying she had died did not reach me until the next morning in New York.

After the first paroxysm of grief, a miracle happened. Instead of feeling that before me lay an unendurable life without her, I felt a sudden new impulse to live for her. She would not have me crushed. I could see her beautiful, smiling face expecting something of me which I must fulfill. That mental image of her stamped indelibly on my soul through half a century is bound to guide my future.

All this happened to me in a few minutes. It must have happened to millions of other lover husbands. But it was almost as amazing an experience to me as was the falling in love with her at sight of her smile through the crack of a door in 1891.

18. *Years Alone*

There were frequent gaps when he didn't write in his diary for weeks at a time, either because he forgot to take it with him on his trips, or simply because he was too busy. As he noted more than once, his diary was "thinnest when events were thickest."

Board meetings, speaking engagements and behind-the-scenes conferences in Washington kept him on the go. For many months after Mother's death he practically lived in his suitcase. Being away so much, it scarcely seemed worth while for him to rent an apartment. Then he found a small house on the outskirts of town which was just what he wanted. It was near the new home of a former Four-sixty laundress, who was delighted to look after his place and cook for him whenever he was in town. On the second floor he had a bedroom and bath adjoining his book-lined study, and on the ground floor the essentials of his office were miraculously condensed into two rooms. There Mrs. Sudela, who had come to work for him as Miss Gutekunst nearly thirty years before, was the sole survivor of the elaborate Four-sixty setup. This combination home and office solved his problem perfectly.

Soon after Wendell Willkie's nomination for the presidency, Father recorded his impressions of the Republican candidate in this diary entry:

NEW YORK, July 4, 1940

A red letter day, not because it's the Fourth, but because I saw Willkie. When I appeared for my appointment I found no other callers, but I could see he was terribly pressed for time. His desk was a terrible mess. I said I hoped he'd give me more time later; but that today I wanted to suggest that in his acceptance speech he avoid tying his hands on the tariff and the money question.

He seemed to agree with me on both. As to the money problem, I said the important thing was stability in purchasing power. I said instability had ruined Hoover and had made Hitler. He agreed and said if it hadn't brought forth Hitler it would have brought forth "some other paper hanger."

I showed him four books, including that in my honor on my Seventieth Birthday, which I explained was to recommend myself. The other three I left with him: *Stable Money, 100% Money* and *How to Live,* explaining that was my hobby and that Wilson had used it.

As I sized him up in those twenty minutes I rated him above Theodore Roosevelt, Taft, Wilson, Hoover, F. D. R., all of whom I have known rather well and still more above Harding and Coolidge whom I scarcely knew. Most of the time he had his feet on the table, and while phoning he lit a cigarette and said over the phone, "Well, he's a darned fool."

By coincidence less than a week after this interview, he visited Willkie's alma mater to speak on "The Establishment of a World Peace." He had entrusted the details of consulting timetables and buying railroad tickets to the porter at the Palmer House in Chicago. So when he alighted from the train he was surprised to find himself in Bloomington, Illinois, instead of Bloomington, Indiana. Fortunately he had allowed an extra day as it required a full eight hours of cross-country train and bus travel to get him to the right Bloomington, where he delivered his address on schedule and "received an ovation."

My wife and I and our three-year-old son spent the summer of 1940 at Whimsy Cot and Father commuted from New Haven for several weekends, but he failed to mention to us one confession which he set down in his diary:

WHIMSY COT, NARRAGANSETT, August 18, 1940
On the way from New Haven yesterday I was held up by State Police for speeding, but was only "warned." The officer said I was going sixty miles per hour, where the limit was thirty. I showed him a

certificate for safe driving from my insurance company. (I had gone 89 miles per hour earlier and on the last trip had gone 91.) The officer said the extreme limit allowed by law in Connecticut was forty-five miles per hour. Hereafter I intend to be more law-observing. . . .

On arriving yesterday, I listened to Willkie's acceptance speech. Good but dull and poorly delivered. I disagreed with what he said on raising wage rates and lowering hours.

Considerable space in his diary was devoted to recording the details of his efforts to recoup his depression losses. In addition to the income from his director's fees he inherited the principal of a small trust fund which had been established for Mother's benefit by her father. He invested two thirds of it in Remington Rand stock, which yielded him enough income to cover living and traveling expenses. But the rest went into new ventures which were so alluring that he borrowed from the banks, using his Remington Rand as collateral, in his vain search for another Index Visible. Only one of these long shots was even partially successful.

His diary recorded many compliments on his youthful appearance—one from a Washington hotel clerk, who said he had scarcely changed from Sugar Hill days, except that his hair was thinner and whiter. Others finding that such flattering remarks struck his Achilles heel, used them to gain his support for their dubious ventures, with no suspicion on his part that the compliments were extended with any ulterior motive. His own forthrightness was so ingrained that it was difficult for him to suspect others of double-dealing.

A great deal of diary space was devoted to his own

health. In this respect his single-track mind became virtually a monorail. His lifelong interest in diet reached its inevitable climax when he fell under the spell of Dr. Max Gerson, whose regime was largely based on the consumption of enormous quantities of fruit and vegetable juices. Salt was absolutely forbidden and vegetables had to be cooked very slowly in their own juices without the addition of one drop of water, so as to preserve every precious mineral and vitamin. Pressure cookers were frowned upon because too rapid breakdown of the minerals was alleged to destroy them. All fats were rigorously excluded, even vegetable fats such as alligator pears, which had ranked high on Father's list of favorites for many years. Thus he completely reversed his previous stand—based on the painstaking work of Dr. Clara Davis of Chicago—that we should eat whatever we crave, provided our appetites are not positively depraved.

During February and March of 1941 he gave a course in the Graduate School of the University of Southern California, where his diary mentioned having to buy a new suitcase and paying for it by check. At sight of the signature the store owner exclaimed: "Are you Irving Fisher of Yale?" and shook Father's hand warmly, saying, "This is the greatest honor I've had in a hundred years! I've read so much of yours. This day has not been in vain!"

Other entries spoke appreciatively of the hospitality of Grant Mitchell, a former pupil, who entertained him several times and put his car constantly at Father's disposal. But his nearest approach to what he considered a newsy letter was to send us a carbon of a long epistle addressed to Dr. Kellogg at Battle Creek, with this pencil notation in the corner: "Here's my first effort to write you, Carol and Uncle Herbert of my happenings, via carbons." The letter consisted chiefly of an account of his long discussion with

313

the explorer, Vilhjalmur Stefansson, regarding some meat-eating experiments. He assumed that the clinical details would fascinate us as much as they did him. For instance, why were the subjects' stools entirely odorless while they ate meat only, then became putrid again when vegetables were reintroduced?

Before leaving Los Angeles he addressed the Pacific Coast Conference of Sales Executives on "Depressions and Money Problems." Some paragraphs from this talk were included in the chapter on the money illusion. He believed that booms and depressions are primarily caused by alternate inflations and deflations: "They are the chills and fever of business. We are just getting out of the chill stage and going into the fever stage. A boom lies before us. . . . Since March, 1933, we've been having inflation—a beneficial inflation. In this case it has done no harm, because it was a corrective for the previous deflation. And inflation from this point onward is real inflation, not simply beneficial reflation, and it is going to be injurious."

To show how this injurious inflation would come about, he spoke of the recently announced seven-billion-dollar appropriation for armaments, and ended with a plug for the 100% plan:

> If we could raise that seven billion dollars out of taxes, or from bonafide savings, it wouldn't raise the price level, and the sanest thing that I've seen come out of Washington recently was a statement from the Secretary of the Treasury that he was going to try to see that this seven billion dollars would be at least partly raised by selling bonds to individuals to be bought out of savings. If that were done completely, we would have no inflation.

Practically all of that seven billion dollars, however,

will I feel be raised by selling these bonds to banks in return for newly created money. If the banks would simply run the printing press and issue bank notes, then people would see why that was inflation. But it's done in a more subtle way, simply by the issue of credit.

When you go to a bank and borrow ten thousand dollars, what really happens is merely that you hand the bank your promissory note and the bank gives you in return a right to draw checks. If you think that you've got ten thousand dollars in the bank as a deposit, you should disabuse your mind. The money isn't there. It isn't money, and it isn't a deposit. All it is is a demand liability of the bank to you.

We've got in this country about thirty billion dollars of obligations of the banks to the public, which circulates as if it were money, and it's ten times as important as the physical money that we carry in our pockets. So, you help inflate the currency when you borrow that ten thousand dollars, and when three months later you pay your debt—at that moment you are helping deflate the currency.

In normal times, when you are borrowing ten thousand dollars, I'm paying ten thousand dollars, and when I'm borrowing you're paying. If the two balance, then there's no inflation or deflation. In normal times, that's what happens and our banking system works fairly well.

But when you have a great mass movement of borrowing in a boom, you raise the volume of money faster than the volume of business and prices go up. And once a depression gets started you get a tail spin, a vicious circle, by which everybody is paying their debts, which means the money of the country is being diminished and it hurts every business man.

If you don't balance up and there is no regulation

of it in any manner, then you have mob movement sometimes one way and sometimes the other way. It was that that made the inflation before 1929 and it was that that made the deflation after 1929, and it's that that is going to make the inflation in the future, because Uncle Sam is going to the Bank, hat in hand, just as you went to get the ten thousand dollars, and he gives his promissory note which is called a government bond.

It would help the bankers if you could give them their job of money-lending, without allowing them to produce or destroy money, which in the end hurts them more than it hurts even the businessman. Some of us economists have a bill in Congress sponsored by a congressman from this state, Jerry Voorhis, and if that idea were realized we could have a central control of the circulating medium of the country.

During that winter he spent several week ends with Aunt Caroline at Santa Barbara. She had retired from the presidency of Wellesley in 1911, because the doctors feared she would not live six months. Instead she was well into her eighty-ninth year when she died in 1945. During a week end which he spent with her at Peace Dale in 1942, Father particiated in a very moving occasion of which he had no fore-knowledge. At the regular Sunday service of the Peace Dale Church he heard the pastor deliver the sermon which his own father had preached at the dedication of the building. In his diary he commented that the sermon seemed as up-to-date as if it had been "written last month rather than seventy years ago."

That fall his final economic book, *Constructive Income Taxation,* came off the press. It was expanded from his 1941 Los Angeles lectures and proposed a spendings tax instead of the current system. His brother Herbert was

316

listed as coauthor, and it was dedicated "To the memory of Ogden L. Mills, the first to draw and introduce a spendings-tax bill." The preface stated: "The root theory of the present book has been in my mind since 1896. It was then that I made my first attempt to formulate a concept of income. The concept was soon seen to be defective and was amended accordingly the next year. Since then I have found no reason for further amendments, as far as fundamental theory is concerned. But how to put the theory into practice still remained a problem; and only recently did a solution occur to me. Still more recently came the realization of how destructive is the present system."

This whole subject loomed so large in his mind that the last two of the five roughly drafted chapters of his projected book, *My Economic Endeavors*, were devoted to its consideration. In a sense, therefore, he appeared to give this book priority over all those which had been written since 1912. They would have been discussed in subsequent chapters, which were not yet blocked out. The reason for this apparent disregard for natural chronology seems to be that his book on a spendings tax harked back to his early investigations in capital and income. These chapters in *My Economic Endeavors* stressed the need for distinguishing between income as he originally defined it, and capital-gains income. Here are his comments on this point:

"Having found few economists willing to accept my proposed exclusion of capital-increase from income, I have, in deference to usage decided (and am sorry I did not do so at the beginning) to propose that we economists employ the term income in *two* senses, one including and the other excluding the disputed element. I have done so in my *Constructive Income Taxation.*

"So far as I can see, the only way for the economist, the accountant, the business man, the tax expert, the tax officials, the judges and the lawyers in the tax disputes to realize it, is specifically to call attention to its inclusion or its exclusion. Just as we distinguish between 'income before taxes' and 'income after taxes.'

"The 'real income' of an individual or a family—the consumption or use of food, clothing, dwellings, amusements, etc., never, in the usage of economists or anyone else adds in capital-increase. On the other hand, the 'income' of a corporation is always taken to include not only what it yields to its stockholders in dividends but what it withholds from them and ploughs back as 'undistributed profits.' Moreover the corporation is taxed on its 'income' in the inclusive sense, while the stockholders are taxed on their 'income' in the exclusive sense. If a corporation is converted into a partnership, its taxable income changes from the inclusive to the exclusive sense!

"In my *Nature of Capital and Income* and in all my writings on the subject prior to *Constructive Income Taxation* I have used the term only in the 'exclusive' sense of yield, while the 'inclusive' concept was called 'earnings.' (Professor Haig proposes 'accretion.') The courts have sometimes used the term 'enrichment.' All three are synonyms of income, including capital-increase. A synonym of income, excluding capital-increase, is 'yield.' The concept, yield of service, is the simpler concept; for it makes income more homogeneous. It is also more fundamental; for the 'earnings' concept cannot be defined before the first is defined.

"It was for these two reasons that, as soon as the yield concept was fully grasped by me (in 1897) I made that my sole concept of income. By conceding (in 1942) that earnings may properly be called by the same name, there is no change of concepts but only a change of terminology, a change made merely to avoid ambiguity.

"While my change in 1942 was only in terminology, I deeply regret that I had not made it forty-five years earlier; for I suspect that I would have convinced many more of my opponents of the correctness of my findings, as to matters far more material than mere terminology. I refer particularly to my findings as to double counting of income and its double taxation, in a certain important sense.

"It seems to me that most of the differences of opinion and misunderstanding and confusions about 'income' are due to the failure to distinguish between income yielded and income earned—in other words to stumbling over the 'savings' element and wondering where to place it. It would be a great mistake, however, to conclude that all the controversy over the role of savings is nothing more than a war of words. On the contrary, the important point is that 'accretion income,' by including savings or capital-increase, thereby includes (reduced by discount) some *future* yield income in addition to the current yield income. Consequently when eventually that future yield is reached, it will be counted a second time. This double counting idea was first expressed by me in an article in the *Economic Journal* for December, 1897:

"To include the rise in value . . . and afterwards count the income which that rise represents . . . would be to count the same things twice, to eat your cake and have it too. . . . To tax the owner both on the rise in value and the subsequent income would be double taxation. . . . There is therefore more justification than economists have usually admitted for the business man's instinct to exempt from taxation unused land rising in value.

319

"From the time these remarks were made to the present I have never ceased my endeavors to get economists to recognize the fact that, whether we call it income or not, the sum of the value of the services flowing from any capital source plus the rise in value of said source, double counts some of the services.

"Until 1938 it was my belief that this double counting idea was original with me. I then learned from Professor [Edwin] Seligman that John Stuart Mill was apparently the first to see clearly this important point. Mill stated that: 'the proper mode of assessing an income-tax would be to tax only the part of income devoted to expenditure, exempting that which is saved.... Unless savings are exempted from income-tax, the contributors are twice taxed on what they save, and only once on what they spend.' In 1942, after most of *Constructive Income Taxation* had been written, I learned from Hans R. L. Cohrssen that Eduard Pfeiffer, a German follower of Mill, wrote a two volume treatise on the subject.

"It is a commentary on how very important contributions to science can be made and forgotten. I remember a talk with Edgeworth, when he visited Yale, in which he expressed great interest in my conclusions on the role of savings in income theory, saying he had himself been puzzled. Though a very learned man, he must have missed as I had Mill's statement, since he made no mention of it.

"Eventually my deep interest in the double-counting and double-taxation of savings led me to advocate an income tax with savings exempted, which in effect means, a spendings tax. This, however, did not take shape until forty-five years had elapsed. The chief reasons for this delay are evident from the following quotation from *Constructive Income Taxation:*

In 1906, in *The Nature of Capital and Income,* the present writer set out to analyze the income concept. At that time there was no federal income tax and little thought was given in that book to the practical problem of devising such a tax.

An unfortunate result of this omission was that, when seven years later, America adopted the Sixteenth Amendment, some of those who then proceeded to consult *The Nature of Capital and Income* gained the impression that its theory of income could not be practically applied. Nor did the author himself then realize how easily a near approximation to real income could be made effective in practice.

John Stuart Mill, Alfred Marshall, and Arthur C. Pigou have held that a pure income tax which should leave savings untouched was impracticable, though theoretically ideal. . . . Apparently the only essential difficulty was that of obtaining an accurate money measure of spendings.

"Although I did not begin the writing of *Constructive Income Taxation* until 1938, nor publish it until 1942, my *Nature of Capital and Income* had indirectly helped Ogden Mills (when in Congress and before he was Secretary of the Treasury) to introduce a bill for a spendings tax on July 20, 1921. Oddly enough he never knew that my book was partly the source of his bill. Nor did I for many years know the connection.

"At a Congressional Hearing in 1932, Mills repudiated his 1921 proposal, testifying: 'I was wrong. . . . I now think that, on the whole, that is uneconomic.' Presumably he was influenced by the prevalent opinion in the depression that spending should be encouraged and that saving should be discouraged. In 1936 he commended an article on the subject by the present author and told him at a luncheon meeting on August 24, 1937: 'the time is now ripe again for a spendings tax.' He also stated that his 1921 bill had been prepared by Professor Thomas S. Adams, who subsequently told me that the bill was based on principles set forth in *The Nature of Capital and Income*. A few weeks before his death on October 11, 1937, Mills wrote a letter favoring the author's present proposal, expressing especial admiration for the plan's simplicity.

"The Mills bill did not provide any workable formula for measuring spendings but merely authorized the tax authorities to examine the tax payer's books. Since practically no one keeps strict account of his spendings, it is not surprising that Congress did not enact the Mills bill. But as stated on the fourth and fifth pages of *Constructive Income Taxation:*

> It is strange that those who recognize that "spendings" are the only fair and logical base for taxable income often fail to realize how practical and simple is its application.
>
> How do we figure what we spend in a day? We need only two data: (1) the amount we had to spend; (2) the amount we did not spend.
>
> Moreover, the data needed for this calculation are considerably more trustworthy than those used in our present income taxes, which often depend on debatable estimates.
>
> We propose, then, to reckon the taxable spendings, not by adding together the separate items spent for food, clothing, rent, amusements, etc. but by adding together the *gross receipts from all sources* and then deducting all items of outgo *other* than "spendings." The chief deductions under this proposal are: investments, taxes paid during the taxable year, and proper exemptions for the taxpayer and his dependents....

322

In this indirect way it becomes very easy for a taxpayer to report his spendings—easier perhaps than to report his "income," according to present law.

"The U. S. Treasury Dept. became deeply interested in the proposal (not, however, as a substitute for all existing income taxes but as an additional thereto). Both the Treasury's tax expert Randolph Paul and Secretary, Henry Morgenthau, Jr. became enthusiastic advocates of this spendings tax."

In Chapter Nine of *Constructive Income Taxation* he quoted Chief Justice Marshall's 1819 decision: "The power to tax is the power to destroy," then continued:

This power to destroy is many times greater when savings are taxed than when merely spendings are taxed. The destructiveness works two ways: *indirectly*, by discouraging the saver from saving, and *directly*, by taking over in taxes some of the savings which he actually makes.

Let us now consider *heavy* taxes on chronic savers. The case of a great new invention is typical of the origin of American capital. To tax the annual growth (which is what savings mean) of such enterprises destroys that growth to an amazing degree—like compound interest in reverse.

A once-for-all tax, at the same rate, on the final total—that is, on the inheritable estate after the accumulator has finished his lifework—would produce far more revenue. At first sight, the opposite result might be expected. But—the higher the tax the lower the revenue!

The automobile industry was essentially established before the American income tax began to put high rates on capital-increase of corporations and before

323

there was any personal income tax. It seems certain that such an income tax as is now in force, and the added taxes which are being proposed, would never have permitted any such industrial developments as have actually occurred in the past. That is a very disconcerting thought.

On the basis of our calculations, we may conclude that, if we were today to repeal all our present taxes on capital-increase—the result would be, in the end, not a reduction of tax revenue but a tremendous increase, as well as a tremendous boost to our whole economy. Our present handling of savings and dissavings is doubly destructive of revenue. It loses immediate revenue by exempting dissavings and it loses ultimate revenue by taxing savings, thereby killing the goose that lays the golden egg.

He testified at hearings on the subject before the House Ways and Means Committee on May 14, 1941 and again on October 11, 1943, but his efforts to bring a spendings tax into being came to naught. In fact, there was so much opposition to his "simple" plan that he prepared a mimeographed brochure, giving detailed answers to the many objections which had been raised, for distribution to anyone requesting it. He felt that all opposition to the proposal would evaporate if its opponents "were not afflicted with the double counting fallacy," which prevented their understanding the problem, just as the money illusion blocked the adoption of the commodity dollar plan.

At the end of a 1947 appreciation of the author of *Constructive Income Taxation,* Dr. Royal Meeker expressed himself on the topic in these words:

If his ideas were followed in revolutionizing our tax systems, Federal, State and Local, our taxpayers would be relieved of several billions of dollars currently being paid in taxes, while the incomes to governments from taxes could be greatly increased. Any doubt about the solvency of the United States would be dissipated, the enormous burden of debts would be on the way to extinction, production would be stimulated and the general welfare would be correspondingly enhanced. However, there is no immediate prospect that sanity will be substituted for lunacy in the framing of tax laws, so my rather sweeping assertions can not be subjected to the acid tests of history for many, many years.

With the coming of the second world war, such events as Pearl Harbor, the Normandy invasion and Hiroshima appeared to affect Father comparatively little. He did take part in a conference on a "durable" peace at Ohio Wesleyan and he delivered an up-to-date version of his 1890-1914 address before a meeting on behalf of Federal Union at St. Louis. He also electrified a dinner of the Newcomen Society in New York with his extemporaneous remarks on the need for a strong United Nations, reciting from memory the passage in Tennyson's *Locksley Hall* about "the Parliament of Man, the Federation of the World," which he had used in his League talks during the twenties. But the incident which brought World War II most sharply home to him was the death of his friend, Sir Josiah Stamp, in a London bombing raid.

During the Bretton Woods monetary conference, he wrote to Lord Keynes, congratulating him on his speech proposing a world bank and asking him to support the 100% money plan "as the best *national* plan to interlock with the *international* plan you are now trying to put over." Here is the meat of Lord Keynes' cordial reply:

Your letter has given me the greatest possible pleasure. You were one of my earliest teachers on these matters and nothing is more satisfactory to any of us than to satisfy one of those from whom we have learned.

On the matter of 100 per cent money I have, however, as you know, some considerable reservations. Possibly they may relate more to British conditions than they would to American conditions; but however that may be it prevents me from coming forward as an advocate.... With us as soon as we make the decision to strengthen our control (which in fact is not too bad already) there are ways with our highly integrated system in which we can do it.

Ever sincerely yours,
KEYNES

A few months later Father received a letter from his twenty-one-year-old grandson, which elicited a six-page dictated reply. Baldwin Sawyer, the recipient of this letter, was at that time a metallurgist in the atomic energy project at the University of Chicago. These excerpts from the letter give some sidelights on the income tax problem and on the question of growing government control:

October 19, 1944

MY DEAR BALDWIN:

I feel flattered to think that my grandson has read two of my books. I have written twenty-nine! I was especially pleased to know that you have read my *Constructive Income Taxation* and have been enough interested to buy the book for yourself. I am glad, also, to find that in your experience with your friends you have found it had a "popular appeal."

I have been more disappointed in this book than in any I have written, because it fell between two stools. Secretary Morgenthau and his legal counsel, Mr. Randolph Paul, adopted the idea and recommended it to Congress, but this proved to be almost the "kiss of death."

The presentation was made when Congress was about to adjourn and the committee resented being rushed into something new at such a time. A business friend of mine who was enthusiastic about the plan, advised the committee to vote against it because it had been recommended as a measure *in addition to* existing legislation instead of *in place of* such legislation.

By the irony of fate it was proposed by the New Dealers, whereas its real friends were on the opposite side. It fell between these two stools. Senator [Robert A.] Taft told me he would have voted for it if it had been "instead of" rather than "in addition to."

I agree with what you say concerning monopoly, tariffs and special interests. I also agree that people should have some say about what happens to them but it is not a healthy situation by which the shiftless people can vote money into their own pockets from the thrifty. One of the reasons for the fall of the Roman Empire was that votes were given to those who had no interest in government except "bread and the circus."

I am actively associated with a movement to try to safeguard private enterprise. I do not believe that socialism or Communism would be good for the masses in the United States. Russia, when rid of the Czar, has leaped forward with the help of the government, but we need no such leap. Moreover, the rise of Russia is largely imitation of our successes, particularly Henry Ford. The so-called planning of Russia is planning to imitate, and when we try to plan here without any model of a country which has progressed beyond ourselves (which doesn't exist) we are getting nowhere.

For the bureaucrats and politicians can never plan as men like Henry Ford could. It would be the greatest possible disaster to this country for the masses if the government should try to run business and to make progress. It would be entrusting the running of the country to people like those who run Tammany Hall, something analogous to developing the automobile as Henry Ford developed it. I think that the government can help but I think Hoover had a better idea of how it could help than Roosevelt does.

A letter written during the following summer to Philip Cortney, President of Coty, climaxed a debate on international monetary matters which they carried on in the columns of the *New York Times*. These paragraphs gleaned from his fifteen-page letter further clarify Father's position with regard to monetary reform:

July 9, 1945

Your way of thinking is substantially the same as that of many other people for whom I have great respect, but whose bases are so unlike mine that the only way we can meet on common ground has been for them to read and digest at least one of my basic books on this subject.

I know this sounds as if I were assuming, too aggressively, my prime role of the schoolmaster. I'm assuming that you earnestly wish to discover any errors you have committed, and are willing to change your mind on evidence, just as Keynes has, and I have, and many other earnest truth seekers.

As to Keynes' views, I have no desire to defend them all; for, as I understand them, I differ in some ways, though not, I think, much in the sphere of money. Incidentally, he told me that my *Purchasing Power of Money* was the first book on money he read which "made sense" to him and on the basis of which all his future work was done.

I am strongly in favor of preserving our American system of free enterprise. I believe that a chief, perhaps the chief, condition which drives us toward the government intervention which you and I deplore is unstable money or inflation and deflation. In 1920 I predicted that unless this condition was remedied, we would have much of what has actually happened.

No permanent and satisfactory solution of the money problem is possible unless, and until, it is international. The Bretton Woods proposal is our opportunity and ought not to be missed. It makes use of gold in the way you approve, as I do. But provision is made for a concerted raising or lowering of the price of gold, which for us means a lowering or raising of the dollar's weight. Such changes in the price of gold may sometimes be necessary if we are to maintain internal stability.

An ounce of gold has *never* been a stable standard. But it is unquestionably the best *medium of exchange* for foreign trade which the world ever saw. The Bretton Woods plan utilizes gold for this, its chief virtue. Its use as a medium is commonly confused with its use as a *standard*. As *medium* it is a carrier of the *standard* of one country to another.

If we revert to the old gold standard, unsupplemented by credit control, we shall enjoy external stability, but shall, with practical certainty, have recurring periods of inflation and deflation. Each such period carries with it the risk of radical political changes, constantly calling for more government control, of all sorts, mostly illegitimate. But government control of money is legitimate and necessary. If we secure such control, we shall not need so much control of other kinds.

A laissez faire monetary policy spells inflation and deflation, booms and depressions, discontent, class hatred, and communism. Gold has *not* "well served humanity" as a standard but only as a medium. A price level and individual prices are as distinct from each other as sea level and individual waves.

Exchange control by government is, I agree, in the long run undesirable, but in the chaotic conditions following this war I can see no better way to effect a steady transition, than that degree of government control provided for in Bretton Woods. Gold will then serve in its best capacity, as a sort of international cement.

Keynes has, I think, always been a stabilizer, though the criterion of absolute stability has shifted with him just as to some extent, it has with me.

I hope I have not tired you out or seemed too "brutally frank" or "pontifical." It would have taken a book to go into all the points which flooded my mind as I read.

The following winter, his diary noted the arrival of still another personal milestone:

NEW YORK, FEBRUARY 27, 1946

My birthday—entering my 80th year! Judging from my feelings, power to work, lack of dopiness or sleepy feeling from morning to night, I'm better than at any time since my breakdown at thirty-one. But my memory isn't as good as at seventy and before. Teeth and hair have diminished. Moreover, my improvement may be more apparent than real owing to my system of resting *before* I'm tired.

Later that year the University of Oslo awarded him an honorary degree, *in absentia*. Up to the last minute he hoped to fly to Norway to accept the award in person, but space was not available to transport him to Oslo in time for the Convocation, so the parchment and signet ring were flown to him instead.

During the summer my wife and I took him on what proved to be his last wholly frivolous carefree outing. We drove him the thirty-odd miles to Ivoryton to see Grant Mitchell perform in *The Late George Apley*. Before the performance we were dinner guests of the star at his Hotel. The play and Grant Mitchell's performance suited Father to perfection, and in the subsequent months he often referred enthusiastically to that memorable evening.

19. *Jumping-off Place*

In the fall of 1946 Father showed the first signs of a general slackening of pace. Two late 1945 diary entries mentioned a mysterious "stoppage," which he attributed to a kink in the intestines, similar to a condition he had experienced fifteen years before. An August, 1946, entry spoke of being X-rayed "for gallstones" by a Chicago physician whom he had first met at Battle Creek; and a month later, when Dr. Tarbell, his former personal physician, returned to New Haven for a visit, another X-ray revealed a "polyp" instead of a "kink." Because of his lifelong tendency toward self-diagnosis, it was hard for Father to place himself unreservedly in the hands of any one physician. He discussed his difficulties with Dr. Gerson, whose attitude was primarily reassuring; and whenever he survived three or four days without any major discomfort, he wrote buoyantly in his diary that his diet regime must have straightened out the kink. During October and November the sleepless nights outnumbered the "good" ones, but he made so light of these danger signals in talking with us, that we felt no real concern until after the start of 1947.

To hedge against possible eventualities, however, he gradually curtailed his activities by resigning from several directorships and declining more speaking engagements than he accepted. In January he was lionized at a dinner of the American Statistical Association at Atlantic City. Replying to Ragnar Frisch's tribute to him, Father spoke of "how embarrassing it is to listen to all the sweet taffy which Professor Frisch has handed me. In fact, since next month I will be eighty, the taffy sounds a little like 'epitaphy!' " From Atlantic City he went to Washington for further conferences regarding monetary legislation, and after his return to New York he commented in his diary: "My trip to Atlantic City and Washington was much too strenuous for me and I have been *much* under par ever since."

We were shocked at the marked change in his appearance when he returned to New Haven in mid-February after an absence of three weeks. According to his diary, the new diagnosis was "gallstones and obstructive jaundice." At the suggestion of a New Haven internist who was never permitted full freedom of action in the case, Father arranged with the top New York surgeon in the field, whose name had been suggested by the Chicago doctor who took X-rays the preceding summer, to have the offending organ removed. He planned to enter a New York hospital for this operation immediately after the testimonial dinner which was to be held at the New York Yale Club on his eightieth birthday.

We did our best to persuade him to cancel the dinner, but nothing would shake his determination to carry through the full program. He felt it was too late to disappoint those who were responsible for planning the event, and he considered it a golden opportunity to put his message across to a distinguished and influential gathering. He would not admit that there could be any valid reason for cancellation.

To prepare himself for the ordeal, he spent the whole of the preceding day incommunicado in his Yale Club room. When he appeared at the gala black-tie affair, few of the hundred men present seemed to appreciate how much weight he had lost, and his complexion looked less jaundiced under the artificial light. The master of ccrc monies called attention to the fact that Father had eaten sparingly and imbibed nothing but milk, while the rest of us guzzled lamb chops and Chateau Poiyeaux 1936. This allusion to his well-known stand on alcohol produced a curious ripple of amusement, which was partly sympathetic and partly a shamefaced snicker.

After Professor Westerfield's graceful introduction Father spoke on "The Inflations and Deflations of My Eighty Years." His delivery was more deliberate than usual and he spoke at greater length than if he had been in prime form. He leaned heavily on the pointer which he used to explain a huge chart, but considering the circumstances his talk was remarkably lucid. Though he would have pooh-poohed the comparison, his last public appearance was on as valiant a level as Cyrano's final effort to keep his white plume aloft.

It was an impassioned summation of his thirty-five year campaign for stabilization, which reviewed the major variations in the purchasing power of the dollar from 1867 to 1947. In only one period—from 1921 to 1929—had there been any lasting stability, which he attributed to the open market operations of Governor Strong of the Federal Reserve Bank of New York. He believed it was the lapsing of this policy after Strong's death which again produced instability. He predicted that unless some way could be found to achieve permanent stability, this country would "fall into the trap of Communism. . . . The Communists will say, 'The system of free enterprise is a failure, and produces depressions and unemployment. Give us Communism and we will see that everybody works.'—If, on the other hand, we solve this problem permanently, we will have the greatest and the least interrupted prosperity this world has ever seen."

After his admission to the hospital on the following day, full examination revealed that he was actually suffering from an inoperable cancer of the colon, which had spread to the liver and produced the jaundice condition. It was much too late for surgery, and the medical problem became one of providing "supportive" treatment—frequent injections of plasma and glucose. Nothing but downhill progress could be expected. It was an ironic fate for one who had so steadfastly obeyed all the health rules and been such a devotee of periodic medical examinations.

In imparting to us his enthusiasm for Dr. Gerson's regime, he had told us confidentially about several cancer cases, where Dr. Gerson had wrought apparent "miracles" when orthodox physicians had abandoned hope. These cases usually followed patterns similar to that of young John Gunther, described in *Death Be Not Proud*. After months—perhaps even a year or two—of apparent improvement under Dr. Gerson's regime, relapse would set in and the spotlight of attention would be focused elsewhere. Who can tell? Perhaps even in Father's case, there may have been an appreciable postponement of the inevitable. As his condition worsened, however, he was more and more reluctant to discuss the situation either with me or with his physician. That he fully appreciated the gravity of his position is shown by this scarcely legible scrawl in his final diary entry, written a month before the end: "Looks desperate to me."

For the first few weeks in the hospital his mind remained as active as ever. He conferred at length with Dr. Max Sasuly, the statistician who had helped him make the intricate calculations for *The Making of Index Numbers*, and who had been collaborating with him for several years on an unfinished project to be entitled *The Velocity of the Circulation of Money*. He kept a secretary in the hospital busy with dictation, including a lengthy letter to President Truman offering unsolicited and unacknowledged advice. He painstakingly corrected the proof of his birthday dinner speech for publication in the *Commercial and Financial Chronicle*. Dr. Solley, who had been best man at his wedding, visited him several times and letters came from Will Eliot and Norman Flagg, with and against whom he had debated in 1884. His dictated replies were affectionate but brief.

One final indignity remained. Three or four years before he had invested a sizable sum with an unscrupulous promoter, on the flimsiest of assurances. About two weeks after Father entered the hospital, this individual disappeared from sight, having apparently absconded with trust funds from another venture in which Father was not concerned. These developments could not be concealed from him because he had a telephone beside his bed, and he was mystified to find the promoter's home and office phones disconnected overnight. The Attorney General's office even tried to find out if Father could shed any light on the promoter's whereabouts. The realization that his own previous investment had presumably gone down the drain was a bitter pill for him to take, as he had regarded that particular item as one of his most likely dark horses.

Several other individuals who had obtained smaller amounts from him at one time or another, also gathered like vultures, trying hard for one final "touch." Thanks to the alertness of his hospital secretary, Miss Isabel Weaver, most of these attempts were nipped in the bud. Then the stock market took a slump and the banks, where he had sizable loans though on a much smaller scale than in 1939, asked for more collateral or a reduction of the loans. As he grew weaker and the pressure from the banks increased, he finally acceded to my suggestion that he give me a power of attorney, thus delegating all these worrisome details. This enabled me to sell enough collateral to pay off the loans at a considerable saving over the prices which prevailed, when I would first have been able to act as his executor.

In our last talk of any consequence, he likened himself to the shoemaker who made fine shoes for everyone except his own barefoot family. Despite all his comprehension of economics, a figurative blind spot corresponding to his physical one had prevented his seeing the total picture in clear enough perspective to protect his own family's best interests. By that time he must have understood that his net estate would not be large enough to require the payment of any Federal tax. From this angle and from the health angle his sufferings were more mental than physical. Fortunately the cancer was not as painfully located as it sometimes is. But it was hard for him to summon the philosophical attitude of his middle years, to "let come what will come," as he neared the jumping-off place.

His early victory over tuberculosis had preternaturally accentuated the yearning for immortality which drives every one of us. The fact that he enjoyed an exceptionally long and productive career was overshadowed by the distress of leaving behind so much unfinished business. When the battle was over, a friend, whose ninety-four-year-old father died at about the same time, remarked to me: "Yes, it always comes too soon" in corroboration of the universal sense of frustration at not being able to live forever. Father lapsed into a merciful coma three days before it came for him on April 29, 1947.

In the *American Economic Review* for September, 1947, Professor Paul H. Douglas (now United States Senator) wrote of him:

> Master of a crystal-clear method of exposition and gifted with mathematical genius, he raised the whole level of our thinking. If we at times smiled over the lack of humor which sometimes accompanied his seriousness of purpose, we could only be reverent towards the total import of his life. Irving Fisher's career gives to us all a living proof of how effective a good man can be when to an able mind is wedded an energetic devotion to the common good.

Of all the other eulogies written following Father's death, the one which would probably have pleased him the most contained these paragraphs, addressed to President Seymour of Yale and signed by Professor Schumpeter and eighteen other members of the Harvard Department of Economics:

No American has contributed more to the advancement of his chosen subject than Fisher. His use of the mathematical techniques in the analysis of economic data was among the first of such applications in this country as it has remained among the best. His *Mathematical Investigations into the Theory of Prices* must, in fact, be recognized as among the best works of its time in any country.

Fisher's *The Nature of Capital and Income* added to his international reputation, to the reputation of Yale University, and to the study of Economics in this country. Together with his masterpiece, *The Rate of Interest*, it established Fisher's position by the side of J. B. Clark and F. W. Taussig as a founder of modern economic study in the United States. That he continued in his *Making of Index Numbers* and in later works the vein of originality so characteristic of his earlier productions is a tribute to his vitality and to the environment in which he worked.

The impulse that Fisher gave to econometric studies, both as a founder of the Econometric Society and as an eminent pioneer in the field, has already yielded a rich harvest and promises to continue to an enduring influence. The name of that great economist and great American has a secure place in the history of his subject and of his country.

In his own seventy-fifth birthday talk at Harvard, from which quotations have been given in the opening chapter as well as in several of the intervening ones, he made this summarization:

My desire to help make economics into a genuine science involved substituting for mere descriptive dictionary definitions, what might be called analytical concepts, such as capital and income. . . . In regard to anticipations, J. Maynard Keynes stated that I had been "the first to publish in book form ideas analogous to those which had been worked out by Marshall at much earlier dates" in his lectures.

One of the points which I look back upon with satisfaction is that I repudiated the idea of Jevons that economics was concerned with a "calculus of pleasure and pain" and I insisted there was a great distinction between desires and their satisfactions and that economics had to do only with desires, so far as the influence of market prices was concerned.

But one should be more interested in truth than in who desires the credit for first reaching it. Ever since my six years of illness I have become much more interested in promoting the truth than in claiming credit or even in adding to knowledge. There is so much knowledge already attained that is not yet applied that I have often set myself to work to bring that knowledge to the attention of others.

Today I would like to see a study, partly economic and partly psychological, showing how the human animal following his desires often misses satisfactions instead of attaining them. The star example is narcotics.

If I can pass on to the younger men a sense of the importance of these economic endeavors, I shall be content.

CHRONOLOGICAL LIST OF PRINCIPAL BOOKS
BY IRVING FISHER

*Mathematical Investigations in the Theory of
Value and Prices*
  Ph.D. thesis, 1891; Yale University Press, New Haven.
  Last printing 1937.

Elements of Geometry (with Prof. A. W. Phillips)
  Harper, New York, 1896. Last printing 1943.

A Brief Introduction to the Infinitesimal Calculus
  Macmillan, New York, 1897. Last printing 1937.

The Nature of Capital and Income
  Macmillan, New York, 1906, 1930.

The Effect of Diet on Endurance
  Yale University, 1907, 1918.

The Rate of Interest
  Macmillan, New York, 1907.

National Vitality (Report of Conservation Commission)
  Government Printing Office, 1909.

Elementary Principles of Economics
  Macmillan, New York, 1910, 1912.

The Purchasing Power of Money
  Macmillan, New York, 1910, 1912.

How to Live (with Dr. Eugene Lyman Fisk)
  Funk & Wagnalls, New York, 1915;
  21st Edition (with Dr. Haven Emerson) 1946.

Why is the Dollar Shrinking?
Macmillan, New York, 1915.

Stabilizing the Dollar
Macmillan, New York, 1920.

The Making of Index Numbers
Houghton Mifflin, New York, 1922, 1927.

League or War?
Harper, New York, 1923.

America's Interest in World Peace
Funk & Wagnalls, New York, 1924, 1926.

Prohibition at Its Worst
Macmillan, New York, 1926.

Prohibition Still at Its Worst (with H. B. Brougham)
Alcohol Information Center, 1928.

The Money Illusion
Adelphi, New York, 1928, 1930.

The Theory of Interest
Macmillan, New York, 1930.
Reprinted by Kelley & Millman, New York, 1954.

The Stock Market Crash—and After
Macmillan, New York, 1930.

The Noble Experiment (with H. B. Brougham)
Alcohol Information Committee, 1930.

Booms and Depressions
Adelphi, New York, 1932.

Stamp Scrip
Adelphi, New York, 1932.

Inflation?
Adelphi, New York, 1933.

After Reflation, What?
Adelphi, New York, 1933.

Stable Money, A History of the Movement
(assisted by Hans R. L. Cohrssen)
Adelphi, New York, 1934.

100% Money
Adelphi, New York, 1935; third edition, 1945.

Constructive Income Taxation (with Herbert W. Fisher)
Harper, New York, 1942.

World Maps and Globes (with O. M. Miller)
Essential, New York, 1944.

INDEX

Index

347

349